Peter Kluska

Landschaftsarchitektur
Landscape architecture

peter kluska

landschafts architektur
Projekte + Wettbewerbe
1970–2010

landscape architecture
Projects + Competitions
1970–2010

HIRMER

Inhalt

- 6 Biographie
- 7 Vorwort
- 8 Freiraum- und Baukultur – Werte der Stadt
- 10 Lebensraum Stadt
- 12 Bäume – der Charme der Stadt
- 14 Die Sprache des Raums
- 16 Landschaftsbilder
- 18 Soziale Gartenkunst
- 20 Gärten – die Kraft der Farbe
- 22 Kompositionen

- 25 **Projekte**
- 27 Zweites Deutsches Fernsehen Sendezentrum Mainz
- 41 Landschaftspark Engelhalde Kempten
- 51 Westpark – IGA 83 Internationale Gartenbauausstellung Metamorphose einer Landschaft München
- 97 Kultur- und Kongresszentrum Max-Reger-Halle Weiden in der Oberpfalz
- 103 Klinikum Dritter Orden München
- 109 Main-Donau-Kanal Berching
- 123 Donaustaustufe Vohburg
- 129 Donau-Glacisbrücke und Querung Luitpoldpark Ingolstadt
- 139 Universität Erfurt Entwicklungsplanung
- 145 Ludwig-Maximilians-Universität Fakultät für Chemie und Pharmazie, Institut Molekularbiologie München
- 151 Einrichtungshaus Theresienhöhe Dachbegrünung München
- 157 Postbank Paul-Heyse-Straße Innenhöfe und Dachbegrünung München
- 163 Bürogebäude der Swiss Re Germany Unterföhring
- 175 Robert-Bosch-Haus Parksanierung Stuttgart
- 187 Bosch-Haus Heidehof Der neue Park Stuttgart
- 197 Pionierkaserne Auf der Schanz Ingolstadt
- 207 Klinikum der Goethe-Universität Medizinische Einrichtungen und städtebauliche Verdichtung Frankfurt am Main
- 211 Kabinettsgarten der Residenz München
- 223 Stadtteilpark Haidenau München
- 227 Palais Holnstein Neugestaltung von Innenhof und Dachgarten München

- 235 **Wettbewerbe**
- 236 IBA Emscher Park Fortbildungsakademie Herne
- 238 Augustusplatz Leipzig
- 242 Rotteck-, Werder- und Friedrichring Freiburg
- 246 Platz der alten Synagoge Freiburg
- 248 Landesmesse Stuttgart
- 250 Würth-Kulturzentrum Garten und Parklandschaft Künzelsau
- 252 Spreebogen Berlin
- 254 Akropolismuseum Athen
- 256 Röthelheimpark Ehemaliges Armeegelände Erlangen
- 260 Güterplatz Frankfurt am Main
- 264 BMW-Werk Neubau Leipzig
- 268 Isar-Amper-Klinikum München-Ost Haar

- 271 **Weitere Projekte und Wettbewerbe 1970–2012**

- 278 Dank
- 279 Text- und Bildnachweis
- 280 Impressum

Contents

- 6 Biography
- 7 Foreword
- 8 The culture of open spaces and buildings – urban values
- 10 The city as living space
- 12 Trees – urban charm
- 14 The language of space
- 16 Landscape pictures
- 18 Social garden art
- 20 Gardens – the power of colour
- 22 Compositions

25 Projects

- 27 Zweites Deutsches Fernsehen Broadcasting Centre
  Mainz
- 41 Engelhalde Country Park
  Kempten
- 51 Westpark – IGA 83
  International Horticultural Show
  The transformation of a landscape
  Munich
- 99 Max Reger Congress Hall
  Weiden
  Upper Palatinate
- 103 Dritter Orden Clinic
  Munich
- 109 Main-Danube Canal
  Berching
- 123 Danube Weir
  Vohburg
- 129 Danube Glacis Bridge and Luitpoldpark Crossing
  Ingolstadt
- 139 University of Erfurt
  Development Planning
- 145 Ludwig Maximilian University
  Faculty of Chemistry and Pharmacy
  Institute for Molecular Biology
  Munich
- 151 Furniture store on Theresienhöhe
  Rooftop greening
  Munich
- 157 Postbank Paul-Heyse-Strasse
  Courtyards and rooftop greening
  Munich
- 163 Office building for Swiss Re Germany
  Unterföhring
- 175 Robert Bosch House
  Park renovation
  Stuttgart
- 187 Bosch House Heidehof
  The New Park
  Stuttgart
- 197 Pionierkaserne Auf der Schanz
  Ingolstadt
- 207 Goethe University Clinic
  Consolidation of medical facilities in an urban setting
  Frankfurt am Main
- 211 Kabinettsgarten of the Residenz
  Munich
- 223 Haidenau District Park
  Munich
- 227 Palais Holnstein
  Redesign of inner courtyard and roof garden
  Munich

235 Competitions

- 236 IBA Emscher Park
  Academy for Further Education
  Herne
- 238 Augustusplatz
  Leipzig
- 242 Rotteckring, Werderring, and Friedrichring
  Freiburg
- 246 Platz der alten Synagoge
  Freiburg
- 248 Trade Fair Centre
  Stuttgart
- 250 Würth Cultural Centre
  Garden and parkland
  Künzelsau
- 252 Spreebogen
  Berlin
- 254 Acropolis Museum
  Athens
- 256 Röthelheimpark
  Former military base
  Erlangen
- 260 Güterplatz
  Frankfurt am Main
- 264 New BMW Factory
  Leipzig
- 268 Isar Amper Clinic Munich East
  Haar

271 Further projects and competitions 1970–2012

- 278 Acknowledgements
- 279 Bibliographical references and photo credits
- 280 Imprint

Biographie
Biography

Peter Kluska, Landschaftsarchitekt in München, war nach dem Studium in Weihenstephan mit Praktikas bei Hans Luz in Stuttgart sechs Jahre Mitarbeiter und Büroleiter bei Walter Rossow in Berlin. Seit 1970 ist er freischaffender Landschaftsarchitekt mit Arbeitsschwerpunkten in der gestaltenden Objektplanung im urbanen sowie im ländlichen Raum und nahm erfolgreich an Wettbewerben teil. In diesem Buch werden 20 seiner realisierten Projekte und 12 Wettbewerbe dokumentiert und vorgestellt, ferner werden Themen wie Schönheit im öffentlichen Raum, Freiraumkultur und Baukultur behandelt.

Peter Kluska war sechs Jahre Mitglied der Stadtgestaltungskommission von München und Preisrichter in vielen Wettbewerben. Er ist Mitglied der Deutschen Akademie für Städtebau und Landesplanung, bekam Auszeichnungen und Wettbewerbspreise. 1977 gewann er den Wettbewerb für den Westpark in München, der Ort der Internationalen Gartenbauausstellung IGA 83 war. Für den Kabinettsgarten in der Münchner Residenz wurde ihm im Jahr 2003 die Ludwig I.-Medaille verliehen: »In Anerkennung für herausragende Verdienste um die Bayerischen Schlösser, Gärten und Seen.«

Er hielt Gastvorlesungen, u. a. 2006 in China bei Xiangrong Wang an der University of Forestry, Beijing.

Peter Kluska is a landscape architect based in Munich. After completing his studies in Weihenstephan, including practical training under Hans Luz in Stuttgart, Kluska worked for six years for Walter Rossow in Berlin as a member of staff and head of office. Since 1970, he has worked as a freelance landscape architect specialising in design and property planning in urban and rural settings. Kluska has participated successfully in a number of competitions. This publication presents twenty of his projects that have been implemented to date and twelve of the competitions that he has taken part in. It also looks at topics, such as beauty in the public space, open-space culture and building culture.

For six years, Peter Kluska was a member of the urban design commission for Munich, and he has also acted as a member of the jury in numerous competitions. He is a member of the German Academy for Town Planning and Rural Development (DASL), and has received various awards and competition prizes. In 1977, he won the competition for the design of Westpark in Munich, which provided the setting for the International Horticultural Show IGA 83. He was awarded the Ludwig I Medal in 2003 for the Kabinettsgarten in the Munich Residenz "in recognition of outstanding services to the Bavarian Palaces, Gardens and Lakes". Kluska's guest lectures have included a visit to China with Xiangrong Wang at the University of Forestry, Beijing in 2006.

Vorwort
Foreword

Freiraumkultur ist Ausdruck der Wertschätzung unbebauter, aber gestalteter Räume, was in einer sich zunehmend urbanisierenden Welt nicht hoch genug eingeschätzt werden kann. In der Verknüpfung der beiden Begriffe »Freiraum« und »Kultur« wird ein Spannungsbogen spürbar, der auf der einen Seite den Freiraum in seiner Gestaltung und Nutzung thematisiert, das Bewusstsein schärft für »Räume unter freiem Himmel« und auf einer zweiten Ebene auf die kulturell bestimmten, ganz unterschiedlichen Ausprägungen menschlichen Gestaltens und Aneignens ebendieser Freiräume hinweist.

Besonders freut mich, dass in dieser Werkschau des Landschaftsarchitekten Peter Kluska zwei Projekte breiten Raum einnehmen, die für die Bosch-Gruppe von herausragender Bedeutung sind, die Freiraumkultur im besten Wortsinn darstellen, ja noch um den Aspekt der Firmenkultur erweitern: Die Restaurierung des historischen Parks der ehemaligen Villa Bosch und die Schaffung eines neuen Parks anlässlich der Errichtung eines multifunktionalen Gebäudes, das den Namen Bosch-Haus Heidehof trägt. Ging es bei Letzterem um die Verknüpfung der von Peter Kulka entworfenen, die Traditionen der Moderne aufgreifenden Architektur mit der historischen Umgebung, war die Hauptaufgabe bei der anschließend realisierten Restaurierung des alten Parks, die teilweise verlorengegangene Qualität des Originals wiederzugewinnen und verschwundene Sichtbeziehungen wiederherzustellen. Entsprach das eine in klassischer Weise den Aufgaben, die sich typischerweise bei historischen Parkanlagen stellen, verlangte der neue Park gleichermaßen Kreativität und Einfühlungsvermögen. Beide Aufgaben wurden so überzeugend gelöst, dass hier ein einzigartiges Ensemble entstanden ist, bei dem die Verknüpfung von Vergangenheit, Gegenwart und Zukunft auf eine überraschende und gleichzeitig unaufdringliche Art und Weise gelungen ist.

Genauso wichtig wie das Erscheinungsbild ist der praktische Nutzen der Anlage, sei es für die Bedürfnisse der hier ansässigen Robert Bosch Stiftung, sei es für bereichs- und länderübergreifende Begegnungen im Rahmen interner Weiterbildungsveranstaltungen für Mitarbeiterinnen und Mitarbeiter, sei es für Empfänge, festliche Veranstaltungen oder Symposien des Konzerns. Eine Funktion, die diese Anlage bestens erfüllt. Man stelle sich nur einen warmen Sommerabend vor, an dem im Anschluss an ein Seminar noch bei einem Rundgang die Geschichte des Ortes lebendig wird, oder ein Buffet im Freien, das als Abschluss einer Veranstaltung die Teilnehmer zu weiteren Diskussionen animiert. Bei solchen Anlässen wird erlebbar, dass hier ein idealer Freiraum im Sinne des oben beschriebenen Spannungsbogens geschaffen wurde.

Franz Fehrenbach
Geschäftsführender Gesellschafter
Robert Bosch Industrietreuhand KG
Vorsitzender des Aufsichtsrats der
Robert Bosch GmbH

The culture of open spaces is an expression of the value we attach to spaces which have not been built on, but which have been planned and designed. In an increasingly urbanised world it is hard to overestimate the importance of such spaces. In the connection established between the two terms "open space" and "culture", we sense an arc of suspension. On one level, it addresses the question of the design and use of open spaces, increasing our awareness of "outdoor spaces" as such, and on a second level refers to the culturally determined, very different forms of man-made design and appropriation of these same open spaces.

I am especially delighted that in this exhibition of works by the landscape architect Peter Kluska, two projects which are of outstanding importance for the Bosch Group have been allotted a prominent place. They represent the culture of open spaces in the best sense of the word; indeed, they extend it by the aspect of corporate culture. They are the restoration of the historic park of the former Bosch Villa and the creation of a new park on the occasion of the construction of a multifunctional building, the Bosch House in Heidehof.

In the case of the latter project, it was a question of establishing the link between the architecture designed by Peter Kulka, which echoes the traditions of Modernism, and its historic surroundings. During the subsequent restoration of the old park, by contrast, the main task was to recreate the quality of the original, which had been partly lost, and to restore visual relationships which had disappeared. While that corresponded with the classic tasks typically involved in historic parks, the new park demanded above all both creativity and sensitivity.

Both tasks were solved so convincingly that the result is a unique ensemble, in which the interplay between past, present and future has been achieved in a surprising and at the same time subtle manner.

The practical use of the complex is just as important as the appearance, not only for the needs of the Robert Bosch Foundation which is located here, but also for the departmental and international encounters within the framework of internal education and training for company employees, including receptions, festive events or corporate symposiums. The complex optimally fulfils this function. We need only imagine a warm summer evening on which the history of the place comes alive during a stroll through the gardens after a seminar; or a buffet in the open air which inspires the event participants to continue their discussions. On such occasions, we can experience directly that here an ideal open space has been created in the sense of the arc of suspension described above.

Franz Fehrenbach
Managing Partner
Robert Bosch Industrietreuhand KG
Chairman of the Supervisory Board,
Robert Bosch GmbH

Freiraum- und Baukultur – Werte der Stadt

The culture of open spaces and buildings – urban values

Freiraumkultur und Baukultur gehören zu den höchsten Werten unseres Lebens. Sie bilden Lebensräume, die von allen Menschen, allen Altersgruppen sowie allen sozialen Schichten täglich genutzt werden und damit die größte soziale Gemeinschaftsebene demokratischen Lebens sind. Freiräume und Architektur sind die Sprache unserer Kultur, unserer kreativen Kräfte, sie lösen Empfindungen aus, Herzens- und Seelenimpulse, Freude und Wohlbefinden.

Fehlen diese Qualitäten der Gestaltung, der Schönheit, so kann das zu Unbehagen, zu sozialen Unruhen, zu Vandalismus und zu Depression führen. Daher ist es eine soziale Aufgabe und eine in die Zukunft weisende Verpflichtung, um die Schönheit und die Qualität der Stadträume täglich zu ringen. Das gilt auch für den ländlichen Raum in dem mit jeder Baumaßnahme die Gefahr besteht, das Landschaftsbild zu verändern, vor allem durch Gewerbegebiete mit mangelnder Durchgrünung. Mit dem Bau des Main-Donau-Kanals wurde eine landschaftsverändernde Trasse für die Schifffahrt in die Landschaft gelegt. In Berching gelang mit der Fuß- und Radwegbrücke über dem Kanal ein signifikantes Zeichen von Baukultur in der Landschaft.

The culture of open spaces and the culture of buildings are among the most valuable elements in our lives. They create living spaces which are used by everyone, every day, by people of all ages and of all social classes, and therefore represent the broadest social level of democratic life. Open spaces and architecture are the language of our culture, our creative strengths. They arouse emotions, impulses of heart and soul, joy and well-being.

If these qualities of design and beauty are missing, their absence can lead to unease, social unrest, vandalism and depression. Thus, it is a social duty and our duty to future generations to strive constantly for the beauty and quality of urban spaces. This also applies to rural spaces, in which each development project threatens to change the appearance of the landscape, especially through industrial estates with inadequate greening. With the construction of the Main-Danube Canal, a shipping route was laid through the countryside and changed it fundamentally. The bridge across the canal for pedestrians and cyclists in Berching is a successful example of building culture in the landscape.

Fuß- und Radwegbrücke über den Main-Donau-Kanal in Berching

The bridge across the Main-Danube Canal for pedestrians and cyclists in Berching

Lebensraum Stadt

The city as living space

Beim Besuch einer Stadt, die man noch nicht kennt, entsteht allmählich ein Bild, das sich aus vielen Wahrnehmungen zusammensetzt: Städtebau und Architektur, die Räume der Stadt, die Straßen, Plätze und Bäume. Die vielen Einzelbilder verdichten sich zu einem Stadtbild, in dem Schönheit lebendig wird. Die städtischen Strukturen sind wie die Partitur einer großen Komposition, an der schon viele geschrieben haben und viele weiterschreiben werden. Beim Durchwandern der Stadtlandschaft kommen Fragen auf: Wie lebt man in dieser Stadt? Gibt es eine Freiraumkultur? Ist es ein schöner Ort, wie fühlt man sich in seinen Räumen?
Die Werte der Stadt sind – neben der urbanen Substanz, den kulturellen Einrichtungen und der städtebaulichen Konzeption – die öffentlichen Freiräume, denn sie bringen ökologische Werte und sinnliche Freude in die Stadt, sozusagen »nachwachsende Energie« für ein nachhaltig positives Lebensgefühl.

When we visit a city which we are not yet familiar with, we gradually form a picture of it composed of a multiplicity of perceptions: town planning and architecture, the urban spaces, the streets, squares and trees. The numerous individual pictures become concentrated to form an image of the city in which the beauty comes alive. The urban structures are like the score of a great composition, to which many have already contributed and in which others will continue to write in the future. As we stroll through the city, we find ourselves asking questions: what is life like in this city? Does it have a culture of open spaces? Is it an attractive place; how does one feel in its spaces?
The values of the city – in addition to the urban substance, the cultural institutions and the design of the town planning – are its public spaces, because they supply environmental values and sensuous pleasure within the city, "renewable energy", as it were, for a sustainable and positive attitude towards life.

Stockholm, Innenhof des Rathauses. Freiräume und Architektur greifen ineinander, von Raum zu Raum entsteht ein neues Bild.

Stockholm, town hall courtyard. Open spaces and architecture are interconnected; a new picture arises as one moves from one space to another.

Bäume – der Charme der Stadt

Trees – urban charm

Die »Durchgrünung« einer Stadt hat einen besonders hohen Stellenwert, sie sorgt – überwiegend durch Bäume gebildet – für einen Aspekt der Lebenskultur. Diese sind nicht nur ein ökologischer Faktor, nicht nur städtebauliches Element, nicht nur Mittel für Raumstruktur und Proportionsausgleich innerhalb der Architektur, Bebauungen und Gewerbegebiete, sondern machen auch den Charme der Stadt aus, sind schönheits- und kulturbildende Elemente, die den Erlebniswert und das Wohlbefinden in einer Stadt wesentlich steigern können. Ohne Bäume wäre die Stadt ein Irrtum. Lebensqualität und sozialer Frieden breiten sich aus, wenn die Räume, die urbanen Freiräume, Orte der Schönheit, Orte der Begegnung und Orte kulturellen Lebens sind. Freiräume zu gestalten, Natur und Form in einer Konzeption zu vereinen, ist ein »Werdungsprozess«. Das Werk ist nie ganz fertig, die Entwicklung geht in Gegenwart und Zukunft weiter. Räume und Proportionsverhältnisse ändern sich, ebenso die Licht- und Schattenverhältnisse, Bäume werden größer. Die Pflege spielt eine entscheidende Rolle. Es muss allumfassend gedacht, geplant, gepflegt werden, damit die Schönheit einer Stadt wachsen und sich in Zukunft weiter entwickeln kann.

The "greening" of a city is extremely important. It is largely created by trees, and it guarantees one aspect of living culture. Trees are not only an ecological factor, not only an urban-planning element, not only a means to structure space and balance the proportions within architecture, building developments and industrial areas; trees also contribute to the charm of the city; they are elements that considerably enhance the experiential value and the feeling of well-being within a city. A city without trees would be a mistake. The quality of life and social harmony are more widespread when the spaces and urban spaces are places of beauty, places of encounter and places of cultural life.
Designing open spaces, uniting nature and form in a single plan, is a "work in progress". The work is never truly finished; the development spills over into the present and the future. The spaces and proportional relationships change, as do the relationships between light and shade; trees grow bigger. Maintenance plays a decisive role. The conception, planning and maintenance must take everything into account so that the beauty of a city can grow and continue to develop in the future.

Weinheim an der Bergstraße, zentraler Stadtplatz. Die Bäume bestimmen das Bild (*Sophora japonica*, dt.: Japanischer Schnurbaum). Eine heitere Atmosphäre unter dem Baldachin der Baumkronen entsteht.

Weinheim an der Bergstrasse, central square. The trees dominate the picture (*Sophora japonica*, Japanese pagoda tree), and their canopy creates a serene atmosphere.

Die Sprache des Raums

The language of space

Als ich zum ersten Mal durch den Park von Sanssouci ging – es war Mitte der sechziger Jahre, Potsdam war damals nur über große Umwege und mit Sondergenehmigung der DDR-Behörden erreichbar – wurde mir klar, welche Bedeutung die Raumbildung und das Raumerlebnis in einem Park haben. Die Weite, die in immer neue Raumbilder mit Bauwerken, Baumgruppierungen und der Wegeführung von Raum zu Raum gegliedert wird: Das ist eine große Komposition.

In diese Epoche der räumlichen Gestaltfindung, wie sie von Friedrich Ludwig von Sckell und Peter Joseph Lenné in Europa und von Frederick Law Olmsted in Amerika praktiziert wurde, verbreitete sich nicht nur der englische Gartenstil, sondern auch eine Kultur des Raums, der Raumfolgen, der rhythmischen Weite, der Verdichtung und der Offenheit, des Schattens und des Lichts. Diese Gestaltkompositionen erzeugen zeitlos schöne Raumbilder und Raumerlebnisse, ihr kultureller Wert wird auch in Zukunft von Bedeutung sein. Man kann in ihnen auch musikalische Merkmale entdecken, wie sie sich aus einem Hauptthema von Satz zu Satz weiterentwickeln und zu einer Komposition entfalten, von einer Idee über Variationen sich zu einem Ganzen zusammenfügen, aus dem die einzelnen Themen herausleuchten. Das ist Klang im Raum, Erlebnis im Sehen, sind Empfindungen, die übergreifen in die Welt der Künste, einen Beziehungszauber von Musik und Landschaft erzeugen.

I first strolled through the park of Sanssouci in the mid-1960s. At that time, Potsdam could only be visited by a very roundabout route and with the special permission of the GDR authorities. I realised at once how important the creation and the experience of space are in a park. The wide expanses are divided up into constantly new impressions of space with buildings, groups of trees and the paths leading from one space to another: the whole is a grand composition.

During that era of the creation of spatial design, practised by Friedrich Ludwig von Sckell and Peter Joseph Lenné in Europe, and by Frederick Law Olmsted in America, it was not only the English garden style which spread but also a culture of space – the sequence of spaces, the rhythmic expanses, the concentration and the openness, the shade and the light. These design compositions create timelessly beautiful spatial images and spatial experiences; their cultural value will continue to be important in the future, too. One can discover in them musical characteristics, in the way that they develop the main theme from movement to movement and unfold as a composition, from an idea through variations to form a whole in which the individual themes shine brightly. It is sound in space, experience in seeing, sensations which overlap into the world of the arts, generating a magical interplay between music and landscape.

Potsdam, Schlosspark Sanssouci. Bäume bilden die Räume. Im Hintergrund Schloss Charlottenhof in der Weite des Raums

Potsdam, Sanssouci Park. Trees form the spaces. In the background Charlottenhof Palace stands in the expanse of the landscape.

Landschafts-bilder
Landscape pictures

Im Landschaftspark Wörlitz erfährt man die große Weite des Raums, der sich mit fließenden Übergängen zur freien Landschaft öffnet. Park, Landschaft und Natur werden zu einem Ensemble, zu einem Gesamtkunstwerk. Wie andere Parks dieser Epoche wurde er zum historischen Erbe und ist auch heute noch Beispiel einer großartigen Freiraumkultur. Die Qualitäten der Raumbildung, die offenen Sichtachsen im Wechsel mit den Strukturen der freien Landschaft ermöglichen das Eintauchen in eine Erlebniswelt, in einen Beziehungszauber von Natur, Landschaft und Gartenkunst. Es sind Sinneseindrücke und Wahrnehmungen, die wie Kunst in Museumsräumen, wie Musik in Konzertsälen erfahren werden können – es sind die Kräfte der Lebensfreude und der sozialen Bildung.

José Antonio Abreu, Gründer der erfolgreichen Musikschulen in Venezuela, hat den Jugendlichen der Straßen- und Drogenszene mit Musik eine neue Lebensperspektive gegeben. Er sagte: »Die Welt der Schönheit, die Welt des Guten, und die Welt der Wahrheit sind unauflöslich miteinander verbunden. Der junge Mensch, der Zugang zur ästhetischen Seite des Lebens und seiner Umwelt hat, der hat auch Zugang zur ethischen Dimension des Daseins.«

In the country park at Wörlitz we can experience the vast expanse of space, which opens up and gives way gradually to the open countryside. Park, countryside and nature combine to form an ensemble, a *gesamtkunstwerk*. Like other parks of this period it has become part of our historic heritage and remains to this day an example of the magnificent culture of open spaces. The qualities of the space formation, the open visual axes alternating with the structures of the open countryside permit us to experience a world in which nature, countryside and landscape gardening form an enchanting symbiosis. These are sensuous impressions and perceptions which can be experienced like art in museum galleries or music in concert halls – the powers of joie de vivre and social culture.

José Antonio Abreu, founder of the successful music schools in Venezuela, gave young people from the streets and the drugs scene a new life perspective through music. He said: "The world of beauty, the world of goodness, and the world of truth are intrinsically linked. The young person who has access to the aesthetic side of life and his surroundings will also have access to the ethical dimension of existence."

Wörlitz, Landschaftspark. Park und freie Landschaft verschmelzen zu einem Gesamtkunstwerk. Bäume in Gruppen bilden die Park- und Landschaftsräume.

Wörlitz, country park. The park and the open countryside are fused together to produce a *gesamtkunstwerk*. Groups of trees create park and landscape spaces.

Soziale Gartenkunst
Social garden art

Die Gartenkunst des 21. Jahrhunderts sind die Gärten in der Stadt. Die neue Liebe zur Stadt, das Wohnen in der Stadt und die Verdichtung der Städte erfordern mehr und mehr freie Flächen, sie erfordern politisches, soziales und wirtschaftliches Engagement für Gärten, Parkanlagen, Grünzüge, aber auch für kleine und kleinste Inseln des Grüns, die sich durch Straßen ziehen, durch Wohn- und Gewerbegebiete, Akzente setzen durch Quartierparks. Und dabei darf nicht übersehen werden, dass auch große Freiflächen, Bürgerparks entstehen müssen. Ein derart vernetztes Mosaik an Grün- und Freiflächen muss nach wie vor Ziel einer sozialverantwortlichen Stadtbaukultur sein. Die Gärten unserer Zeit sind soziale Gartenkunst, die alle Menschen erreichen soll.

Es gibt eine Art von Sehnsucht nach Schönheit im öffentlichen Raum und Städte werden danach beurteilt. Ein Glücksfall für eine Stadt ist es, wenn auch private Initiativen einen Beitrag zur Vermehrung von Stadtqualität leisten.

Der Dirigent Claudio Abbado setzte ein Zeichen für die baumlose Innenstadt von Mailand. Für ein Engagement an der Scala verlangte er die Pflanzung von 500 Bäumen unter Verzicht auf sein Honorar. Ein weitsichtiger Impuls für das Erscheinungsbild und die Lebensqualität einer Stadt.

The garden art of the twenty-first century lies in town gardens. The new love of the town, of city living and the concentration of the cities demand increasing numbers of open spaces, demand political, social and economic commitment to gardens, parks, green spaces, and to small, even tiny, oases of green which are carried through streets, through residential and industrial areas, setting accents with district parks. Nor should we forget, however, that large open spaces, public parks, must also be created. The creation of an interconnected mosaic of green and open spaces must continue to be one of the aims of a socially responsible urban town planning. The gardens of our time are social garden art which should reach everyone.

There is a sort of longing for beauty in the public space, and cities are judged according to this criterion. Fortunate is the city in which private initiatives make a contribution to the increase of urban quality.

The conductor Claudio Abbado pointed the way in the treeless city centre of Milan. He agreed to appear at La Scala without payment in return for the planting of 500 trees. It was a far-sighted gesture for the appearance and quality of life in the city.

Stockholm, Zentrum. Ein Hain von Blütenbäumen (*Prunus sargentii 'Accolade'*, dt.: Zierkirsche) bildet das Grundgerüst für Stadtraumatmosphäre und somit für eine soziale Gartenkunst des 21. Jahrhunderts.

Stockholm, city centre. A grove of blossoming trees (*Prunus sargentii 'Accolade'*, flowering cherry) forms the basic framework for the atmosphere within the urban space and hence for "social garden art" in the twenty-first century.

Gärten – die Kraft der Farbe

Gardens – the power of colour

Die Schönheit von Gärten war für viele Maler Inspiration ihrer Werke. Angeregt von der Atmosphäre, dem Licht, den Farben und dem Raum malten sie Gärten. Kunstwerke entstanden, die ihren Ursprung in den Erscheinungsbildern der Gärten haben, das Gesehene war dabei gleichzeitig durchdrungen von Empfindungen, die übergingen in Kunst. Claude Monet, Camille Pissarro, Auguste Renoir, Vincent van Gogh und viele andere waren von diesen Bildern der Gärten und der Landschaft fasziniert, sie haben uns »Garten-Kunst« geschenkt, gemalte Gärten, die wir in den Museen bewundern können.

Van Gogh schrieb in einem Brief an seine Schwester: »Ich weiß nicht, ob Du verstehen kannst, dass man Poesie durch nichts weiter als durch gute Anordnung der Farben auszudrücken vermag, wie man Tröstendes durch Musik sagen kann. Das Bild soll nicht den Garten in seiner gewöhnlichen Ähnlichkeit wiedergeben, sondern ihn für uns nachzeichnen, wie im Traum gesehen, zugleich in seinem wahren Charakter und doch seltsamer als in der Wirklichkeit.«

Der Maler Giovanni Segantini formulierte seine Empfindungen mit den Worten »In meinen Werken ist das Sehen die natürliche Erfahrung des Lichts, hier erfüllt mich eine große Freude, meine Augen begeistern sich am Blau des Himmels, dem zarten Grün der Weiden und an der Farbe als harmonischer Schönheit.«

Many artists were inspired in their paintings by the beauty of gardens. Attracted by the atmosphere, the light, the colours and the space they painted gardens. Artworks were created whose origins lay in the appearance of gardens, but what the painters saw was also filled with emotions which were transformed into art. Claude Monet, Camille Pissarro, Auguste Renoir, Vincent van Gogh and many others were fascinated by these pictures of gardens and landscapes. They have given us "Garden Art", painted gardens which we can admire in museums.

Van Gogh wrote in a letter to his sister: "I don't know if you can understand that it is possible to express poetry through nothing more than an attractive arrangement of colours, just as you can say something comforting through music. The picture is not intended to portray the garden in its usual similarity, but to depict it for us as in a dream, both in its true character and yet stranger than reality."

The painter Giovanni Segantini described his feelings as follows: "In my works, seeing is the natural experience of light; here I am filled with great joy; my eyes are delighted at the blue of the sky, the delicate green of the meadows and colour as a harmonious beauty."

Keukenhof Holland. Bilder der Farbe und des Lichts leuchten und erfüllen den Betrachter in jedem Frühling neu: Es ist die Poesie der Bilder, die Kunst sind, das Sehen harmonischer Schönheit.

Keukenhof, Netherlands. Pictures of colour and light glow and delight the viewer anew every spring: It is the poetry of pictures that are art, the sight of harmonious beauty.

Kompositionen
Compositions

Musik und Gartenkunst haben das gemeinsame Ziel, die Menschen innerlich zu erreichen, zu bereichern, »Be-Geisterung« zu erzeugen. Den Beziehungszauber von Landschaft und Musik definierte der Dirigent Philippe Auguin mit den Worten »Bekannte Musik ist wie eine geliebte Landschaft, die man immer wieder gerne bereist, eine Reise durch diese Landschaft ist immer eine glückliche Balance zwischen Entdecken und Wiedererkennen. Die Italiener haben dafür vielleicht den besten Ausdruck, das Wort »sentire«, das heißt »zuhören-hören«, »empfinden-spüren«.
Diese Leidenschaft zu Musik und Landschaft lebt in allen Künsten, das Zuhören und Hören, das Empfinden und Spüren ist der Weg, den José Antonio Abreu meint, um die ästhetische Seite des Lebens zu erfahren und damit den Zugang zur ethischen Dimension des Daseins zu finden. Diese »Be-Geisterung« für die Künste ist ein Lebensimpuls, man darf nie aufhören, ihn zu suchen.

Music and garden art have the common aim of reaching men's souls, of enriching and delighting them.
The enchanting spell of landscape and music was defined by the conductor Philippe Auguin thus: "Familiar music is like a beloved landscape which we love to travel through again and again; a journey through this landscape is always a happy balance between discovery and recognition. The Italians have the best word for it, the word 'sentire', which means 'hearing oneself listening', 'feeling oneself experiencing'".
This passion for music and landscape exists in all forms of art: listening and hearing, feeling and experiencing is the path that José Antonio Abreu believes that we should follow in order to experience the aesthetic side of life and hence to access the ethical dimension of existence. This delight for the arts is the spark of life itself. We must never stop searching for it.

München, Seebühne im Westpark. Musik, Park, Kultur und Kunst: Das Münchner Kammerorchester spielt zur Eröffnung der IGA 83. Skulptur »Wasserfall« von Alf Lechner

Munich, Lakeside stage in the Westpark. Music, park, culture and art: The Munich Chamber Orchestra is seen playing at the opening of the IGA 83. Sculpture *Waterfall* by Alf Lechner

Projekte
Projects

Zweites Deutsches Fernsehen
Sendezentrum
Mainz
Zweites Deutsches Fernsehen
Broadcasting Centre
Mainz

Landschaftspark Engelhalde
Kempten
Engelhalde Country Park
Kempten

Westpark – IGA 83
Internationale Gartenbauausstellung
Metamorphose einer Landschaft
München
Westpark – IGA 83
International Horticultural Show
The transformation of a landscape
Munich

Kultur- und Kongresszentrum
Max-Reger-Halle
Weiden in der Oberpfalz
Max Reger Congress Hall
Weiden, Upper Palatinate

Klinikum Dritter Orden
München
Dritter Orden Clinic
Munich

Main-Donau-Kanal
Berching
Main-Danube Canal
Berching

Donaustaustufe
Vohburg
Danube Weir
Vohburg

Donau-Glacisbrücke und Querung
Luitpoldpark
Ingolstadt
Danube Glacis Bridge and Luitpoldpark
Crossing
Ingolstadt

Universität Erfurt
Entwicklungsplanung
University of Erfurt
Development Planning

Ludwig-Maximilians-Universität
Fakultät für Chemie und Pharmazie
Institut Molekularbiologie
München
Ludwig Maximilian University
Faculty of Chemistry and Pharmacy
Institute for Molecular Biology
Munich

Einrichtungshaus Theresienhöhe
Dachbegrünung
München
Furniture store on Theresienhöhe
Rooftop greening
Munich

Postbank Paul-Heyse-Straße
Innenhöfe und Dachbegrünung
München
Postbank Paul-Heyse-Strasse
Courtyards and rooftop greening
Munich

Bürogebäude der Swiss Re Germany
Unterföhring
Office building for Swiss Re Germany
Unterföhring

Robert-Bosch-Haus
Parksanierung
Stuttgart
Robert Bosch House
Park renovation
Stuttgart

Bosch-Haus Heidehof
Der neue Park
Stuttgart
Bosch House Heidehof
The New Park
Stuttgart

Pionierkaserne Auf der Schanz
Ingolstadt
Pionierkaserne Auf der Schanz
Ingolstadt

Klinikum der Goethe-Universität
Medizinische Einrichtungen und
städtebauliche Verdichtung
Frankfurt am Main
Goethe University Clinic
Consolidation of medical facilities
in an urban setting
Frankfurt am Main

Kabinettsgarten der Residenz
München
Kabinettsgarten of the Residenz
Munich

Stadtteilpark Haidenau
München
Haidenau District Park
Munich

Palais Holnstein
Neugestaltung von Innenhof und
Dachgarten
München
Palais Holnstein
Redesign of inner courtyard and
roof garden
Munich

Zweites
Deutsches
Fernsehen

Sendezentrum
Mainz

Zweites
Deutsches
Fernsehen

Broadcasting Centre
Mainz

Vom Acker zur Hochtechnologie: der Sendebetrieb des ZDF

Das Zweite Deutsche Fernsehen war nach seiner Gründung 1962 zunächst dezentral an mehreren Orten in Mainz und Wiesbaden verteilt. Der erste Intendant Kurt Holzhammer begann mit dem Aufbau einer zentralen Sendeanstalt in Mainz-Lerchenberg. Das 100 Hektar große Grundstück, das die Stadt Mainz bereitstellte, war bis dahin landwirtschaftlich genutzt worden. Das baumlose Gelände bildete eine leichte Kuppe mit Weitsicht nach Wiesbaden und auf die Höhenzüge des Taunus.
Die Planungsaufträge für den ersten Bauabschnitt wurden 1967 an Johannes Krahn für die Architektur, an Hellmut Schubert für die Verkehrserschließung und an Walter Rossow für die Landschaftsplanung erteilt. Die städtebauliche Konzeption, die Verkehrserschließung, das Bebauungskonzept und die Freiraumplanung wurden unter Mitwirkung von Peter Kluska gemeinsam erarbeitet. Ziel war ein weiträumiges, offenes Erscheinungsbild für eine Sendeanstalt des öffentlichen Rechts, die sich einer demokratischen Gesellschaft verpflichtet fühlt.
Die ersten Baumaßnahmen 1971 beinhalteten einen großflächig angelegten Erdbau, die Sicherung des Oberbodens und den Abtrag der Geländekuppe für ein ebenes Baufeld, das für einen langfristigen Bebauungsprozess ausgelegt war. Für die Freiraumplanung wurde das Prinzip der linearen Gliederung der umgebenden Felderteilung aufgegriffen und nach innen übertragen. Dieses Ordnungsprinzip stand auch Pate für die Vorgabe der Positionierung der Bauten im ersten Bauabschnitt mit Verwaltungshochhaus, Filmtechnik, Kantine und Ü-Wagen-Station.
Die Einbindung einer großen Anzahl von Parkplätzen für Mitarbeiter und Gäste sowie die räumliche Gliederung der Freiflächen durch Baumpflanzungen folgte diesem linearen Prinzip. Mit alternierenden Baumreihen, Hainen und offenen Räumen entstand eine wechselvolle Raumwirkung von intimer Gartenstimmung bis hin zum offenen Landschaftsbezug.
1976/77 wurde mit dem zweiten Bauabschnitt begonnen, für die Freianlagenplanung wurde auf Empfehlung von Walter Rossow Peter Kluska beauftragt. Die Architektengruppe Stieldorf war mit einem Rundbau, der drei Sendestudios beinhaltete, als Sieger aus einem Wettbewerb hervorgegangen. Das wichtigste Gebäude, das den Sendebetrieb ermöglicht, fand einen durch Form und Fassadenfarbe ganz eigenständigen Ausdruck innerhalb des baulichen Ensembles ZDF.
Die Architektursprache hatte sich mit diesem Bauabschnitt geändert und damit auch die Freiraumplanung in seinem Umfeld. Darin war ein Freiraumstudio zu integrieren, der sogenannte Sommergarten, von dem aus Sonntags-Matineen live gesendet werden.
Im Rahmen von Kunstwettbewerben wurden Skulpturen ausgewählt und in das Freiraumkonzept integriert, darunter Arbeiten von Otto Herbert Hajek, Goepfert/Hölzinger, Ursula Sax, Ernst Joseph Stahl und Otto Wesendonck. Sie bilden zusammen mit den Arbeiten von Matschinsky-Denninghoff und Horst Antes das Ensemble »Kunst im ZDF«. So wurde in mehrjähriger Bauzeit aus einer baumlosen Agrarfläche eine Komposition aus Bauten, aus Freiräumen, Bäumen und Hainen, die eine Kultur des Raums bilden, in dem verwaltet, gearbeitet, kreativ gestaltet und technisch geschaltet wird.

———————

Projektbeteiligte
Walter Rossow, Landschaftsarchitekt, Berlin
Johannes Krahn, Architekt, Frankfurt
Heinz Laubach, Architekt, Frankfurt
Helmut Schubert, Verkehrsplaner, Hannover
Sendebetriebsgebäude:
Planungsgruppe Stieldorf, Architekten
Fritz Eichler, Leiter der Bauabteilung

From farmland to high technology: the ZDF broadcasting centre

Founded in 1962, Zweites Deutsches Fernsehen was initially scattered across various locations in Mainz and Wiesbaden. The first director, Kurt Holzhammer, initiated the establishment of a central broadcasting institute in Mainz-Lerchenberg. The site provided by the City of Mainz extended across 100 hectares and had been used for agricultural purposes up to that time. The treeless plot of land formed a gentle hill affording views of Wiesbaden and the peaks of the Taunus in the distance.
In 1967, the planning contracts for the first building phase were awarded to Johannes Krahn for the architecture, to Hellmut Schubert for the traffic infrastructure and to Walter Rossow for the landscape planning. The urban planning design, traffic infrastructure, land-use concept and open-space planning were developed jointly in cooperation with Peter Kluska. The aim was to create a spacious, open appearance for a public-service broadcasting institute committed to serving democratic society.
The first building measures in 1971 included extensive earthworks. These were designed to preserve the topsoil while levelling the raised ground in order to produce a flat site for a long-term building process. The open-space planning for the site copied the principle of linear segmentation evident in the division of the surrounding fields. This organising principle was also the basis for the guidelines governing the position of the buildings during the first building phase, which included the administrative block, the film technology building, the canteen and the parking spaces for the outside broadcasting vans.
The inclusion of a large number of parking spaces for staff and visitors as well as the spatial subdivision of the open spaces through the planting of trees followed this linear principle. The alternating rows of trees, copses and open spaces resulted in a varied spatial impact – reminiscent of a private garden which was integrated into the open countryside.
The second building phase began in 1976/77. Upon the recommendation of Walter Rossow, Kluska was commissioned to plan the open spaces. Stieldorf the architects had won the competition with their design for a round building containing three broadcasting studios. In both its form and façade colour, the ZDF's most important building for broadcasting purposes thus acquired its own independent character within the architectural ensemble.
The architectural language changed with this building phase, and accordingly, so, too, did the open-space planning in its vicinity. An open-air studio was to be integrated here, the so-called Summer Garden, from which matinees were to be broadcast live on Sundays.
Art competitions were held and sculptures selected for integration into the open-space concept. They included works by Otto Herbert Hajek, Goepfert/Hölzinger, Ursula Sax, Ernst Joseph Stahl and Otto Wesendonck. Together with the works by Matschinsky-Denninghoff and Horst Antes they form the ensemble "Art at ZDF".
Over the course of several years, a building project thus transformed treeless farmland into a composition of buildings, open spaces, trees and copses which together create a culture of space in which people carry out administration, work, produce creative designs and operate the latest technology.

———————

Project Team
Walter Rossow, landscape architect, Berlin
Johannes Krahn, architect, Frankfurt
Heinz Laubach, architect, Frankfurt
Helmut Schubert, traffic planner, Hanover
Broadcasting centre:
Planungsgruppe Stieldorf, architects
Fritz Eichler, head of the building department

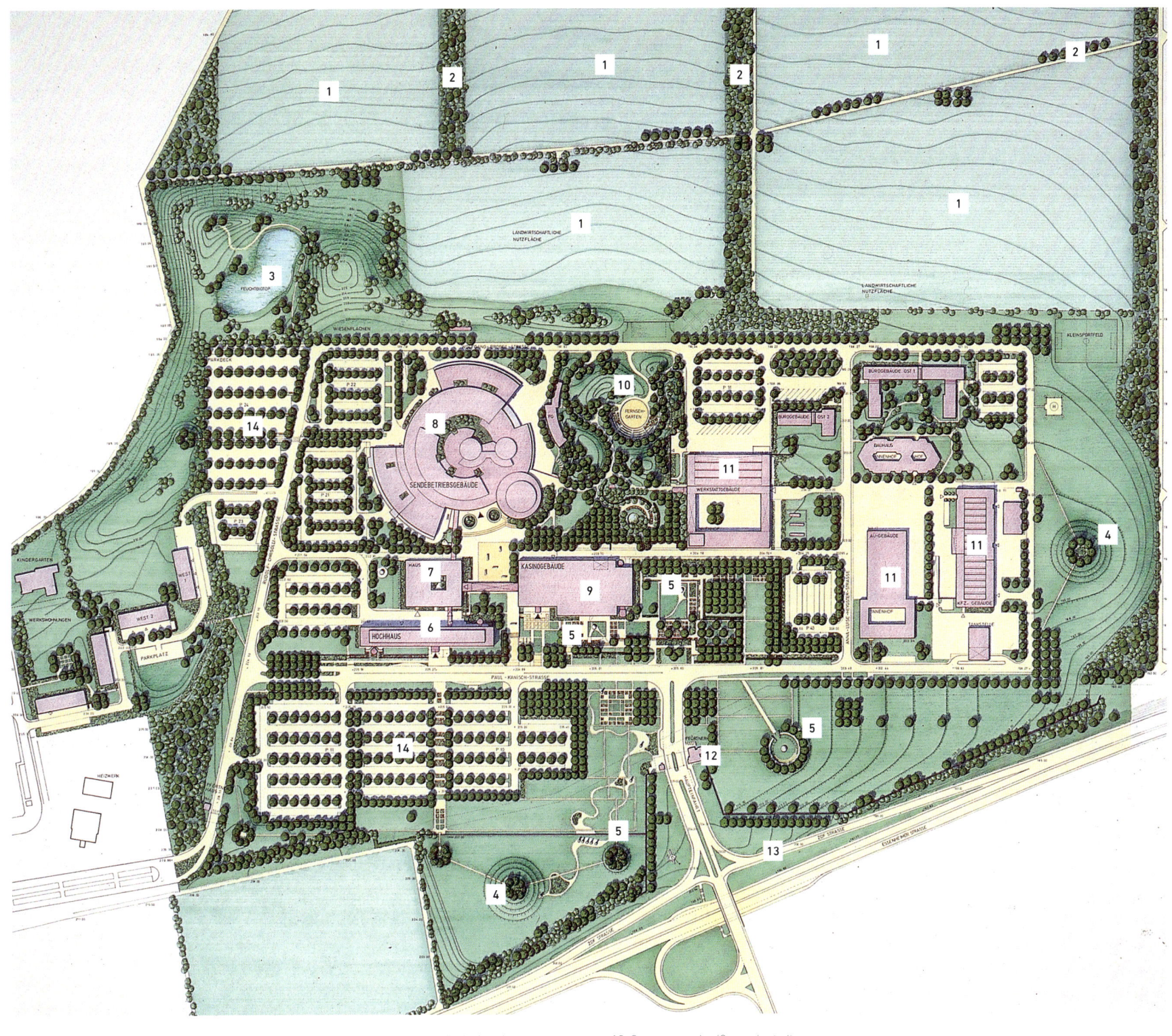

1 Landwirtschaftliche Nutzung	10 Sommergarten/Open-Air-Studio	1 Agricultural use	10 Summer garden/Open-air studio
2 Windschutzhecken	11 Technik/Ü-Wagen	2 Hedges forming windbreaks	11 Technology/Outside broadcast vehicles
3 Feuchtbiotop	12 Pforte	3 Wetland biotope	12 Gate
4 Baumhügel	13 Zufahrt	4 Forested hill	13 Access road
5 Kunst	14 Mitarbeiterparkplätze	5 Art	14 Staff car park
6 Hochhaus, Verwaltung		6 High-rise, administration	
7 Technik/Schnitt		7 Technology/Cutting	
8 Sendebetriebsgebäude		8 Broadcasting building	
9 Kantine		9 Canteen	

Linke Seite oben: Gesamtgelände: 100 Hektar, davon ca. 60 % landwirtschaftliche Nutzung im Norden, Feldwege, Obstbäume, Windschutzhecken
Linke Seite unten: Lineare Gliederung des Geländes analog zu den vorhandenen Feldstrukturen außen, im Innenbereich Verdichtung der Raum- und Flächenstrukturen zu Park- und Gartenräumen

Left top: Total site area: 100 hectares, of which about 60 % is used for agriculture in the north, country paths, fruit trees, hedges as windbreaks
Left bottom: Linear division of the site, which mirrors the shape of the fields beyond; on site, concentration of spatial and areal structures to create park and garden areas

Kunstprojekt Landmarke »Wolken« von Matschinsky-Denninghoff, Komposition aus Stahl im Dialog mit Bäumen und Landschaft

Right: Art project landmark: *Wolken* (clouds) by Matschinsky-Denninghoff; composition of steel in dialogue with the trees and landscape

Kunst im ZDF: »Platz der Köpfe«, Skulpturengruppe, Horst Antes

Art at ZDF: *Platz der Köpfe* (Place of Heads), sculpture group, Horst Antes

Erbauung

Als visuelles Medium besitzt das Fernsehen eine besondere Nähe zu allem Optischen, Bildhaften und also auch zur Bildenden Kunst. Speziell das künstlerische Herz- oder Kopfstück des ZDF-Sendezentrums, der »Platz der Köpfe« von Horst Antes, als Verbindung von Hochhaus und Sendebetriebsgebäude, von Verwaltung und Technik, Programmentwicklung und Programmausstrahlung, steht symbolisch für die Verbindung beider Organisationsbereiche: »Es sind Köpfe – von innen und von außen gesehen. Es sind Köpfe mit Inhalten, offene Köpfe, bewohnbare Köpfe. Sie sind transparent zu den sie umgebenden Bauten«, beschreibt der Künstler selbst seine Grundabsicht.

Analog sollten in der modernen Mediengesellschaft die Köpfe der Zuschauer offen sein für die Vielzahl der Ein- und Ausblicke sowie die Vielfalt der Informationen und Visionen von Fernsehbildern, die über das Auge Einlass und gelegentlich auch Wohnung in uns finden.

Auch wenn gerade die zeitgenössische Kunst, die durch die Kunst-Initiativen des ZDF mitgefördert werden soll, manchem Betrachter ein gewisses Kopfschütteln verursachen kann, so legen es die für das ZDF ausgewählten Werke nicht auf irgendeine Anstößigkeit oder Provokation an, im Gegenteil: Durch den kritischen Umgang mit unkonventionellen, ungewohnten Formen und Bildern soll der Betrachter nicht abgestoßen, sollen vielmehr seine Phantasie, aber auch sein Verständnis und seine Toleranz angestoßen werden. Kultur ist nicht, wenn man Kunstwerke besitzt, sondern wenn diese auch in unseren Köpfen arbeiten und unser Einfühlungs- oder auch Urteilsvermögen beleben.

Dieter Stolte
Intendant des ZDF

Edification

As a visual medium, television has a special affinity with everything visual, pictorial and, of course, with the fine arts. In particular, the artistic heart of the ZDF broadcasting centre, the *Platz der Köpfe* (Place of Heads) by Horst Antes, forms the link between the high-rise and the broadcasting office, the administration and the technology, the programme development and programme broadcasting. It represents symbolically the link between the two areas of the organisation. The artist described his basic intention thus: "They are heads – seen both from the inside and from the outside. They are heads with content, open heads, inhabitable heads. They are transparent to the buildings which surround them."

In the same way, in a modern media society the heads of the viewers should also be open to the countless insights and views, as well as the wealth of information and visions provided by the television pictures which we take in through our eyes and then sometimes absorb.

The modern art in particular, which is also fostered by the art initiatives of ZDF, may cause some viewers to shake their heads. Nonetheless, the works selected for ZDF were not chosen with the express purpose of upsetting or provoking anyone. On the contrary: the intention is not to offend the viewer with the critical study of unconventional, unfamiliar forms and pictures, but rather to encourage him to bring his imagination, his understanding and his tolerance into play.

Culture is not a matter of possessing artworks, but arises rather when they make us think and when they spark off our sensibilities and our sense of judgement.

Dieter Stolte
Director of ZDF (1982–2002)

»Platz der Köpfe« (Detail), Skulpturengruppe, Horst Antes

Platz der Köpfe (Place of Heads; detail), sculpture group, Horst Antes

Landmarke »Wolken«, Skulpturengruppe, Brigitte und Martin Matschinsky-Denninghoff

Landmark *Wolken* (Clouds), sculpture group, Brigitte and Martin Matschinsky-Denninghoff

»Licht-Wasser-Objekt« (Detail), Hermann Goepfert und Johannes Peter Hölzinger

Licht-Wasser-Objekt (Light-Water Object; detail), Hermann Goepfert and Johannes Peter Hölzinger

»Spiralzeichen«,
Otto Wesendonck

Spiralzeichen (Spiral Sign), Otto Wesendonck

»Rotation«,
Ursula Sax

Rotation,
Ursula Sax

Rechte Seite: Die Entwicklung der ZDF-Parklandschaft nach 25 Jahren

Right: The development of the ZDF parkland setting after 25 years

Sendebetriebsgebäude
Architekten:
Gruppe Stieldorf
- Technischer Sendeablauf
- drei Großraumstudios
- Nachrichtenstudio
- Fernsehtechnik
- Redaktionsräume
- Filmarchiv
- Programmabwicklung

Broadcasting building
Architects:
Gruppe Stieldorf
- Technical broadcasting procedures
- Three large studios
- News studio
- Television technology
- Editorial department
- Film archive
- Programme implementation

Rechte Seite: »Sommergarten«, Open-Air-Studio für sommerliche Live-Sendungen. In der Ferne das Rheingau und die Berge des Taunus

Right: *Sommergarten* (Summer Garden), open-air studio for live broadcasts in summer. The Rheingau and the Taunus mountains can be seen in the background.

Landschaftspark Engelhalde
Kempten

Engelhalde Country Park
Kempten

Die Heilung einer landschaftlichen Wunde

Auf einem ca. 20 Hektar großen Gelände, unmittelbar hinter dem Hochufer der Flusshangkante der Iller wurde über Jahrzehnte Kies abgebaut. Es entstand eine riesige Kiesgrube mit 12 bis 15 Meter hohen steilen Abbrüchen: ein unwirtliches Gelände, ein Loch in der Landschaft, abgeschieden hinter der Iller-Hangkante und ohne jeglichen Bezug zur Stadt.

Ein Landschaftspark sollte daraus werden, der Stadtrat hatte beschlossen, die erste Bayerische Landesgartenschau 1984 unter Einbeziehung der Stadträume und Plätze auf diesem Gelände zu realisieren. Ein offener Wettbewerb für den Park mit Schwimmbad wurde zusammen mit Architekt Peter Seifert gewonnen. Nach Monaten langer Diskussionen entschied der Stadtrat, die Landesgartenschau doch nicht durchzuführen, aber den Park zu realisieren und lediglich den Bau des Schwimmbads zurückzustellen.

Das entscheidende Merkmal dieser erfolgreichen Arbeit war die Öffnung der Iller-Hangkante mit Sichtbeziehung zur Stadt und mit neuer Fußwegverbindung zum Fluss. Das war ein gewagter Eingriff in die Landschaftsstruktur der Flusslandschaft, es war aber auch die einzige Möglichkeit, den neuen Park mit der Stadt in Verbindung zu bringen. Nach intensiver Höhenlinienplanung für das neue Relief wurden die steilen Kieswände an den Rändern weitläufig ausmodelliert, ein Quellbach an tiefster Stelle zu einem Teich ausgeweitet, Tal- und Höhenwege zu einem Erholungswegenetz gestaltet. So wurde aus der landschaftlichen Wunde wieder ein artifizielles Stück Allgäuer Landschaft, ein viel genutzter Park.

Projektbeteiligte
Peter Seifert, Architekt, München, Vorentwurf Schwimmbad (nicht realisiert)

A wound in the landscape is healed

For many years, gravel was quarried on a site measuring about 20 hectares immediately behind the fluvial terrace along the edge of the river bank of the Iller. The result was a vast gravel pit with steep sides of 12 to 15 metres in height: an inhospitable place, a gaping scar in the landscape, tucked away behind the river bank and without any connection to the town.

It was to become a landscape park. In 1984, the town council had decided to stage the first Bavarian Garden Show on this site, also incorporating the urban spaces and squares. A public competition for the park including a swimming pool was won in cooperation with the architect Peter Seifert. After months of protracted discussions, the town council decided not to hold the garden show after all, but nonetheless to create the park. Only the construction of the swimming pool was postponed.

The main characteristic of this successful project was the opening of the Iller incline to provide a visual link with the town, together with a new footpath linking it to the river. It was a daring intervention in the structure of the river landscape, but it was the only possible way of connecting the new park to the town. After intensive planning of the contours for the new profile the steep gravel walls were extensively reshaped along the edges, a spring at the lowest point was widened to create a pond, and footpaths along the top and bottom were laid out to form a network of leisure paths. In this way, the scar on the landscape was transformed into a stretch of Allgäu countryside again, a popular and much used park.

Project Team
Peter Seifert, architect, Munich, preliminary design for swimming pool (not realised)

Lageplan, Planungsstand 1984. Modellierung und neue Raumbildung waren das Planungsziel.

Site plan showing the layout in 1984. The planning aims were landscaping and the creation of new spaces.

Eine ausgeräumte, 12 Meter tiefe Kiesgrube an der Hangkante zur Stadt war die Ausgangssituation für einen neuen Park: Steilhänge und keine Bäume.

An empty gravel pit 12 metres deep on the slope side towards the town was the starting point for the new park: steep slopes and no trees.

Die Öffnung zur Stadt war die entscheidende Grundidee zum Wettbewerbserfolg.

The opening up of the site towards the town was the fundamental idea behind the successful competition entry.

Mit Hilfe der Reliefplanung und Modellierung, den Bäumen und Baumgruppen, den Wasserflächen und einer neuen Raumbildung wurde aus der Kiesgrube ein Landschaftspark.

By planning the relief and contouring, as well as adding trees, copses, areas of water and new open spaces the gravel pit was transformed into a country park.

Rechte Seite: Planungsstand Entwurf 1982 – Relief- und Höhenlienienplanung. Eine sehr differenzierte Höhenplanung mit 1-Meter-Höhenlinien war die Grundlage für das neue Relief im Park.

Right: Layout sketch of 1982 showing the planning of the relief and the contouring. The basis for the relief within the park was detailed planning of the contours using one-metre contour lines.

Spielen unter Bäumen, spielen am Wasser – Licht und Halbschatten erzeugen eine heitere Atmosphäre im Park.

Playing beneath the trees, playing by the water – light and half-shade create a cheerful atmosphere in the park.

Rechte Seite: Menschen im Park unter Bäumen im Schatten. Das musikalische Thema *ombra mai fu* von Georg Friedrich Händel wurde hier zu einem realen Motiv.

Right: People in the park in the shade of the trees. The musical theme "Ombra mai fu" by George Frideric Handel assumes real form here.

Westpark – IGA 83

Internationale
Gartenbauausstellung
Metamorphose
einer Landschaft
München

Westpark – IGA 83

The International
Horticultural Show
The transformation of a
landscape
Munich

Urteil der Jury

Aus dem Wettbewerbsprotokoll vom 10. Februar 1977, 1. Preis

Eine Tallandschaft als Gesamtidee ist überzeugend und wird über beide Teile des Wettbewerbsbereiches hinweg konsequent durchgehalten. Hier wird ein gesteigertes Landschaftserlebnis geboten, das in seiner Eigenart unverwechselbar ist. Diese Arbeit ist in der formalen, gestalterischen und künstlerischen Qualität herausragend.
Die Bodenmodellierung ist in Verbindung mit den Pflanzungsvorschlägen ausgezeichnet gelöst und unterstreicht die Raumbildung konsequent, ohne sich in Details zu verlieren. Die konsequente Verwendung von zwei Vegetationsformen, nämlich den hochstämmigen wegebegleitenden Bäumen und Gruppen und den geschlossenen Gehölzpartien ist sehr gut.
Die Einordnung der Wasserflächen im westlichen Teil im Kontrast zur raumbildenden Erdmodellierung entspricht in der formalen Durchbildung dem Gesamtkonzept. Hervorzuheben ist der Erlebnisgehalt der durch Wege erschlossenen Wasserflächen.
Die baulichen Anlagen ordnen sich wohltuend in das landschaftsplanerische Gesamtkonzept ein. Das gilt im besonderen Maße für das Restaurant, das sowohl in seiner Lage und Erreichbarkeit als auch in der Zuordnung zu den Freiräumen gut situiert ist. Der Rahmen für eine IGA-Nutzung ist wie selbstverständlich vorgegeben.

Projektbeteiligte
zuständig für den temporären Ausstellungsteil Mollgelände:
Eckart Brülle, Landschaftsarchitekt, Technischer Leiter IGA-Baubüro
Gottfried und Anton Hansjakob, Landschaftsarchitekten, München
Büro Brunken, Landschaftsarchitekten, Stuttgart, Rosengarten
Ortrun Wippermann, Landschaftsarchitektin, München, Kräuter- und Apothekergarten
Gerhardt Teutsch, Landschaftsarchitekt, München, Staudengarten
Buro Stern, Landschaftsarchitekten, Zürich, Farntal und Feuchtbiotop
Klaus Wittke, Landschaftsarchitekt, München, Koordination Ostasiatischer Gärten
Projektteam FKC, Spielplatz Regenbogen
Obermeyer Ingenieurbüro München, Fußgängerbrücke über den Mittleren Ring (Auszeichnung Deutscher Betonpreis)
Bruno Leipacher, Landschaftsarchitekt, Kleingartenanlage
Paul Lutz, Landschaftsarchitekt, Spielplatz »am Jackl« (westlicher Parkteil)
Werkmeister Martin Heimer, Landschaftsarchitekt, Hannover, Wasserspielplatz (östlicher Parkteil)
Karl Kagerer, Otto-Albrecht Bertram, München, Landschaftsarchitekten, Bauerngarten am Bayerwaldhaus

The Jury's Verdict

From the minutes of the competition of 10 February 1977, First Prize

A valley landscape as the overall idea is convincing and is pursued consistently across both sections of the competition site. It offers an enhanced scenic experience which is unique in character. The work is outstanding in form, design and artistic quality.
The design for the terrain in connection with the planting suggestions offers a very satisfactory solution. It underlines the space creation logically without losing itself in details. The consistent use of two forms of vegetation, the trees bordering the paths and planted in groups and the denser groups of shrubs has been planned very well.
The arrangement of the expanses of water in the western part in contrast with the space-creating contouring of the ground corresponds with the overall concept in its formal design. Special mention should be made of the experiential value of the areas of water, which are linked by paths.
The buildings fit in harmoniously within the overall landscape concept. This applies in particular to the restaurant, which is very well placed both as regards location and accessibility.
The framework of use for the IGA is provided in a most straightforward manner.

Project Team
in charge of the temporary exhibition section on Moll site:
Eckart Brülle, landscape architect, Technical Manager IGA-Baubüro
Gottfried and Anton Hansjakob, landscape architects, Munich
Büro Brunken, landscape architects, Stuttgart, rose garden
Ortrun Wippermann, landscape architect, Munich, herb and medicinal herb garden
Gerhardt Teutsch, landscape architect, Munich, herbaceous borders
Buro Stern, landscape architect, Zurich, ferns and wetland biotope
Klaus Wittke, landscape architect, Munich, coordination East Asian Garden
FKC project team, Rainbow play area
Obermeyer Ingenieurbüro Munich, pedestrian bridge over the Mittlerer Ring (German Concrete Prize)
Bruno Leipacher, landscape architect, allotments
Paul Lutz, landscape architect, play area "am Jackl" (western section)
Foreman Martin Heimer, landscape architect, Hanover, water playground (eastern section)
Karl Kagerer, Otto-Albrecht Bertram, Munich, landscape architects, cottage garden in Bayerwaldhaus

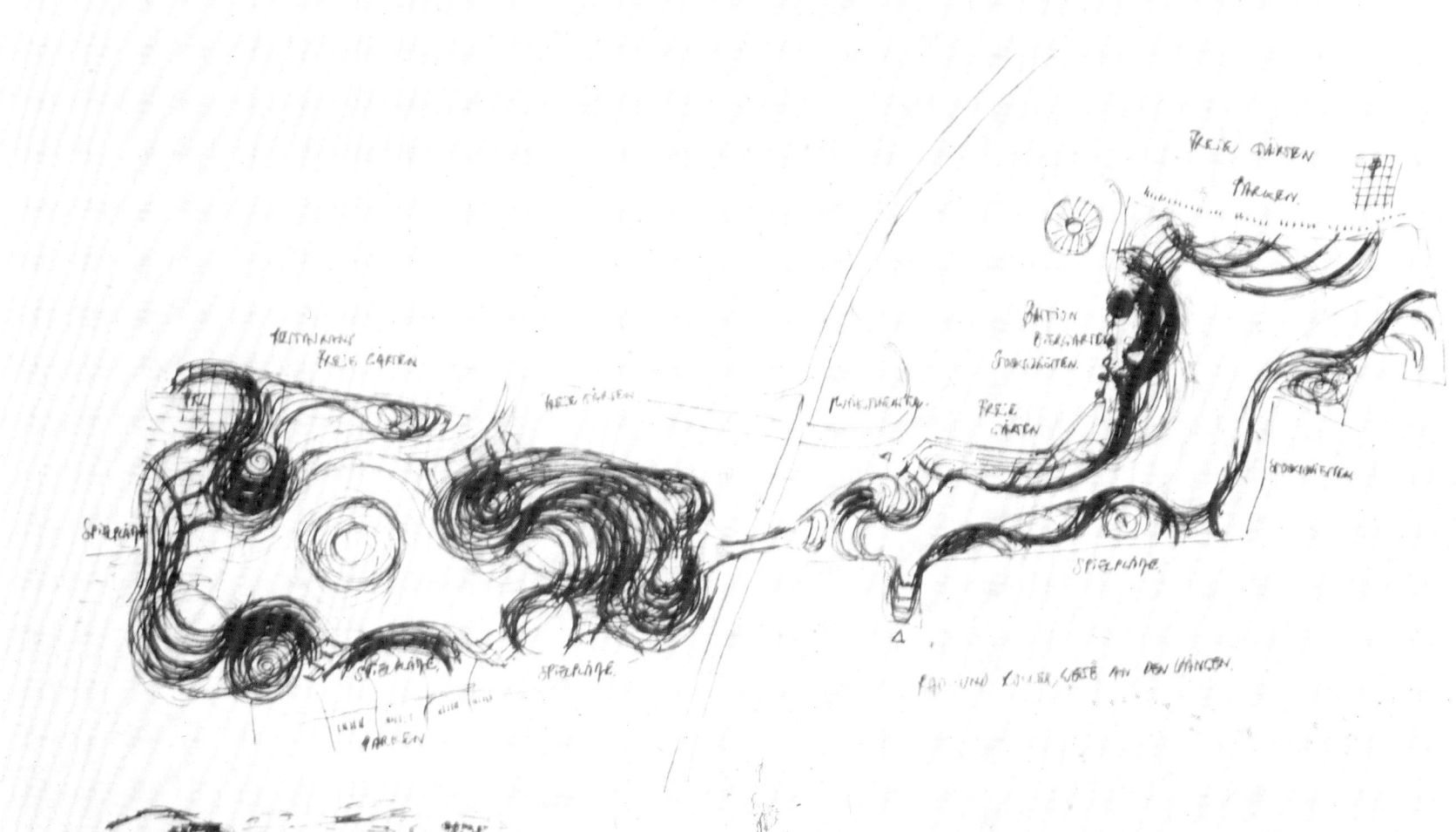

Die erste Skizze

The first sketch

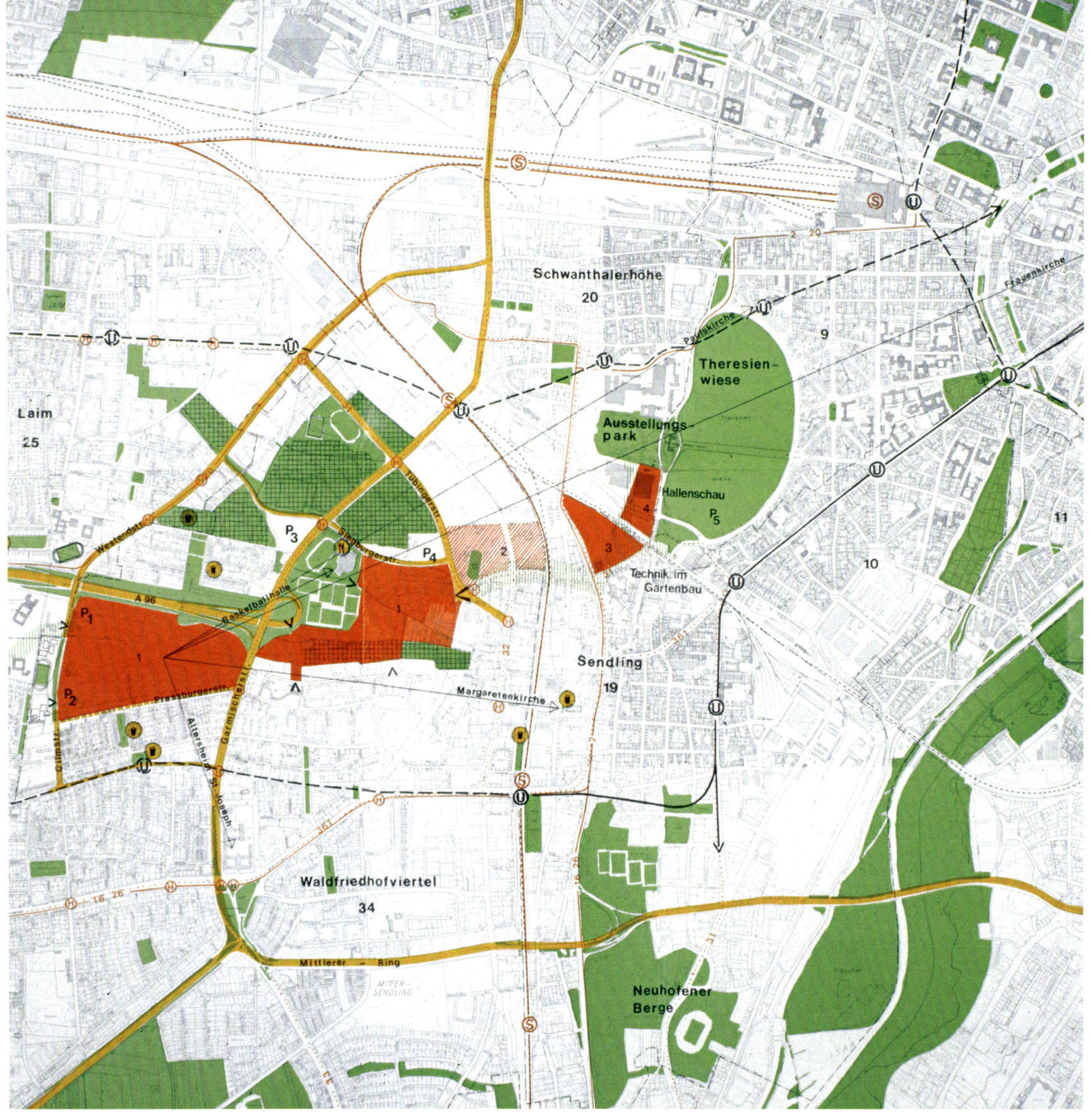

Linke Seite: Städtebauliche Position des Parks im Westen der Stadt mit Verbindung zur Innenstadt

Left: The location of the park in the west of the city with connections to the city centre

Das Gelände 1977 vor Baubeginn: vollständig ebene städtebauliche Restflächen ohne Bäume

The site in 1977 before construction started: a completely flat urban wasteland without trees

Entstehungsdokumentation

1976 wurde der Wettbewerb für den Park ausgeschrieben. 60 Hektar Fläche waren in zwei Teilen zu bearbeiten, die über den Mittleren Ring hinweg miteinander verbunden werden sollten. Sie waren auf beiden Seiten vollständig eben, mit einer hohen Lärm-, Abgas- und Feinstaubbelastung. Es gab auf dem gesamten Gelände mit zwei alten Eichen auf der Ostseite nur zwei Bäume. Ein ehemaliger Kiesabbau hatte ein ausgedientes Kiesquetschwerk hinterlassen, dazu kamen eine Restgrube und Brachflächen, außerdem ein letztes Feld der ehemaligen Landwirtschaft.

Die Inspiration zu diesem Park entstand am Fensterplatz eines Flugzeugs, das sich im Landeanflug auf den Flughafen Riem befand. Ganz unerwartet tauchte unter mir das Wettbewerbsgelände auf, die heterogenen Stadtstrukturen, die Verkehrsstränge vom Mittleren Ring und der Autobahn nach Lindau. Während der kurzen Betrachtung der Situation von oben war die Idee einer Tallandschaft entstanden, einer Einheit von Raumbildung und Lärmschutz. Noch am Abend, unmittelbar nach der Landung, entstand im Büro die erste Skizze, die am nächsten Morgen auf dem Gelände kritisch überprüft wurde. Beim Abstieg in einen kleinen Teil noch nicht verfüllter Kiesgrube wurde es immer stiller. Es war die Bestätigung der Idee einer Tallandschaft, die den Lärm bei gleichzeitiger Erhöhung der Ränder ausgrenzen konnte.

Damit begann eine intensive Höhenlinienplanung, um eine prägnante Erdskulptur zu erarbeiten, eine modellierte Gesamtkomposition, mit Absenkungen von 8 und Aufschüttungen von bis zu 17 Höhenmetern. Neben den Wettbewerbsplänen war auch ein Modell im Maßstab 1:1000 gefordert. Dieses Modell mit 2 Metern Länge war bestens geeignet, die Planungsidee der Tallandschaft räumlich sichtbar werden zu lassen.

Am 10. Februar 1977 entschied sich die Jury des Gestaltungswettbewerbs einstimmig für diese Tallandschaft. Das Jury-Mitglied Richard Boedecker brachte seine Begeisterung für den Entwurf mit den Worten »Dann steh' ich auf dem Berge und Schau ins Paradies« zum Ausdruck. Damit war der erste Preis besiegelt.

Nach einjähriger Planung markierte im Januar 1978 der erste Spatenstich den Baubeginn einer faszinierenden Umwandlung des völlig ebenen Geländes in eine neue Raumgestalt. Der Präsident des ZVG-Zentralverbands Gartenbau, Karl Ley, sagte später immer wieder in einer Mischung aus Staunen und Bewunderung, er hätte nicht gedacht, dass diese große Umwälzung des Geländes möglich sei. 12 000 Höhenpunkte wurden auf der Grundlage meiner Höhenplanung nach X-, Y- und Z-Achsen eingemessen und ausgesteckt, damit 1 Million Kubikmeter Boden bewegt und das Relief so ausgeformt werden konnten.

Mit der Reliefveränderung und der Realisierung der großzügigen Talräume, der Seitentäler, der Abfolge von Räumen, der Hierarchie von breiten Talwegen, Höhenwegen und schmalen Bergwegen, der Wasserflächen in den Talsenken, mit diesen Prinzipien wurden die Grundstrukturen für ein sehr differenziertes Nutzungspotential gelegt. Die waldartigen Baumpflanzungen an den Rändern, die wegebegleitenden Bäume und die freien Gruppierungen von Einzelbäumen sollten die Raumbildung noch verstärken sowie die Nutzungsräume definieren.

Mit dem ehemaligen Mollgelände, das im Osten des Parks die temporären Teile der Gartenschau, vor allem den Gärtnermarkt aufnehmen sollte, kam nach einem Wettbewerb noch ein weiterer Baustein der IGA hinzu, den die Kollegen Gottfried und Toni Hansjakob gestalteten. Das Planungsbüro Obermeyer übernahm die technische Ausarbeitung meines Brückenvorschlags über den Mittleren Ring, der mit dem Deutschen Betonpreis ausgezeichnet wurde. Der Torbogen des Künstlers Otto Leismüller wurde zu einer ergänzenden Bereicherung und zu einem Zeichen zwischen den beiden Parkteilen.

Damit waren auch die Voraussetzungen für eine erfolgreiche Bewerbung um die IGA 83 geschaffen.

The construction documentation

The competition for the park was announced in 1976. An area extending over 60 hectares was to be dealt with in two sections which were to be linked together across the Mittlerer Ring. Both sections were completely flat and were badly polluted by noise, exhaust fumes and particulate matter. There were only two trees on the entire site: two old oaks on the east side. Since gravel had previously been quarried here, there was an obsolete gravel crushing station, together with the remains of a pit and abandoned areas, as well as one last field from the former farmland.

The inspiration for the park came as I was sitting looking out of a plane window on its descent towards Munich's former airport at Riem. Unexpectedly the competition site appeared beneath me, together with the heterogeneous structures of the city, the traffic arteries of the Mittlerer Ring and the motorway to Lindau. This brief glimpse of the location from the air was what made me think of a valley landscape, a unity of space creation and noise insulation. That very evening, immediately after landing, I sat down in my office and produced the first sketch, which I then appraised critically the next morning on site. As I climbed down into a small section of gravel pit which had not yet been filled in, things became progressively quieter. It was an endorsement of my idea of creating a valley landscape which could block out the noise if the edges were raised at the same time. That marked the start of a detailed period of planning the contours in order to create a distinctive sculptural earthwork, a three-dimensional overall composition, by lowering the level of the land by up to eight metres and carrying out earthfill works of up to 17 metres. In addition to the competition plans, we were also required to produce a model to the scale of 1:1,000. The model was two metres long and represented an ideal way of demonstrating the planning idea of a valley landscape visually and spatially.

On 10 February 1977 the competition jury decided unanimously in favour of this valley landscape. Voicing his enthusiasm for the design, one member of the jury, Richard Boedecker, said that it would be like looking into Paradise. The first prize was a foregone conclusion.

After a year's planning, the ground-breaking ceremony in January 1978 marked the beginning of the construction phase. It was fascinating to see the completely flat site take on its new form. The president of the central gardening association (ZVG), Karl Ley, said later – with a mixture of amazement and admiration – that he would never have thought that such a complete realignment of the site was possible. 12,000 triangulation points were measured out and positioned along their X, Y and Z axes on the basis of my contour planning; one million cubic metres of earth were moved in order to create the desired relief.

The changes in relief and the formation of the spacious lowland areas, the side valleys, the sequence of spaces, the hierarchy of broad paths through the valleys and along the hilltops, the narrow mountain paths and the expanses of water in the hollows provided the basic structures for a varied range of uses. The planting of trees around the edges like a forest, the trees bordering the paths and the random groups of individual trees were intended to underline the creation of spaces as well as define the purposes to which the spaces were to be put.

Following another competition, a further section of the IGA was added on the former Moll site on the eastern side of the park, which was chosen to house the temporary parts of the Horticultural Show, such as the gardener's market. My colleagues Gottfried and Toni Hansjakob were in charge of the design. The Obermeyer planning office was responsible for the technical design of the bridge I suggested over the Mittlerer Ring; it was subsequently awarded the German Concrete Prize. The archway by the artist Otto Leismüller complemented and enhanced the design, becoming a symbol of the link between the two parts of the park. We had thus fulfilled the requirements for a successful application for the IGA 83.

Rechte Seite: Eben, baumlos, lärmüberflutet, ohne Räumlichkeit: das Gelände vor Baubeginn

Right: Flat, treeless, noisy, without three-dimensionality: the site before construction

baumgruppe

stelen aus granit

58

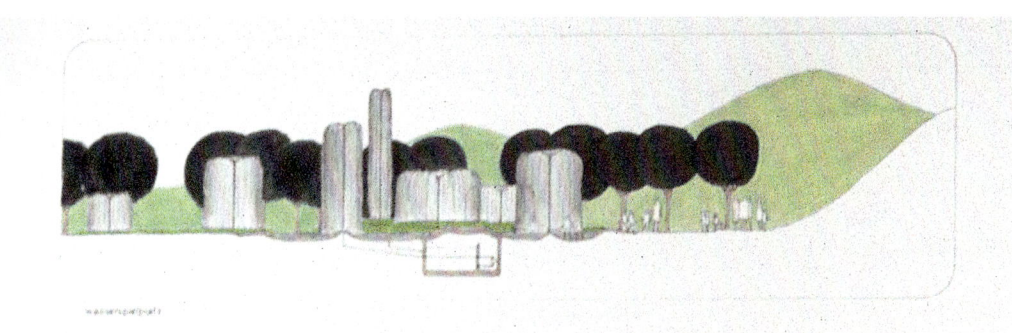

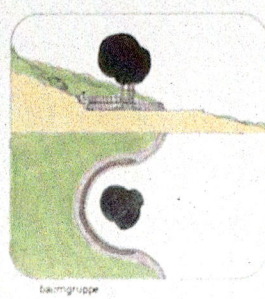

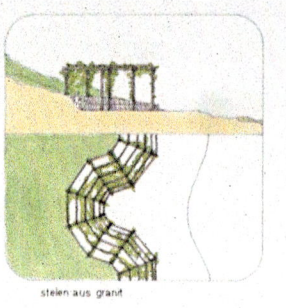

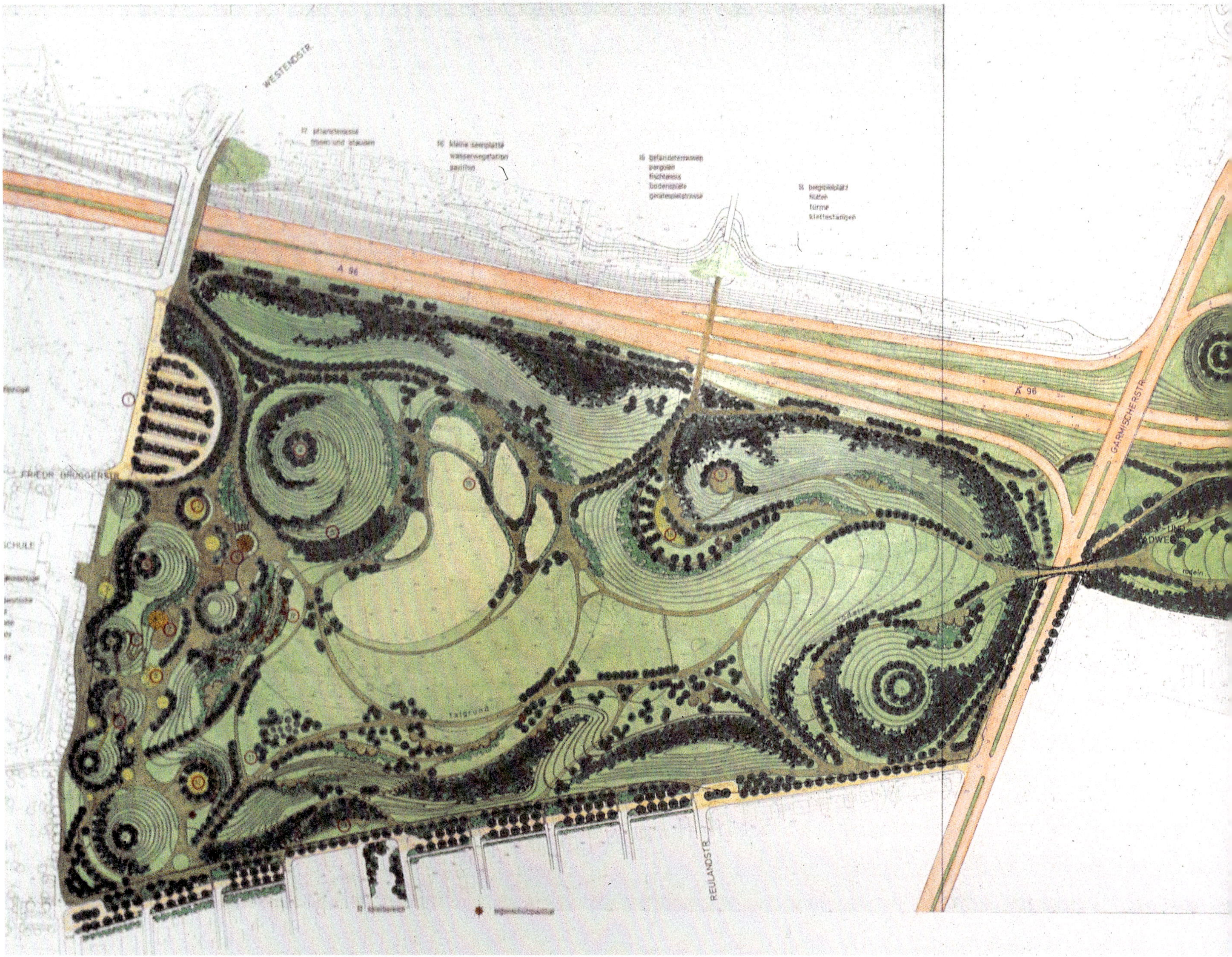

Wettbewerbsplan, 1977, die Vision einer Tallandschaft

Competition plan, 1977: the vision for a valley landscape

Wettbewerbsmodell, Maßstab 1:1000, westlicher Teil

Competition model; model to the scale of 1:1,000, western section

Entwurfsmodell, Maßstab 1:500: Die Idee der Tallandschaft mit Seitentälern wird sichtbar.

The draft model to the scale of 1:500 visualises the idea for a valley landscape with tributary valleys.

Entwurfsplanung Daueranlage, mit Seebühne im Westen und Erdkegel in der Autobahnschleife

Draft planning: Permanent installations with lakeside theatre in the west, and earth cone in the motorway bend

Höhenplanung mit 1-Meter-Höhenlinien. Insgesamt 12 000 Messpunkte für das Relief und 6000 Höhenpunkte für die Standorte der Bäume wurden auf XYZ-Achsen festgelegt und eingemessen.

Contour planning with one-metre contour lines. A total of 12,000 measuring points for the relief and 6,000 altitude points for the location of the trees were determined using XYZ axes and then surveyed.

Im Januar 1978 begann die Umwandlung des Geländes mit dem Aushub und den ersten Aufschüttungen.

The transformation of the site began in January 1978 with the excavation and the start of the earthfill works.

Der Erdbau auf dem Westgelände: Bodenabtrag minus 8 Meter, Bodenauftrag plus 17 Meter, Bodenbewegung von insgesamt 1 Million Kubikmeter, Umformung des ebenen Geländes zu einer Erdskulptur und Raumstruktur

The earthworks on the western site: Soil was removed to a depth of 8 metres and deposited to a height of 17 metres. A total of one million cubic metres of soil were moved and the site was reshaped to create an earth sculpture and space structure.

Rechte Seite: Die Ausformung des Geländes wurde zu einem sehr wirksamen Lärmschutz. Hinter dem Hügel verläuft die Autobahn A96 mit gewaltigem Lärm, der ausgeblendet wurde. Die ersten Bäume sind angekommen.

Right: The contouring of the site proved a very effective noise protection measure. Behind the hill, the A96 motorway roars past. The first trees have arrived.

Winterliche Poesie im Park 1980

Wintry poetry in the park, 1980

Fortschreitende
Baustelle mit
Reliefausformung und
Baumpflanzungen

Progress on the building
site with the contouring
of the landscape and
the planting of trees

Ausstellungsplan, Studie 3, IGA 83, Grundlage zur Integration der IGA-Themen

1 Autobahn A96 Lindau
2 Restaurant am Rosengarten
3 Rosengarten
4 Spielplatz West
5 Staudengarten
6 Internationale Gärten
7 Kneippgarten
8 Biergarten Ost mit Sommerstockbahn
9 Seecafé
10 Sommerblumen
11 Farntal
12 Feuchtbiotop
13 Spielplatz Regenbogen
14 Sardischer Garten
15 Große Spielzone Ost
16 Rhododendrontal
17 Kleingartenanlage
18 Gärtnermarkt
19 Übergang Mollgelände

Exhibition plan, Study 3, IGA 83, basis for integration of the IGA themes

1 A96 motorway towards Lindau
2 Rose Garden restaurant
3 Rose garden
4 Western play area
5 Herbaceous garden
6 International gardens
7 Kneipp garden
8 Eastern beer garden with summer curling pitch
9 Lakeside café
10 Summer flowers
11 Fern valley
12 Wetland biotope
13 Play area Rainbow
14 Sardinian garden
15 Large play area (east)
16 Rhododendron valley
17 Allotments
18 Gardeners' market
19 Crossing point Moll site

Eröffnung,
28. April 1983

Opening,
28 April 1983

Impressionen des IGA-Sommers

Am 28. April 1983 eröffnete der damalige Bundespräsident Karl Carstens den Park und die IGA. Nach der Eröffnungsfeier begann der erste offizielle Rundgang. Mit dabei waren der bayerische Ministerpräsident Franz Josef Strauß, der Oberbürgermeister von München Erich Kiesel sowie Minister des Kabinetts.

Das Konzept, den Park mit der Ausstellung zu verflechten, hat sich als richtig erwiesen, bei den Besuchern war ein großes Staunen und Begeisterung zu vernehmen, 50 000 Besucher kamen bereits am ersten Tag. Auch die Presse war voll des Lobes: »die Münchner sind ganz verliebt ins Blumenparadies«, schrieb die AZ. Der Münchner Merkur frohlockte: »München ist um ein Juwel reicher«. 11 Millionen Besucher wurden gezählt, damit war das Westpark-IGA-Ereignis die erfolgreichste Gartenschau, die es je gab.

Zu dem Erfolg der IGA haben natürlich sehr viele kreative Menschen beigetragen. Der Planungsstab der IGA, meine Mitarbeiter im Büro und der Bauleitung, die Büros der Kollegen, die Einzelthemen zur IGA geplant haben, die Mitarbeiter aus dem damaligen Gartenamt, die Firmen des Garten- und Landschaftsbaus, die vielen Gärtner und ganz am Anfang die Erdbaufirmen. Sie alle zu nennen, ist in diesem Rahmen nicht möglich. Ihnen allen zu danken ist mir aber ein großes Anliegen. Namentlich erwähnen möchte ich die Gartenamtsdirektoren Joseph Wurzer und Ernst Rupp, den damaligen Präsident des ZVG Karl Ley und meinem Kollegen im Planungsteam der IGA Eckhart Brülle. Ihnen sei in Würdigung ihrer Verdienste und der guten Zusammenarbeit besonders gedankt.

Nach der IGA dankte mir der Oberbürgermeister Georg Kronawitter bei einer Schlussveranstaltung mit den Worten: »Der Landschaftsarchitekt Kluska war ein Glücksfall für uns«.

Impressions of the IGA summer

On 28 April 1983, the President of the Federal Republic, Karl Carstens, opened the park and the IGA. After the opening ceremony the first official tour of the park began. The dignitaries included the Prime Minister of Bavaria Franz Josef Strauss, the Lord Mayor of Munich Erich Kiesel, and various cabinet ministers.

The idea to integrate the park into the exhibition turned out to be the right one. The design was received with admiration and enthusiasm; 50,000 visitors came on the first day. The press was also full of praise: "The citizens of Munich have fallen in love with their floral paradise," wrote the *Abendzeitung*, Munich's local evening newspaper. The *Münchner Merkur* commented gaily: "Munich can boast another jewel". A total of eleven million visitors attended the IGA in Westpark, making it the most successful Horticultural Show ever.

Of course, a lot of highly creative people contributed to the success of the IGA. They included the planning team of the IGA, the members of staff at my office and the building contractors, my colleagues and their staff who planned individual themes at the IGA, not to mention the staff members of the parks and gardens department of the time, the horticultural and landscape gardening firms, the countless gardeners and, at the beginning, the earthwork contractors. It is not possible to name them all here, but I should very much like to thank them all. I should, however, like to mention in particular the directors of the parks and gardens department, Joseph Wurzer and Ernst Rupp, the president of the ZVG Karl Ley and my colleague Eckhart Brülle in the planning team of the IGA. I should like to pay tribute to their achievements and thank them for the congenial cooperation.

At the closing ceremony, after the IGA, I was touched when the Lord Mayor of Munich, Georg Kronawitter, thanked me in his speech and said: "We were very fortunate to have the landscape architect Peter Kluska".

Der Westpark am
Tag der Eröffnung
der IGA 83

Westpark on the day
of the opening of the
IGA 83

Linke Seite: Die Sehnsucht nach grünen Räumen

Left: The longing for green spaces

11 Millionen Besucher kamen

11 million visitors came to the IGA 83.

Impressionen eines IGA-Sommers

Impressions of an IGA summer

Der vertikale Garten: Gedanken über den Westpark

Beim Münchner Westpark war es wie bei vielen anderen Glücksfällen der (Garten-)Architektur: Je schlechter die Rahmenbedingungen für ein Haus oder – in diesem Fall – einen Park sind, desto triumphaler ist der Erfolg, wenn das Gebaute die widrigen Umstände vergessen lässt, ja wenn die Planer aus den Zwängen heraus zu ganz außergewöhnlichen Lösungen vorstoßen, die unter normalen Voraussetzungen nie angedacht worden wären.

Der Westpark und die IGA 83 wurden, als 1976 der Wettbewerb für sie ausgeschrieben wurde, in eine extrem ungünstige stadträumliche Situation hineinprojiziert. Doch dem Sieger des Wettebewerbs, dem Münchner Landschaftsarchitekten Peter Kluska, ist es gelungen, die Schikanen des Geländes so zu beantworten, dass etwas ganz Eigenes, Charakteristisches, ja Unvergleichliches entstehen konnte, das dem Unort hohe räumliche Qualitäten abgewinnt. Heute, 23 Jahre nach der Eröffnung des Parks, kann man die gestalterischen Ideen, da sie von der nachgewachsenen Natur überformt sind, als subtile Landschaftsereignisse genießen, ohne an die Gewaltsamkeit der ursprünglichen »Bodenarbeit« erinnert zu werden. Ja an einigen Aussichtspunkten auf dem nördlichen Hang des Westteils kann man sich, wenn man in das Tal mit dem See und dem gegenüberliegenden Waldhang hinunterschaut, der Illusion hingeben, dass die künstliche Senke tatsächlich ein Stück Ländlichkeit, ein natürlich gewachsenes Stück Tal in einer süddeutschen Hügellandschaft sei.

So kann man ein Fazit ziehen: Fast alle Parks, die anlässlich von nationalen oder internationalen Gartenschauen in Deutschland angelegt wurden, haben nach der Herausnahme der Schau-Attraktionen viel von ihrem Reiz verloren. Bei Kluskas Münchner Westpark ist es genau umgekehrt.

Kluska ist es also gelungen, die unschönen Zwänge des Geländes mit einer Steigerung des räumlichen Ausdrucks zu kompensieren, wie es unter normalen Bedingungen kaum möglich gewesen wäre. Ja er hat unter dem Druck der Verhältnisse vertikale Dimensionen in die sonst fast ausschließlich der Horizontalen verpflichtete Gartenkunst eingeführt. Sein künstlicher Talpark mit den bewaldeten wulstigen Rändern kann also sicher nicht als Vorbild für Grünanlagen in anderen – normalen – städtischen Situationen dienen, doch wie Kluska die räumlich eingeschränkten Parkteile durch Bodenmodellierungen partiell verdichtet und so in der Mitte vor allzu dichter Bestückung bewahrt hat, das ist in der reichen Geschichte der Park- und Gartenschau-Planungen in der Bundesrepublik ohne Beispiel.

Gottfried Knapp
Redakteur der Süddeutschen Zeitung

The vertical garden: thoughts about Westpark

Westpark in Munich was like many other strokes of luck in garden and building design: the worse the framework conditions for a house or – in this case – a park are, the more triumphant is the success, when the finished result makes one forget the unfavourable circumstances, indeed when the planners overcome the constraints to arrive at extraordinary solutions which no one would ever have thought of under normal circumstances.

When the competition was announced in 1976, Westpark and the IGA 83 were projected onto an extremely unfavourable urban location. But the winner of the competition, the Munich landscape architect Peter Kluska, succeeded in countering the fickleness of the site in such a way that something unique, characteristic, even incomparable was created, something that extracted remarkable spatial qualities from this non-place.

Today, 23 years after the opening of the park, we can enjoy the creative ideas, transformed by the continued growth of nature, as subtle landscape features without being reminded of the violence of the original "groundwork". Indeed, from some viewpoints on the northern slope of the western section, as you look down into the valley with its lake and the wooded slope on the other side, you can even allow yourself to be carried away by the illusion that the artificial hollow is actually a piece of rural landscape, a naturally formed valley section in a hilly landscape in South Germany.

We can draw a conclusion, too: almost all the parks created in Germany on the occasion of national or international horticultural shows, have tended to lose much of their charm once the event attractions have been removed. In the case of Kluska's Westpark in Munich, the very opposite is true.

Kluska succeeded in compensating for the unattractive constraints of the site by increasing the spatial expression, something which would scarcely have been possible under normal conditions. Indeed, under the force of circumstances he introduced vertical dimensions into the landscape gardening, which is otherwise largely a horizontal art. His artificial valley park with its forested uneven edges can certainly not serve as a model for green spaces in other – normal – urban situations, yet the way in which Kluska partly condensed the spatially restricted sections of the park by contouring the ground, thereby preserving it in the middle from too great a density, is unparalleled in the extensive history of park and horticultural show planning in the Federal Republic.

Gottfried Knapp,
Editor, Süddeutsche Zeitung

Rechte Seite: Der Park als grüne Erdskulptur. Modellierte Höhen und Tiefen bilden Räume der Regeneration.

Right: The park as a green earthwork sculpture, the moulded hills and valleys creating spaces for regeneration.

| IGA – Rückbauplan – Erhaltungsbereiche, Übernahme in das Dauerkonzept | 1 Parkplatz
2 Restaurant
3 Rosengarten
4 Spielzone West
5 Seebühne
6 Ostasiatische Gärten
7 Bauernhaus | 8 Biergarten
9 Seecafé
10 Wasserlauf
11 Farntal
12 Feuchtbiotop
13 Spielplatz
14 Sardischer Garten | 15 Große Spielzone Ost
16 Rhododendron und Azaleen
17 Kleingärten | IGA – Renaturation plan – Areas to be retained, adoption into the permanent concept. | 1 Parking space
2 Restaurant
3 Rose garden
4 Play area (west)
5 Lakeside stage
6 East Asian garden
7 Farmhouse | 8 Beer garden
9 Lakeside café
10 Water course
11 Fern valley
12 Wetland biotope
13 Play area
14 Sardinian garden | 15 Large play area (east)
16 Rhododendron and azaleas
17 Allotments |

83

Landschaft zum Aufatmen – Menschen im Park

Nach der Gartenschau blieben dem Park die wertvollsten Gartenschaubeiträge – die Rosen- und Staudengärten, das Ensemble asiatischer Gärten, die Spielzonen und die Seebühne – erhalten. Das führte zu einer Aufwertung des Parks durch ein breit gestreutes Interesse der Besucher und damit zu sozialer Balance.
Es gibt keine Interessenkonflikte, sondern ein Nebeneinander von Rosen- und Staudengärten mit Biergärten, das Spielen auf den großen Wiesenflächen, Fußball, Volleyball, Drachensteigen, die Meditations- und Gymnastikgruppen, die hier täglich üben, stören sich nicht. Familien verschiedener Nationalitäten verbringen den ganzen Tag im Park, sie essen und trinken miteinander. Es sind andere Menschen als die Restaurantbesucher. Zwei große Spielzonen sowie ein Spieltal mit Bachlauf sind immer von Kindern besetzt. Auf der Seebühne gibt es Musik, Theater und Open-Air-Kino. Nach Zählungen ist der Westpark der meistbesuchte städtische öffentliche Garten in München, seine Beliebtheit ist groß, er zeigt, dass Schönheit und Raumerlebnisse zum friedlichen Neben- und Miteinander gehören, zur bewussten oder unbewussten Freude, die ein Park seinen Besuchern bieten kann. Das Miteinander und die Begegnungen der Menschen sind die Werte dieser multikulturellen »Parkgesellschaft«. Es ist ein Park für alle.
Was für die meisten Besucher der IGA 83 noch nicht richtig vorstellbar war, das sieht man jetzt, fast drei Jahrzehnte später. Es ist die geplante räumliche Dimension, die, durch den Wuchs der Bäume entstanden ist und sich noch weiterentwickeln wird.
Wer diesen Park besucht, verlässt die Stadt und taucht in die Räume des Parks ein, die, wie vorhergesagt wurde, für ein paar Stunden ein kleines Paradies der Erholung sind.

Landscape for leisure moments – people in the park

After the Horticultural Show the most valuable contributions to the show – the rose garden and shrub garden, the ensemble of Asian gardens, the play areas and the lakeside theatre – were all retained. They enhanced the park by providing a wide range of interesting features for visitors, thereby creating a social balance.
There are no conflicts of interest; the rose and shrub gardens exist side by side with the beer gardens. Games take place on the large expanses of lawn: football, volleyball and kite-flying. The meditation and gymnastics groups who practise here daily do not interfere with each other. Families of various nationalities spend entire days in the park, eating and drinking together. They are different groups from those who visit the restaurants. There are always children to be seen in the two large play areas and the play valley with its stream. Music, drama and open-air cinema performances take place in the lakeside theatre.
Surveys indicate that Westpark is the most popular public municipal garden in Munich. It is so popular because it demonstrates that beauty and the experience of space are part of the peaceful coexistence, and contribute to the conscious and unconscious joy which a park can offer its visitors. The coexistence and encounters of these people are the values propagated by this multicultural "park society". It is a park for everyone.
For most visitors to the IGA 83 it would have been hard to imagine, but almost three decades later we can see the results of the planned spatial dimension which has been created by the growth of the trees; it is a development which will continue in the future, too.
Those who visit this park and allow themselves to be immersed in its spaces will experience the way it becomes a miniature paradise for a few hours – which was how it was seen from the start.

Seite 85–87: Menschen im Park. 25 Jahre nach der IGA

Pages 85–87: People in the park. 25 years after the IGA

25 Jahre Westpark – Interview mit Radio Lora

Gespräch mit Ulrich Schneider, Leiter der Hauptabteilung Gartenbau im Baureferat München, und Wolfgang Czisch, Stadtrat und Mitglied des Preisgerichts, sowie Peter Kluska, Landschaftsarchitekt. Gesprächsleitung: Ursula Ammermann, Münchner Forum.

Ammermann: Schauen wir einmal in die Vergangenheit. Herr Czisch, wie war das damals in München?
Czisch: Dem damaligen Oberbürgermeister Georg Kronawitter wurde das Gelände gezeigt und gesagt, wie viele Menschen um dieses Gelände herum wohnen, 200 000, die darauf warten, endlich einen Park zu bekommen und er war begeistert von der Idee. Das war der Startschuss für das große Unternehmen Westpark.

Ammermann: Welchen Stellenwert hatte die vorgesehene Gartenbauausstellung, war das eine Art von Beschleunigung des Ganzen?
Czisch: Wenn die IGA kommt, so sagten wir uns, dann haben wir einen Termin, IGA 83, zu dem alles 1983 fertig sein muss. Die Ausschreibung des Westparks sollte so sein, dass wir zu jeder Zeit eine IGA in den Westpark einlegen können.

Ammermann: Dann kamen Sie ins Spiel, Herr Kluska. Wie ging es dann weiter?
Kluska: Ja, ich habe den Westparkwettbewerb 1977 im Februar mit der Idee der Tallandschaft gewonnen. Die Idee war, aus dem Gelände eine Erdskulptur zu formen, eine Tallandschaft mit Überhöhungen an den Rändern, um daraus die Struktur für die Räume des Parks vorzugeben. Es sollte ein großer, zentraler Erlebnisraum werden, der sich durch den ganzen Park zieht, mit Seitentälern und mit einer Abfolge von Räumen, die stets etwas Neues bringen. Mit diesem Konzept hat sich die Landeshauptstadt um die IGA beworben und den Zuschlag bekommen. Die Stadt hat daraufhin beschlossen, die IGA auf der Grundlage der Westparkplanung auszurichten. Damit waren die Weichen zur Integration der vielen Gartenschauthemen im Westpark gestellt. Das war meines Erachtens der Grund, warum die Gartenschau mit 11 Millionen Besuchern so erfolgreich war – da sich Park und Ausstellung durchdrungen haben und zu einer Einheit werden konnten.

Ammermann: Herr Dr. Schneider, Sie haben etwas Wunderbares geerbt, wie stellt sich denn der Westpark heute dar?
Schneider: Auf jeden Fall kann man das sagen, dass es ein ganz wunderbarer Park ist für die Münchnerinnen und Münchner. Der Westpark bietet im Prinzip alles, wonach das Herz begehrt, egal ob Jung oder Alt, er hat alles, was man sich von einem innenstädtischen Park wünscht und das immerhin schon seit 25 Jahren.

Ammermann: Herr Kluska, wie kommt ein Landschaftsarchitekt zu dieser Idee, wie kamen Sie zu der Berg-Tal-Idee?
Kluska: Es ist die Idee gewesen, den Verkehrslärm auszuschließen, das wollte ich nicht mit üblichen Lärmschutzwällen, wie das an den Autobahnen der Fall ist. Ziel war es, eine Gesamtkonzeption zu entwickeln, also Abtragen des Geländes in der Mitte bis 8 Meter Tiefe und Auftragen an den Rändern bis 17 Meter Höhe. Dies sollte eine Erdskulptur ergeben, in der die neue Gestalt mit den Nutzungsanforderungen zu einer Einheit wird und ausreichend Lärmschutz bietet. Das war der Grund für die Modellierung.
Eine Brücke über den Mittleren Ring, der die beiden Parkteile Ost und West trennte, sollte aus der Erdmodellierung »herauswachsen« und den Besucher ganz selbstverständlich von den einen in den anderen Parkraum führen. Das wollte ich aus der Geländeformung heraus entwickeln, bis hin zu den Wasserflächen an den tiefsten Stellen des Parks.
Die höchsten Stellen des Parks sind sieben kreisrunde, markante Erdkegel mit Bäumen auf den Kuppen, die das Höhenprofil des Parks noch dynamischer werden ließen. Von dort oben kann man bei Föhn ein Stück Alpenpanorama, die Kampenwand, die Zugspitze sehen. Ein Erdkegel wurde außerhalb des Parks im Kreis der Autobahneinfahrt A9, in den Mittleren Ring positioniert. Damit entstand an der schmalsten Stelle eine optische Erweiterung des Parks und ein signifikantes Zeichen am Ende der Autobahn.
Die Entwicklung des Reliefs mit der Erarbeitung der Höhenlinien, die manuell gezeichnet wurden, war ein ganz entscheidender Prozess für die Gestalt des Parks. Ganz wichtig war dann noch das Wegesystem, in mehreren Hierarchien abgestuft, mit breiten Talwegen, mit Höhenwegen und mit schmalen »Bergwegen«. Dieses Wegenetz war wohl auch der Grund, warum die vielen Besucher der IGA sich auf mehreren Ebenen sehr gut verteilen konnten.

Czisch: Ich war in dem Wettbewerbspreisgericht mit dem Oberbürgermeister als Sachpreisrichter dabei. Wir sind gemeinsam durch die Ausstellung gegangen, da fiel dieser Entwurf sofort auf – und zwar nur deswegen, weil er für sich gesehen ein geschlossenes, klares Konzept hatte, das so zwingend war für den so schwierigen Raum, dass er wie geschaffen schien, für einen Park mit der IGA – und alle anderen Entwürfe verblassten dagegen ganz stark. Das war für uns alle auf den ersten Blick überzeugend.

Schneider: Ich halte auch diese Raumbildung im Westpark für sehr gelungen, diese, sagen wir einmal voralpine Moränenlandschaft. Ich glaube, dass der Besucher gar nicht so sehr merkt, warum er sich so wohl fühlt, wenn er im Tal steht. Weil nämlich kein Lärm mehr da ist und weil das einfach alles stimmig ist. Was für den Besucher dann besonders attraktiv ist, das sind Einrichtungen, die aus der Zeit der IGA stammen, wie die Seebühne, Rosengarten, Staudenflächen, Biergarten, Seecafé und die großen Spielplätze, das Asienensemble mit dem chinesischen und dem japanischen Garten, der Thai-Sala und der Nepal-Pagode. Was besonders attraktiv ist, ist das viele Wasser; die Seen, die kleineren Teiche, der Gebirgsbach, der Wasserspielplatz etc.
Zur Parkpflege haben wir Herrn Kluska beauftragt, ein Parkpflegewerk für uns auszuarbeiten, denn in diesem Werk wird auch beschrieben, welche Sichtbeziehungen auf Dauer zu erhalten sind. Solche Hinweise sind uns wichtig, denn die Natur verändert sich, die Bäume wachsen.

Ammermann: Was ist denn geblieben von der IGA?
Kluska: Es gab nach der IGA eine große Diskussion darüber, was einen besonderen Wert hat für ein breites Publikum. Die Vielfalt und der Blütenreichtum der Stauden und Rosenpflanzungen ist für mich ein ganz wichtiger Teil des Parks, weil dies uns mithilft, die soziale Balance im Park zu halten. Die unterschiedlichen Interessen, die Vielschichtigkeit der gesellschaftlichen Gruppierungen zu erhalten, ist sehr wichtig. Dazu ist es aber auch notwendig, den Park, die Rosengärten, die Staudengärten gut und kompetent zu pflegen, damit sie immer neue Freude bringen und das kostet natürlich auch einen finanziellen Aufwand, der aber gerechtfertigt ist, wenn man sieht, was der Park für eine Ausstrahlung auf die Menschen hat. Der Park ist zu einem Park für alle geworden.

Ammermann: Ich möchte Ihnen zum Schluss noch die Frage stellen: Was ist denn für Sie die Seele des Westparks?

Schneider: Für mich ist die Seele des Westparks der Herr Kluska und darüber hinaus noch die tolle Atmosphäre, die der Park ausstrahlt.

Rechte Seite: Der Park in seiner weiteren Entwicklung, 25 Jahre nach der IGA

Right: The development of the park, 25 years after the IGA

25 years Westpark – Interview with Radio Lora

Conversation with Ulrich Schneider, director of the department of parks and gardens in the building directorate in Munich; Wolfgang Czisch, a municipal councillor and member of the prize committee; and Peter Kluska, landscape architect. Moderation: Ursula Ammermann, Münchner Forum.

Ammermann: Looking back to the beginning of the project, Mr Czisch, what actually happened here in Munich?
Czisch: The Lord Mayor of the time, Georg Kronawitter, was shown the site. He was told how many people lived in the vicinity of the site – 200,000, and that they were hoping to be given a park at last. Kronawitter was delighted with the idea. And that was the go-ahead for the huge project of Westpark.

Ammermann: How important was the proposed horticultural exhibition – did that help to speed up things?
Czisch: Well, we said to ourselves, if the IGA comes to Munich we've got a deadline – IGA 83, and then everything must be finished by 1983. The tender for Westpark was to be such that we could put the IGA into Westpark at any time.

Ammermann: And then you appeared on the scene, Mr Kluska. Where did things go from there?
Kluska: Yes, I won the Westpark competition in 1977, in February, with the idea of the valley landscape. The idea was to transform the site into an earth sculpture, a valley landscape with the ground rising at the edges, in order to create a structure for the spaces within the park. It was to become a large, central urban experience space which extended through the entire park, with tributary valleys and a succession of spaces which constantly offer new experiences. The capital of Bavaria presented this concept in its application to stage the IGA and won. As a result, the city decided to stage the IGA on the basis of the planning for Westpark. That set the course for the integration of the various themes of the horticultural show into Westpark. And in my view that is the reason why the horticultural show was so successful and attracted eleven million visitors – because the park and the show interacted with each other so seamlessly.

Ammermann: Dr. Schneider, you inherited something wonderful. So what does Westpark look like today?
Schneider: Well, we can definitely say that it is a wonderful park for the citizens of Munich. Westpark basically provides everything you could wish for – for young and old. It has everything you would expect to see in an urban park – and that is how it has been, basically, for the past 25 years.

Ammermann: Mr Kluska, how does a landscape architect come up with an idea like this? What gave you the idea of creating a mountain and valley landscape?
Kluska: The idea was to shut out the noise of the traffic. I didn't want to put up the usual noise protection barriers like the ones you have along motorways. My aim was to develop an overall concept, involving the removal of the ground in the middle down to a depth of up to eight metres, and raising the edges by up to 17 metres. I wanted to produce an earth sculpture in which the new form perfectly matched the requirements and also provided sufficient noise protection. That was the reason for the contouring of the site.
A bridge across the Mittlerer Ring, which separated the eastern and western sections of the park, was to "grow out of" the contouring and lead the visitor quite naturally from one section of the park to the other. I wanted to develop that from the sculpturing of the terrain, right down to the areas of water at the lowest points in the park.
The highest points are seven round, prominent cones of earth with trees on their summits. They add a dynamic element to the silhouette of the park. From the top, when the Föhn wind is blowing, you have a view of the Alps with the Kampenwand and the Zugspitze. One cone of earth was placed outside the park on the roundabout at the point where the A9 motorway joins up with the Mittlerer Ring. That extends the park optically at its narrowest point and also serves as a landmark at the end of the motorway.
The development of the relief and the calculation of the contour lines, which were drawn manually, was one of the decisive elements in the design of the park. The network of footpaths is also very important. They are organised with a distinct hierarchy, from the broad valley paths to the paths along the hilltops and the narrow "mountain paths". This network of paths was in fact the reason why the many visitors to the IGA could spread out so well across the various levels.

Czisch: I was one of the members of the competition committee with the Lord Mayor as expert judge. We walked together through the exhibition, and the design caught our attention immediately – purely and simply because it had a cohesive, clear concept, which was absolutely essential for the difficult site. It seemed to have been tailor-made for a park with the IGA – and all the other designs paled by comparison. That was what convinced us all from the very start.

Schneider: I also consider the space creation in Westpark – this pre-alpine moraine landscape, as we can refer to it – to be highly successful. I think the visitor doesn't really notice why he feels so at ease when he stands there in the valley. It's because the noise has disappeared, and because everything just fits together. And what the visitor finds particularly attractive is the facilities which hark back to the time of the IGA, like the lakeside theatre, the rose garden, the areas of shrubs, the beer garden, the lakeside café and the spacious play areas, as well as the Asia ensemble with the Chinese and Japanese gardens, the Thai pavilion and the Nepalese pagoda. What is especially attractive is the abundance of water: the lakes, the little ponds, the mountain stream, the water playground and so on.
As regards park maintenance, we asked Mr Kluska to create a park service manual for us, because in it he has described which vistas must be permanently preserved. These tips are very important for us because nature changes; the trees keep growing.

Ammermann: What has remained of the IGA?
Kluska: After the IGA there were great discussions about what the general public would find particularly attractive. The diversity of shrubs and the variety of blossoms, and the rose beds, form a very important part of the park in my view, because they help us to maintain the social balance in the park. It's very important to cater to the various interests and the wide range of social groups. To do that we have to maintain the park, the rose gardens and the herbaceous gardens at a high standard, so that they continue to give people pleasure – and that, of course, entails expense, which is justified when you see the effect the park has on people. It has become a park for everyone.

Ammermann: And finally, I should like to ask you one last question: What, in your opinion, constitutes the spirit of Westpark?

Schneider: For me, Mr Kluska embodies the spirit of Westpark, and so does the fantastic atmosphere which the park radiates.

Rechte Seite: Der Park, östlicher Teil. Aus der früheren Kiesgrube ist hier mit der Stille des Wassers eine neue Räumlichkeit entstanden.

Right: The park, eastern section. The tranquillity of the water has transformed the former gravel pit into a new open space.

Sommer im Park

Der Park ist ein Ort der Selbstwahrnehmung: Er ermöglicht die Austreibung des falschen, entfremdeten, des erschöpften Selbst. Der Parkbesucher versucht, seinem Alltags-Ich – ausgebucht mit Erwartungen und Ansprüchen, träumend und seelenschweifend – zu entkommen, ebenso dem Lärm, den Anmaßungen, Zumutungen und Fremdbestimmungen des Alltäglichen. Menschen im Park sind andere, nachdenkliche. Sie werden zugänglich für sich. Sie entdecken sich aufs Neue, graben sich frei aus dem Seelenschutt der Erwerbsbiographie. Und wenn die Ruhe den Stadtmenschen erreicht, ergibt er sich der ästhetischen Kraft des Parks, ahnt die Schönheit des Seins in einem kleinen Nu, das zum großen Luxus wird.

Dieser Park hat gar nichts von der Noblesse anderer, herrschaftlicher Parks, deren Eitelkeit oder Mystik einen ablenkt oder herausfordert. Dieser Park ist keiner, der ein Faible hätte für eine Gehaltsklasse oder Kaste, keiner, in dem permanent Aufgeplustertes in den öffentlichen Raum stelzt wie im Englischen Garten, der Geltungsgalerie Münchens.

Der Westpark ist der Park von nebenan und noch vielmehr ist er die Oase des Westens, wo früher Schotter war und wildes, verwahrlostes Kraut, das lieblose Vorspiel der Großstadt.

Vor der Seebühne ist ein Schwanennest, dort biegt der Weg nach links, vier Bänke stehen dort, wo das Wasser künstlich fällt, und auf einer Bank sitzt, mit den nackten, rot lackierten Zehen spielend, Ina Janson, Jura-Professorin aus Riga. Sie möchte, sagt sie, jetzt mal richtig Deutsch lernen. In Ihrem Schoß liegt der russisch-deutsche Langenscheidt, nach dem sie greift, um das nötige Wort zu suchen: »Zukunft«. Sie plane hier ihr weiteres Leben, hier im Westpark, den sie, die nach Frankreich und England und überallhin reist und dort die Parks der Welt zur Erholung besucht, für einen der schönsten Europas hält. Das ist ein Plädoyer, und das Urteil hat Ina Janson bereits gefällt: Immer wieder kam sie her, jetzt will sie in München bleiben. Hier wird sie leben, an der Universität lehren und wohnen – ohne Zweifel dort drüben oder da hinten, auf jeden Fall in der Nähe des Westparks. Auf Wiedersehen!

Der Stadtmensch im Park ist innerhalb der Stadt außerhalb derselben. Er hat in diesem, mit etwas Glück und Geduld, ein überirdisches Refugium gefunden, wo der äußere Blick in die Himmelsweite mit dem inneren verschmilzt. Seltsam genug: Im Park fliegt einen das an, was man sich im verwalteten Leben kaum gestattet: Einsamkeit, Melancholie, die Langeweile, und all das tut wohl.

»Verzeihen Sie, ist das Lesen im Park ein anderes?« Der Unbekannte lacht und legt das Buch zur Seite: ›Die Wittelsbacher – Geschichte einer Familie‹. »Setzen Sie sich. – Sie wirken so, na ja, sagen wir … sind Sie im Park gelassener?« – »Exakt. Und Sie?«

»Ich habe hier gleich nebenan, bei der Kriegersiedlung, eine kleine Stadtwohnung, und wenn ich ungestört sein will, radle ich in den Westpark.« – »Kommen Sie also in den Park, um Ihre Stimmung zu heben?« – »Der Park ist ein Luxus, der jedermann zur Verfügung steht, man kommt sich so fürstlich vor …«

Der unbekannte Freund beugt sich vor und sagt: »Man empfindet so etwas wie Gnade und Dankbarkeit, diese Schönheit hier erleben zu dürfen.« – »Sie sprechen von Transzendenz?« – »Auch wenn ich Buddhist bin, ja, es hat etwas Absolutes, man findet zur gemeinsamen Mitte.« Ein Lachen, ein Handschlag, das Versprechen, in Kontakt zu bleiben.

Am Wochenende ist hier ein Trubel, eine Ausgelassenheit, ein anderer Park. Die Grillzonen wurden grade ausgeweitet und manche Anwohner protestieren noch immer heftig. Am Montagmorgen aber atmet der Park wieder frei, die Besucher verlieren sich in ihm. Dann harren die Menschen aus, minutenlang stieren sie auf den Wellenschlag des Schwanes, in Traumwelten gefangen. Dann sitzt man da, spürt die Rosen, hört den Kies knirschen, sieht das Schloss, das es nicht gibt.

Christian Schüle
Das evangelische Magazin Chrismon plus

Rechte Seite: Der Park in seiner weiteren Entwicklung, 25 Jahre nach der IGA

Right: The development of the park, 25 years after the IGA

Summer in the park

The park is a place of self-awareness. It permits us to banish the false, alienated, exhausted self. The visitor to the park attempts to escape his everyday self – overwhelmed by expectations and claims, dreaming and letting his soul ramble freely. He tries to escape the noise, the pretensions, the impositions and the heteronomy of everyday life.

People in the park are different, more contemplative. They are open to their own selves. They rediscover themselves; dig themselves out of the emotional rubble of their career biography. And when the peace reaches the town dweller, he surrenders to the aesthetic power of the park, senses the beauty of being in a brief moment that becomes a great luxury.

This park has nothing of the nobility of other, more sophisticated parks, whose vanity or mysticism distracts or challenges the visitor. This park has no weakness for a particular salary bracket or caste; it is not a place where permanently puffed-up individuals stalk around as they do in the Englischer Garten, Munich's status gallery. Westpark is the park next door, and even more than that it is the oasis in the west, where previously there was gravel and wild, neglected weeds, the loveless antechamber of the big city.

In front of the lakeside theatre you will see a swan's nest. The path winds to the left there, and there are four benches where the water falls artificially, and on one of the benches sits Ina Janson, professor of law from Riga. She is playing with her naked red-varnished toenails. She says that she wants to learn German properly. In her lap lies Langenscheidt's Russian-German dictionary, which she takes up in order to find the right word: "*Zukunft*", future. She is planning her future life here, in Westpark, which she considers one of the loveliest in Europe, having travelled to France and England and all over the place, visiting the world's parks by way of recreation. It is an impassioned final speech, and Ina Janson has already passed judgment. She has kept returning here, and now she wants to remain in Munich. She will live here, teach at the University and live – no doubt over there or back there, at any rate near Westpark. *Auf Wiedersehen!*

The city dweller in a park is in the city, but yet outside it. With a bit of luck and patience he will have found here a super-terrestrial refuge where the view outwards, towards the expanse of heaven, fuses with the view inwards. It is very strange: in the park you will find all those emotions which you refuse to allow into your strictly ordered life: solitude, melancholy, boredom; and they are very comforting.

"Excuse me, is reading a different experience in the park?" The stranger laughs and puts down his book: '*Die Wittelsbacher – Geschichte einer Familie*' (The Wittelsbachs – History of a Family). "Do sit down. – You look so, well, how shall I put it? ... Are you more relaxed in the park?" – "I am indeed. And what about you?"

"I have a little town flat nearby, near the Kriegersiedlung, and when I don't want to be disturbed I cycle to Westpark." – "So do you come to the park to cheer yourself up?" – "The park is a luxury which is available for everyone; you feel like a prince ..."

The unknown friend bends forward and says: One feels something like grace and gratitude for being allowed to experience this beauty. – "Are you speaking of transcendency?" – "Although I am a Buddhist, yes, it has something absolute. You can discover your common centre." A laugh, a handshake, and the promise to stay in contact.

At the weekend it is bustling, relaxed – a different park. The barbecue areas have just been extended and some people from the houses nearby are still protesting vigorously. However, on Monday morning the park breathes freely again, and visitors can lose themselves here. People stand stock still, staring for minutes on end at the ripples left by the swan, caught up in their own imaginary world. Then you sit there, sensing the roses, hearing the crunch of the gravel, and gazing at the castle which does not exist.

Christian Schüle
The Protestant magazine Chrismon plus

Rechte Seite: Alle sozialen Schichten besuchen den Park, die Freude im Staudengarten und das Interesse an den blühenden Pflanzen ist groß.

Right: All social classes visit the park. Everyone enjoys the herbaceous garden and takes an interest in the flowering plants.

Kultur- und Kongresszentrum Max-Reger-Halle
Weiden in der Oberpfalz

Max Reger Hall Cultural and Congress Centre
Weiden, Upper Palatinate

**Kunst und Kultur –
Musik und Architektur**

Die Stadt Weiden begann 1990 mit dem Bau einer Kultur- und Kongresshalle. Der Architekt Peter Kaup erhielt nach einem ersten Preis im Architektenwettbewerb den Planungsauftrag. Das Bauwerk bekam den Namen Max-Reger-Halle, zu Ehren des Komponisten, der ein Bürger dieser Stadt gewesen war. Die Gestaltung der Außenanlagen ergab sich aus zwei wesentlichen baulichen Eigenschaften des Konzerthauses: Dem Zugangs- und Vorplatzbereich sowie dem kleinen Park am Foyer.

Der ca. 60 Meter lange Zugangsbereich, der gradlinig von der Straße zum Eingang führt, wurde als Promenade und langgestreckter Vorplatz gestaltet. Eine markante Baumhecke aus kastenförmig geschnittenen Linden gibt dem Platz eine räumliche Führung. Bodenlicht erhellt am Abend die Baumkronen, und es entsteht am Haupteingang eine gewisse Festlichkeit durch die Edelstahl-Skulptur von Otto Wesendonck in der Mittelachse.

Der Foyergarten mit großer Wasserfläche flankiert seitlich den Konzertsaal. Er bildet das Außenfoyer bei Veranstaltungen und wird in der warmen Jahreszeit gerne neben dem Innenfoyer genutzt. Er schafft Distanz zum Straßenverkehr und steht den Bürgern als Stadtteilpark zu Verfügung. Mit dieser Freiraum- und Baukultur wurde das kulturelle Leben der Stadt wesentlich bereichert.

Projektbeteiligte
Peter Kaup und Partner, Architekten, München

**Art and culture –
music and architecture**

In 1990, the town of Weiden began to build its congress centre. The architect Peter Kaup was commissioned with the planning of the project after winning first prize in the architects' competition. The building was named the Max Reger Congress Hall in honour of the composer, who was a local citizen. The design of the grounds was based on two important features of the congress centre: the access area and forecourt, and the little park by the entrance. The access area is about 60 metres long and leads straight from the road to the entrance. It was designed as a promenade and extended forecourt. A prominent hedge of trees consisting of box-shaped pruned lime trees gives the area spatial direction. At night, lights set into the ground illuminate the treetops, and the stainless-steel sculpture by Otto Wesendonck in the central axis lends the main entrance a festive air.

The entrance garden with its expanse of water lies to one side of the concert hall. It serves as an outdoor foyer for events and is often used in summer together with the indoor foyer. It helps to increase the feeling of space between the road traffic and the hall and it is open to the public as a local district park. The creation of this open space and building complex has considerably enriched the cultural life of the town.

Project Team
Peter Kaup and Partners, architects, Munich

Skulptur von Otto Wesendonck

Sculpture by Otto Wesendonck

Lageplan
Freiraumgestaltung

1 Vorplatz-Promenade mit geschnittenen Linden
2 Begrünte Parkplätze
3 Haupteingang
4 Pflanzterrassen
5 Teich
6 Konzertpark
7 Anlieferung

Site plan showing leisure areas

1 Forecourt promenade with pruned lime trees
2 Landscaped car park
3 Main entrance
4 Plant terraces
5 Pond
6 Concert park
7 Deliveries

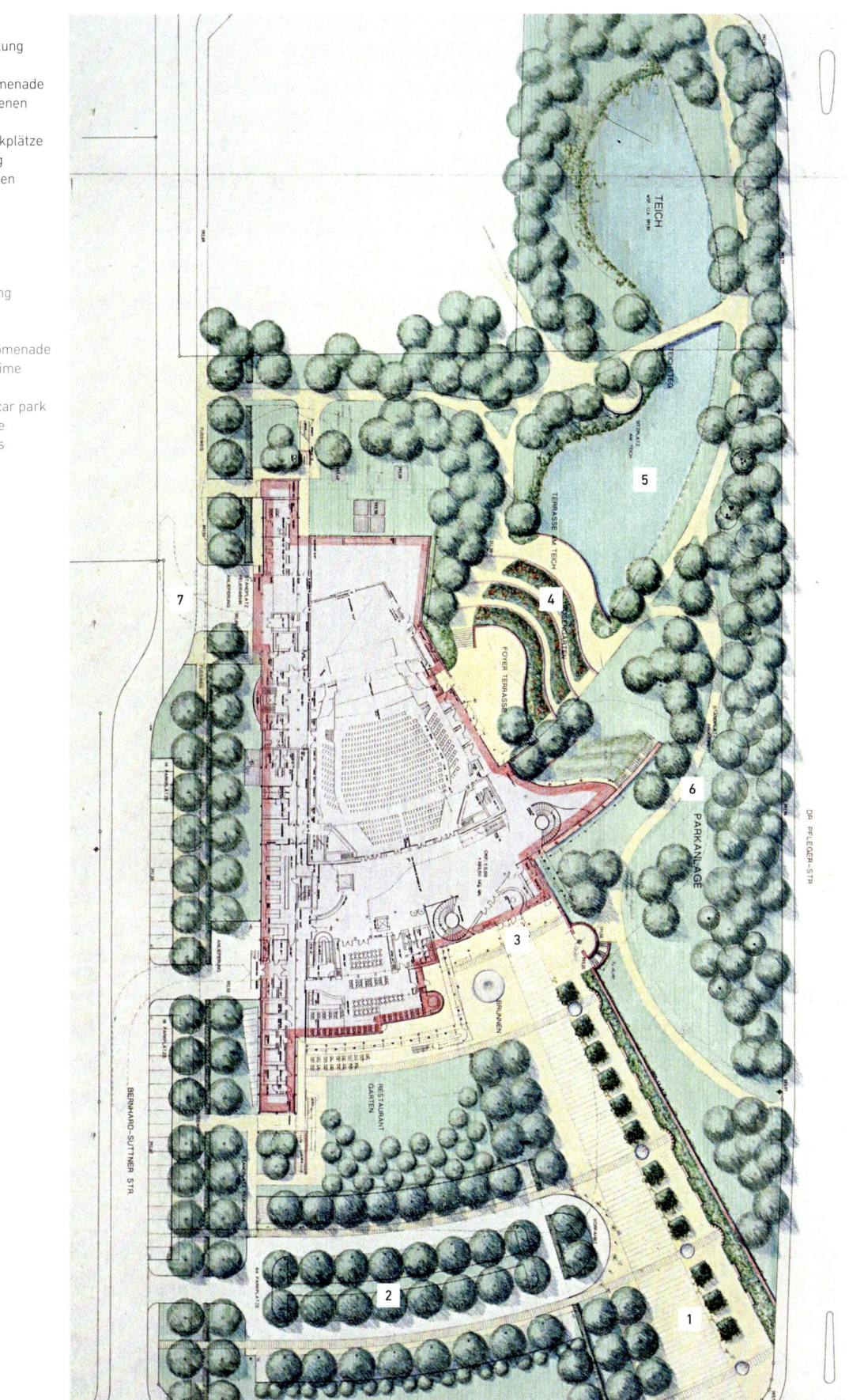

Linke Seite: Das Foyer wird durch Terrassen am Wasser erweitert, die bei Veranstaltungen auch am Abend gern genutzt werden.

Left: The foyer is extended by terraces beside the pond which are also used during evening events.

Der Park ist öffentlich, ein städtebauliches Ensemble von Freiraum- und Baukultur.

The park is public, an urban ensemble of open spaces and buildings.

Klinikum Dritter Orden
München

Dritter Orden Clinic
Munich

Das »Gartenkrankenhaus« der Schwesternschaft

The "Garden Hospital"

Mit einer bewundernswerten Energie hat die Schwesternschaft des Dritten Ordens über Jahrzehnte dieses traditionsreiche Krankenhaus kontinuierlich ausgebaut. Eine Erweiterung folgte der nächsten und diese Neubauten legten sich wie ein Perlenkranz um das sogenannte Mutterhaus. Die Planung der Freiräume begann 1983. Mit erstem und zweitem Bauabschnitt im Osten sowie die Zufahrt zum neuen Eingang begannen umfassende Bautätigkeiten. Trotz der engen Grundstücksverhältnisse gelang es dabei, grüne Freiraumstrukturen zu entwickeln. Es wurden unter anderem Baumkulissen aufgebaut, Freiräume als Patientenpark und Patientengarten gestaltet, eine Gartenachse vom Mutterhaus zur neuen Kinderklinik gebaut sowie ein zweigeschossiges Parkdeck in die neuen Baumkulissen integriert.
Im Verlauf der Zeit wurde das Klinikum Dritter Orden zu einem »Gartenkrankenhaus«, in dessen Schönheit sich Patienten und Pflegepersonal eingebunden fühlen.

Over the past decades, a lot of energy has been invested into expanding this long-standing hospital. A succession of extensions in the form of new buildings have been added like a string of beads around the so-called mother house.
The planning of the open spaces began in 1983. The extensive building activity started with the first and second building phases in the east together with the approach to the new entrance. In spite of the limited space available on the site it was possible to develop green open-space structures. For example, rows of trees were planted; open spaces were laid out as a park and garden for patients; a garden axis was established between the mother house and the new children's clinic; and a two-storey parking deck was integrated into the new rows of trees.
Over the years the Dritter Orden Clinic became a "Garden Hospital", and patients and nursing staff are able to benefit from its beauty.

Projektbeteiligte
Ott Geiselbrecht Beeg und Partner, Architekten, München

Project Team
Ott Geiselbrecht Beeg and Partners, architects, Munich

Oben: Kleiner Patientengarten – »Intensivstation« zur Regeneration
Unten: Parkdeck, in den Lärmschutzwall und in die Baumkulisse integriert. Das Untergeschoss ist natürlich belüftet und belichtet.

Top: The little garden for patients – an "intensive care unit" for regeneration.
Bottom: Parking areas, integrated into the noise protection embankment and the backdrop of trees. The lower floor has natural ventilation and light.

Lageplan, östlicher Teilbereich der Klinikgärten

1 Ein- und Ausfahrt
2 Vorfahrt mit Brunnen
3 Haupteingang
4 Parkdeck
5 Patientenpark
6 Patientengarten
7 Begrünte Innenhöfe

Site plan, eastern section of the clinic gardens

1 Entrance and exit
2 Forecourt with fountain
3 Main entrance
4 Parking area
5 Patients' car park
6 Patients' garden
7 Greened inner courtyards

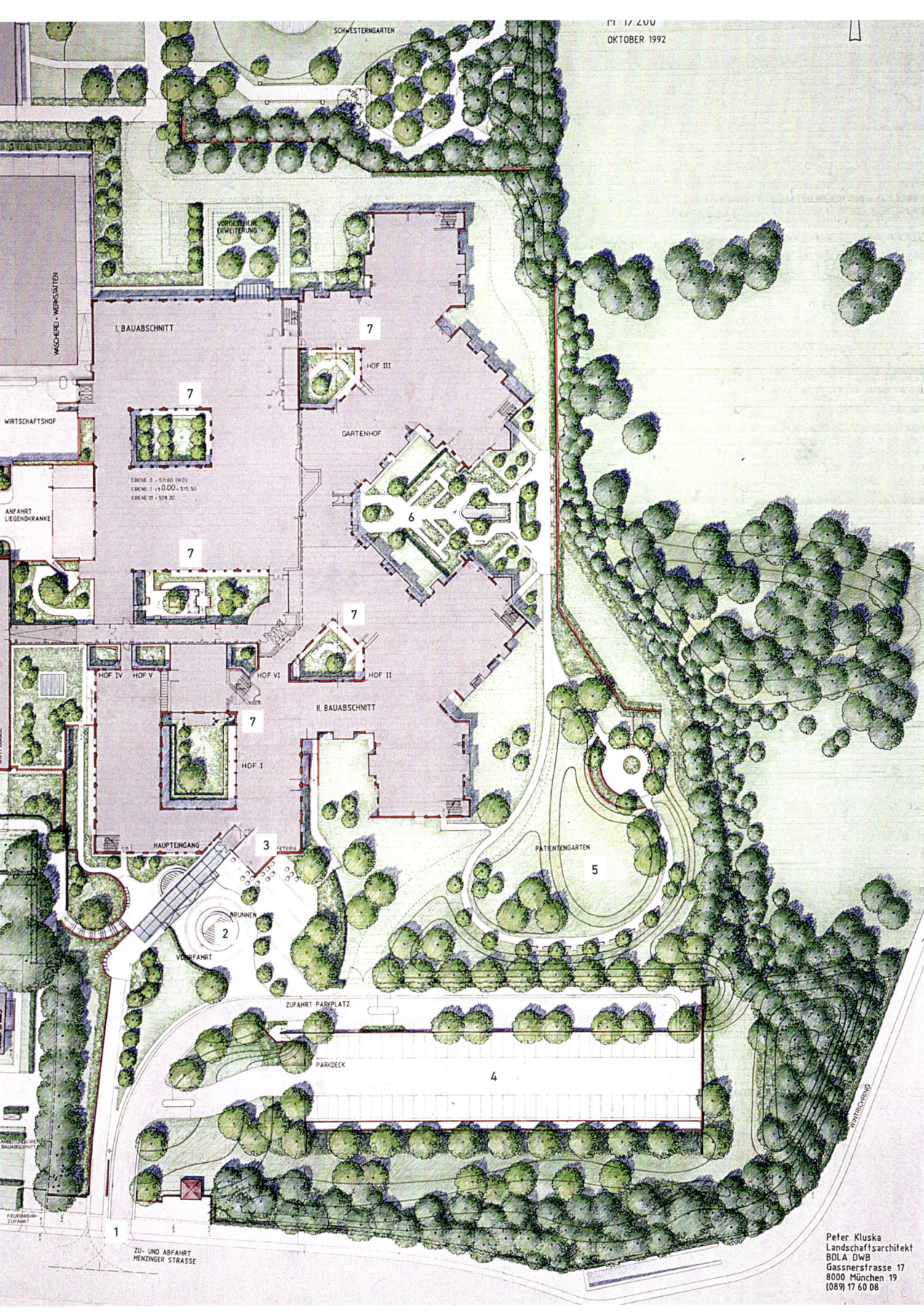

Bettenhaus, zum Park hin orientiert. Naturerlebnis vom Krankenbett aus

Ward block overlooking the park. Views of nature from the sickbed

Rechte Seite: Rosen, Stauden, viel Blühendes und Wasser beleben den Garten in den Sommermonaten.

Right: Roses, shrubs, an abundance of flowers and water brighten up the garden in the summer months.

Main-Donau-Kanal
Berching

Main-Danube Canal
Berching

Eine neue Identität für einen alten Ort – Berching und der Main-Donau-Kanal

Ein Jahrhundertbauwerk, so wurde sie genannt, die Wasserstraße von der Nordsee bis zum Schwarzen Meer, die Verbindung von Main und Donau. Jahrzehntelang wurde dieses letzte Teilstück geplant und in zwei Richtungen an ihm gebaut, von Norden kommend über die Scheitelhaltung von Hilpoltstein hinweg, von Süden kommend über Kelheim und durch das Altmühltal. Berching war das Ziel beider Richtungen. Hier wurde das letzte Teilstück, der Zusammenschluss, gebaut sowie die Fertigstellung des Kanals festlich begangen und dieser für die Schifffahrt frei gegeben.
Die Schwierigkeit dieses letzten Teilstücks lag darin, dass die Kanaltrasse in nur 40 Metern Abstand zu der historischen Stadt und zu der unter Denkmalschutz stehenden Stadtmauer lag und alle Fahr- und Fußweg-Verbindungen auf der Westseite der Stadt abschnitt.
Ein städtebaulicher Wettbewerb, kombiniert mit einem Realisierungswettbewerb sollte Klarheit bringen, wie diese Probleme gelöst werden könnten. Gefordert waren eine nördliche und eine südliche Umfahrung des Ortskerns mit Brücken über dem Kanal sowie eine Fuß- und Radwegquerung im zentralen Bereich und eine Zufahrtsmöglichkeit zum westlichen Stadttor.
Die Trassenführung für die neuen Straßen wurde mit dem jeweils größtmöglichen Abstand zu beiden Ortsrändern gewählt und damit der Verkehr in weitem Bogen um die Stadt geführt, so dass die Rahmenbedingungen für eine weitere städtebauliche Entwicklung mit einem Sportzentrum im Süden und einem Schwimmbad mit Parkplatz im Norden klar definiert wurden.
Der geringe Abstand der Kanalkante zur Stadtmauer und zum westlichen Stadttor ergab die Chance einer 600 Meter langen Uferpromenade und einer Fußgängerzone mit eingeschränkter Zufahrtsmöglichkeit zum Stadttor. Das Kanalgeländer wurde durch Steinlamellen rhythmisch gegliedert, so dass die Schifffahrt in der Längssicht nicht geblendet werden kann. Das Geländer selbst erlaubt eine freie Durchsicht auf das Wasser. Mit Bäumen und Sitzplätzen auf der neuen Uferpromenade entstand eine sehr charakteristische »Stadtterrasse« am Wasser mit angegliederter Schiffsanlegestelle und einem Anlegesteg für Sportboote.

Für die Fußgängerbrücke quer über den Kanal konzipierte Jörg Schlaich eine an einem Pylonen aufgehängte Seilkonstruktion, die sich durch ihre Leichtigkeit konfliktfrei in die neue städtebauliche Situation einfügt und mit den historischen Stadttürmen ein überzeugendes Ensemble von Alt und Neu bildet.
Die Wasserfläche vor der Stadt wurde zu einem großen Gewinn für Berching und der Eingriff in die Landschaft nördlich und südlich des Ortskerns durch Geländemodellierung und Neupflanzungen wieder geheilt. Das Erscheinungsbild der Stadt mit der westlichen Stadtmauer, ihren Türmen, dem Stadttor, der Uferpromenade am Kanal und der Fußgängerbrücke wurde aufgewertet und attraktiver – ein Beispiel für ein gelungenes Miteinander von Erhalten und Gestalten.

Projektbeteiligte
Schlaich, Bergermann und Partner, Tragwerksplaner, Stuttgart (Fußgängerbrücke)
Kurt Ackermann und Partner, Architekten, München (Beratung)

A new identity for an old town – Berching and the Main-Danube Canal

The waterway from the North Sea to the Black Sea, the link between the Main and the Danube, was described as one of the construction projects of the century. For decades, this final section was planned and the construction work proceeded in both directions; from the north across the summit level by Hilpoltstein, and from the south via Kelheim and through the Altmühltal. Berching was the goal in both directions. It was here that the final section, the link, was built, and it was here that the completion of the canal was celebrated and the waterway was declared open to shipping.
The difficulty of this final section was that the stretch of canal lay only 40 metres away from the old town and the town walls, which were a protected monument. It also cut across all roads and footpaths to and from the western side of the town.
It was hoped that a town-planning competition combined with a realisation competition would bring clarity as to how these problems could be solved. The requirements were for a northern and southern bypass for the town centre with bridges over the canal as well as a crossing point for a footpath and cycle track in the central area, together with an access point by the west town gate.
The routing for the new roads was selected to afford the greatest possible distance from the two town boundaries. This led the traffic in a wide arc around the town, so that the framework conditions for further urban development with a sports centre in the south and a swimming pool and car park in the north were clearly defined.
The narrow area between the canal bank and the town wall and the western town gate provided enough space for a 600-metre-long canal-side promenade and a pedestrian zone with restricted vehicle access to the town gate. The canal balustrade incorporates skilfully placed stone "ribs" so that boats are not dazzled by the lights as they go past. The balustrade itself permits an unobstructed view of the water. The trees and benches along the new canalside promenade form a very characteristic "town terrace" by the water with an integrated shipping pier and a jetty for sports boats.

For the footbridge across the canal, Jörg Schlaich designed a cable construction suspended from a pylon. Thanks to its lightness it is absorbed happily into the new urban situation, forming with the historic town towers a convincing ensemble of old and new.
The area of water outside the town proved to be a tremendous gain for Berching and the intrusion into the landscape to the north and south of the town centre has been repaired by landscaping and replanting.
The appearance of the town, with its western town wall, its towers and town gate, the canalside promenade and the footbridge, was upgraded and made more attractive – an example of the successful integration of existing features and new design.

Project Team
Schlaich, Bergermann and Partners, structural engineers, Stuttgart (pedestrian bridge)
Kurt Ackermann and Partners, architects, Munich (consultants)

Rechte Seite: Zentraler Bereich Altstadt. Östliches Vorfeld mit Uferpromenade, Schiffsanlegestelle, Festplatz, neuer Zufahrt zum Westtor, Fußgängerbrücke

Right: Central district of the Old Town centre. Eastern approach with riverside promenade, shipping pier, fairground, new approach to the Western Gate, pedestrian bridge

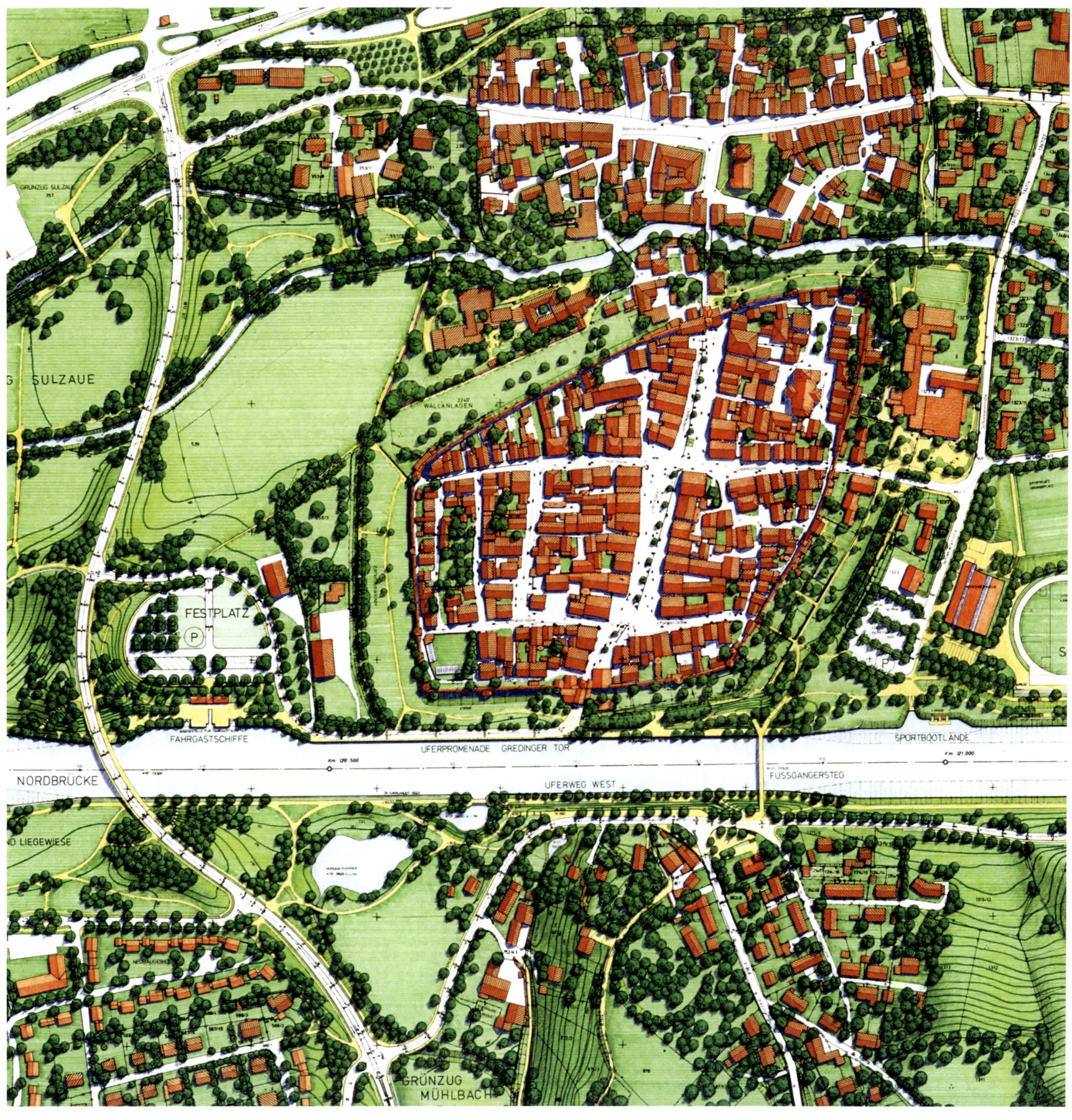

Landschaft nördlich von
Berching vor Baubeginn

Landscape north
of Berching before
construction started

Landschaft südlich von Berching vor Baubeginn

Landscape south of Berching before construction started

Die Baustelle vor der Altstadt mit Blick nach Süden. Das Trogprofil des Kanals zeichnet sich bereits ab.

The building site in front of the Old Town, looking south. The trough profile of the canal is already visible.

Die Baustelle mit Blick nach Norden. Im Hintergrund die neue Straßenbrücke zur Nordumfahrung

The building site looking north. In the background one can see the new road bridge for the northern bypass

Linke Seite: Altstadt und Kanal, ein neues Ensemble im ländlichen Raum

Left: The Old Town and canal form a new ensemble in a country setting.

Die östliche Uferpromenade ist urban geprägt: mit Bäumen und Sitzplätzen am Ufer.

The eastern riverside promenade has an urban air with trees and benches along the river bank.

Die Uferbegrenzung mit Steinlamellen als funktionaler Blendschutz für die Schifffahrt und Gestaltungselement der Uferpromenade

Strips of stone mark the edge of the river bank, serving as a functional glare shield for the ships and a design element on the riverside promenade.

Rechte Seite: Das westliche Ufer mit höher liegender Umgehungsstraße und Fuß- und Radwanderweg am Wasser

Right: The western bank lies at a lower level than the bypass and includes a footpath and cycle track beside the water.

Linke Seite: Schichtwasser aus den westlichen Hängen wird vor der Einleitung in den Kanal in einem Teich gestaut.

Left: Formation water from the western hill slopes is dammed in a pond before being channelled into the canal.

Technik, Baukultur und Landschaft ergänzen sich

Technology, buildings and landscape complement each other to form an ensemble.

Donau-
staustufe
Vohburg

Danube Weir
Vohburg

In den Fluss gebaut – Wasserkraft und Landschaftsenergie

Die Flussgestalt der Donau hat eine lange Veränderungsgeschichte hinter sich. Bis vor 200 Jahren war sie ein Wildfluss, der sich mäandernd über mehrere Kilometer Breite hinzog und sich permanent veränderte. Auwälder waren ihre typische Begleitvegetation.
Die ökologischen Bestandsqualitäten wurden von der Baumaßnahme stark betroffen. Das Konfliktpotential war beträchtlich. Die Planung wurde von einer interdisziplinären Arbeitsgruppe unter Einbeziehung der Naturschutzbelange aktiv begleitet. Die Integration des Bauwerks in das neue Landschaftsbild konnte nur mit landschaftlichen Maßnahmen erreicht werden. Auf beiden Uferseiten, an den Schnittstellen von Bauwerk und Landschaft wurden daher Baumhaine mit Eschen gepflanzt, die eine Art Brückenköpfe bilden, die das Bauwerk flankieren, und mit zunehmendem Wachstum die Integration der Staustufe in das Landschaftsbild fördern.
In dieser architektonischen Anordnung erhielt das Bauwerk einen klaren Abschluss, aber auch einen vermittelnden Übergang zu den anschließenden Naturräumen durch Anpflanzung von Bäumen der gleichen Art. Die Wunden sind weitgehend geheilt, das Landschaftsbild mit Ober- und Unterwasser, mit dem tangierenden Altwasser-, Bach- und Vegetationsstrukturen wurde in eine neue Balance von Natur- und Technik gebracht. Die Pflanzung von Solitärbäumen auf dem Dach über den Turbinen trägt dazu ebenfalls bei.

Projektbeteiligte
Fred Angerer und Gert Feuser, Architekten, München

Built into the river – Hydropower and landscape energy

The course of the Danube has been changed frequently over a long period of time. Until 200 years ago it was an untamed river which meandered over a width of several kilometres and kept changing. Alluvial forests formed the typical vegetation along its banks.
The quality of the ecological populations suffered greatly as a result of the construction project. There was considerable conflict potential. The planning was actively accompanied by an interdisciplinary workgroup which took the nature conservation aspects into consideration. The integration of the building structure into the new countryside image could only be achieved with landscaping measures. On both river banks, at the interfaces between the building structure and the landscape, groves of ash trees were planted. They form a sort of bridgehead flanking the structure, and as they grow they encourage the integration of the weir into the landscape.
With this architectural arrangement the building structure was given a clearly defined boundary, but at the same time a mediating transition to the adjacent natural spaces through the planting of trees of the same type. The wounds are largely healed, the landscape countenance with headwater and tailwater, with the nearby oxbow lakes, stream and vegetation structures have been adjusted to create a new balance between nature and technology. The planting of single trees on the roof over the turbines also contributes to the harmonious appearance.

Project Team
Fred Angerer and Gert Feuser, architects, Munich

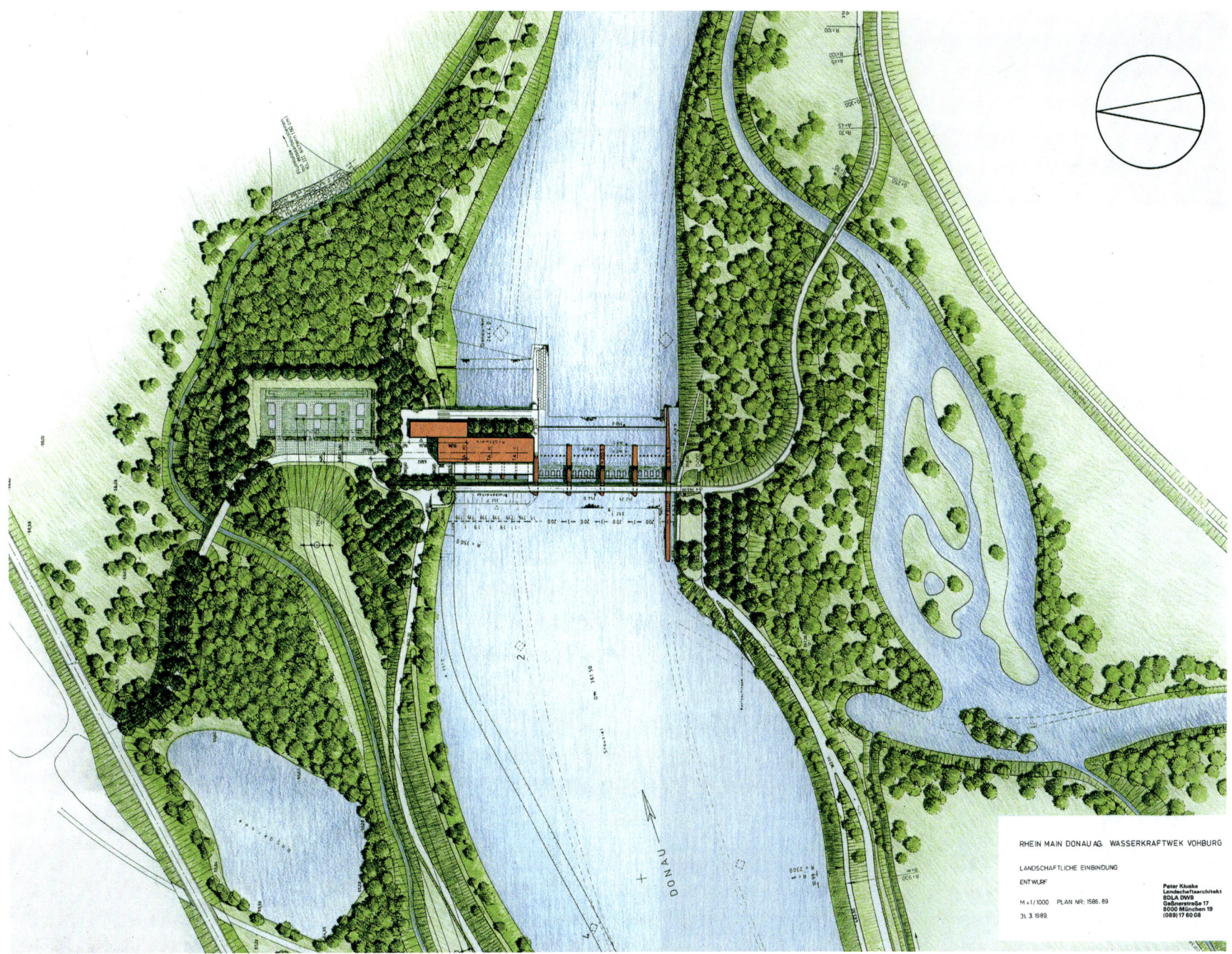

Lageplan mit Ober- und Unterwasser. Baumgruppierungen auf beiden Uferseiten aus Eschen als Maßnahmen des Naturschutzes zur Wiederherstellung des ökologischen Gleichgewichts

Site plan with headwater and tailwater. Groups of ash trees were planted on both banks as nature protection measures to restore the ecological balance.

Bäume über den Turbinen im Flussbereich – Kunstobjekt als Symbol der Wasserkraft, Hans Wurmer

Trees above the turbines in the vicinity of the river – art object as symbol of water power, Hans Wurmer

Rechte Seite: Das Staustufenbauwerk mit Oberwasser, ästhetisch-schön, zur Energieerzeugung sinnvoll, ökologisch problematisch

Right: The weir structure with headwater: an aesthetically attractive and useful way of generating power, but ecologically problematic

Donau-Glacisbrücke und Querung Luitpoldpark

Ingolstadt

Danube Glacis Bridge and Luitpoldpark Crossing

Ingolstadt

Eine Brücke über die Donau, eine Brücke über dem Verkehr

Die neue Glacisbrücke ist die dritte Donaubrücke in Ingolstadt. Sie entstand als Ergebnis eines beschränkten Realisierungswettbewerbs. Bei der Übergabe der Brücke 1999 sagte der Tragwerksplaner Jörg Schlaich: »Der Erfolg einer so komplexen Aufgabe hängt immer von einer guten und die gegenseitigen Belange respektierenden Zusammenarbeit des Entwurfsteams ab; dem Bauingenieur, dem Landschaftsarchitekten und dem Architekten.«

Im Rahmen dieser ganzheitlichen Konzeption waren vom Landschaftsarchitekten mehrere Teilbereiche zu lösen, um die baulichen Eingriffe zu einem neuen Landschaftsbild zu formen.

Am nördlichen Brückenkopf konnte der motorisierte Verkehr vom Fuß- und Radwegverkehr getrennt werden. Mit einer Unterführung wurde die verkehrsfreie Verbindung zwischen Glacis und Donauufer hergestellt. Mit der Pflanzung von über 100 Einzelbäumen entstand ein den Verkehr überspielender räumlich wirksamer Brückenkopf.

An den beiden Ufern ordnen sich die Tragstützen der Spannbandbrücke in die Reihe der mächtigen Weidenstämme, die schräg aus der Uferzone herauswachsen, ganz selbstverständlich ein. Die Brückenkonstruktion schwebt ohne weitere Stütze über dem Fluss. Technik und Natur finden eine Einheit von Freiraum- und Baukultur.

Bei der Trassenführung der Straße durch den Park konnten die raumbildenden alten Baumbestände und -gruppierungen weitgehend berücksichtigt werden, so dass nicht nur die Eingriffe gering gehalten, sondern auch die Straße durch Baumbestände räumlich gut integriert wurde. Die notwendigen Rodungen wurden durch 290 Neupflanzungen kompensiert.

Mit der 35 Meter breiten Grünbrücke bleibt eine wesentliche Lebensader des Luitpoldparks erhalten, die trennende Wirkung ist aufgehoben. Durch die Tieflage der Straße wird der Verkehrslärm im Park erheblich vermindert.

Das Gesamtkonzept wurde 1999 mit einer Würdigung des Deutschen Landschaftsarchitekturpreises ausgezeichnet.

Projektbeteiligte
Schlaich, Bergermann und Partner, Tragwerksplaner, Stuttgart (Brückenbau)
Kurt Ackermann und Partner, Architekten, München (Beratung)

A bridge over the Danube, a bridge over the traffic

The new Glacis Bridge is the third bridge over the Danube in Ingolstadt. It was constructed as the result of a restricted implementation competition. When the bridge was officially handed over in 1999, Jörg Schlaich, who planned the supporting structure, commented: "The success of a task as complex as this one is always dependent on a good standard of cooperation and mutual respect for the concerns of the other on the part of the design team: the civil engineer, the landscape architect and the architect."

Within the framework of this integrated conception, the landscape architect was required to provide solutions for several sections in order to combine the building measures and to create a new appearance for the landscape.

Around the northern bridgehead it was possible to separate the motorised traffic from the pedestrian and cycle traffic. A traffic-free underpass was constructed to provide a link between the glacis and the banks of the Danube. The planting of over 100 separate trees created a spatially effective bridgehead which hides the traffic.

On both banks the supporting pillars of the stressed ribbon bridge blend in naturally with the trunks of the mighty willow trees, which grow at an angle out of the bank area. The bridge construction hovers over the river without further support. Technology and nature combine in a unity of leisure and building culture.

For the routing of the road through the park, it was largely possible to include the space-defining mature stock and groups of trees, so that interference was kept to a minimum and the road was well integrated by the stock of trees. The necessary clearing was compensated by the planting of 290 new trees.

The 35-metre-wide green bridge remains an important artery of the Luitpoldpark, thereby removing the impression of a separation between the two sections. Since the road lies at a low level the traffic noise in the park is considerably reduced.

The concept was awarded a commendation by the organisers of the German Landscape Architecture Prize in 1999.

Project Team
Schlaich, Bergermann and Partners, structural engineers, Stuttgart (bridge construction)
Kurt Ackermann and Partners, architects, Munich (consultants)

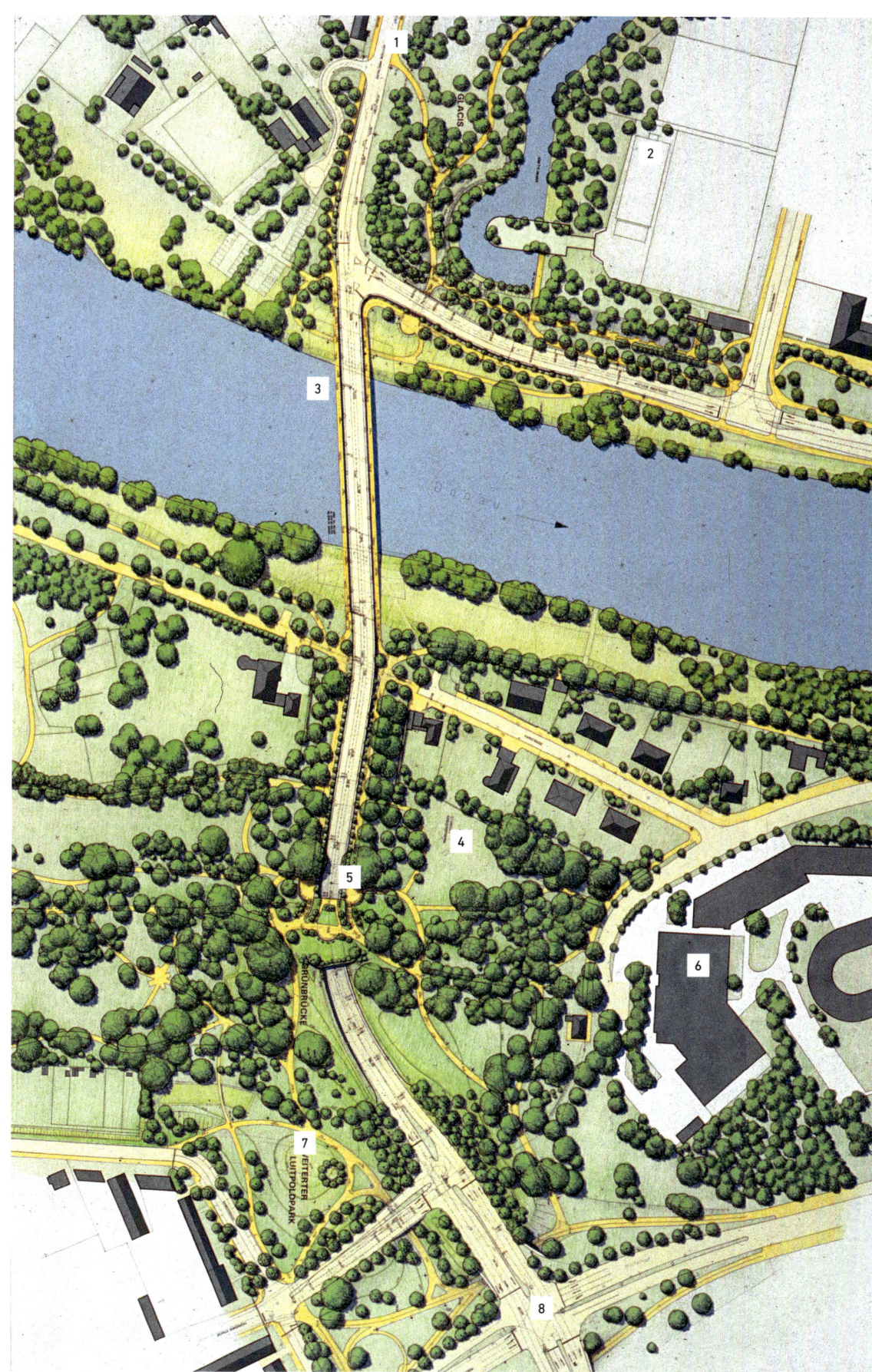

Gesamtlageplan
Glacis, Donaubrücke,
Luitpoldpark

1 Westliche Ringstraße
2 Glacis
3 Glacisbrücke
4 Luitpoldpark
5 Grünbrücke
6 Historische
  Wehranlage
7 Erweiterung
  Luitpoldpark
8 Südliche Ringstraße

General plan of the
Glacis, Danube Bridge
and Luitpoldpark

1 Western ring road
2 Glacis
3 Glacis Bridge
4 Luitpoldpark
5 Wildlife crossing
6 Historical fortifications
7 Luitpoldpark extension
8 Southern ring road

Südliche Donau mit Blick auf das Schloss

Southern Danube looking towards the Castle

Nördliche Donau, von der neuen Brücke aus gesehen

Northern Danube, seen from the new bridge

Rechte Seite: Die neue Spannbandbrücke (Ansicht von Süden) mit aufgeständerter Fahrbahn und dem auf den Spannbandseilen liegenden Fuß- und Radweg ordnet sich mit dieser Technik optimal in die Flusslandschaft ein. Technik und Natur ergänzen sich.

Right: The new stress ribbon bridge (seen from the south) with raised carriageway and the footpath and cycle track located on the stress ribbon cables blends in very well with the river landscape. Technology and nature complement each other.

Die Brücke in der Ansicht von Norden. Unter der Brücke erkennbar das Überspannungsauflager

The bridge, from the north. The tension support under the bridge can be clearly seen.

Rechte Seite: Die Tieflage der Straße ermöglicht eine grüne Verbindung zwischen den beiden Parkteilen

Right: The low positioning of the road permits a green link between the two sections of the park.

Die von der Glacisbrücke kommende Straßentrasse führt in Tieflage durch den Park.

The road from the Glacis Bridge runs at a low level through the park.

Die Grünbrücke verbindet beide Parkteile, die Fahrbahntrasse verläuft im Kurvenschwung unter der Grünbrücke.

The wildlife crossing links the two sections of the park, and the roadway curves down beneath the wildlife crossing.

Rechte Seite: Die Wegetrassen im Park führen auf die Grünbrücke zu. Die Fahrbahntrasse kann gefahrlos überquert werden.

Right: The footpaths in the park lead towards the wildlife crossing, which enables the carriageway to be crossed safely.

Universität Erfurt
Entwicklungsplanung

University of Erfurt
Development planning

Universität Erfurt – Vision und Konzeption einer Entwicklung

Mit der Erweiterung und Aufwertung der Pädagogischen Hochschule zur Universität Erfurt begann eine Neuordnung, die auch architektonische Folgen hatte. Ein städtebaulicher Wettbewerb mit Realisierungswettbewerb für die Bibliothek war der erste Schritt.

Der städtebauliche Grundgedanke war, das architektonische Programm der neuen Universität an einen vorhandenen Feldweg, den alten »Gärtnerweg«, anzugliedern. Auf diesem Areal bauten die ehemals weltberühmten Samenhändler Benary ihre Pflanzensortimente an und züchteten Gemüse- und Blumensamen. Das war ein historischer Leitpfad, mein Ziel war es, ihn als Entwicklungsachse städtebaulich einzubeziehen.

Der erste Bauabschnitt war der Neubau der Bibliothek, des geistigen Zentrums der neuen Universität. Sie steht zeichenhaft an einer städtebaulich wirksamen Position.

Die vorhandene Bausubstanz der ehemaligen Pädagogischen Hochschule, Bauten der DDR-Zeit, steht unter Denkmalschutz. Dieser Komplex wird im Westen durch die neue Bandstruktur der Bebauung räumlich gefasst, somit ergibt sich ein langgestreckter Campus von der Bibliothek bis zur Mensa und in Ergänzung bis zur Sporthalle mit freiem Sportgelände.

Die gesamte Zone ist frei von Kraftfahrzeugverkehr. Die Parkplätze sind als Parkharfe linear geschwungen im Westen angeordnet, so dass die kurzen Querwege durch einen Grünzug direkt auf den Campus führen.

Projektbeteiligte
Koch + Partner, Architekten und Stadtplaner, München

University of Erfurt – vision and conception of a development

The extension and upgrading of the Teaching College of the University of Erfurt marked the beginning of a reorganisation which also had architectural consequences. An urban planning competition and a competition for the construction of the library represented the first step.

The basic idea behind the town planning was to arrange the architectural programme of the new university along an existing footpath, the old "Gärtnerweg". On this site Benary, the formerly world-famous seed merchants, cultivated their ranges of plants and grew fruit and vegetable seeds. It was a historic pathway and it was my goal to integrate it as a development axis into the urban planning concept.

The first building phase was the construction of the new library, the intellectual centre of the new university. It stands symbolically in an effective location from an urban planning point of view.

The existing buildings of the former teaching college, buildings dating from GDR times, are listed buildings. This complex is framed spatially in the west by the new ribbon structure of the building development, thereby creating a strung-out campus from the library to the dining room, continuing to the sports hall and the open sports grounds.

The entire zone is free of vehicle traffic. The parking spaces are arranged in the west in an arching curve so that the short cross paths through the green space lead directly towards the campus.

Project Team
Koch + Partners, architects and town planners, Munich

Zielplanung, Universitätscampus

1 Bibliothek, 1. Bauabschnitt
2 Vorhandenes Ensemble der Pädagogischen Hochschule
3 Mensa
4 Institutsbauten
5 Hörsäle
6 Parkharfe
7 Bachlauf
8 Grünzug
9 Kleingärten
10 Alter Gärtnerweg, Fußweg zur Stadt

Planning overview, university campus

1 Library, 1st building phase
2 Existing ensemble of the Teaching College
3 Canteen
4 Institute buildings
5 Lecture theatres
6 The curve of the car park
7 Course of the stream
8 Wildlife crossing
9 Allotments
10 Old "Gärtnerweg", footpath to the town

Linke Seite: Städtebaulicher Gesamtentwurf

Left: General urban plan

Vorplatz der Bibliothek, 1. Bauabschnitt. Im Hintergrund die Felder der Samenzüchter

Forecourt in front of the library, first building phase. In the background are the fields of the seed growers.

Rechte Seite: Zugangsachse zur Bibliothek, rechts Bauten der Pädagogischen Hochschule (unter Denkmalschutz)

Right: Approach axis for the library; on the right the buildings of the Teaching College (protected buildings)

Ludwig-Maximilians-Universität
Fakultät Chemie und Pharmazie, Institut für Molekularbiologie
München

Ludwig Maximilian University
Faculty of Chemistry and Pharmacy, Institute for Molecular Biology
Munich

Chemie, Pharmazie, Molekularbiologie – eine Wissenschaftsmeile

Auf einem schmalen Grundstück wurde eine architektonische Komposition entwickelt, in der eine Abfolge von Räumen mit Verengungen und platzartigen Erweiterungen eine gute Struktur für die Freiraumgestaltung ergaben. Eine Magistrale führt von der Molekularbiologie an den Instituten der Pharmazie und Chemie vorbei bis zu dem Zentrum am Hörsaalgebäude – Freiraum für Aufenthalt, Begegnung und Kommunikation.

Der Campus ist durch Wege funktional mit den Zugangsbereichen aus dem öffentlichen Raum und der U-Bahn vernetzt. Besondere Akzente auf dem Campus sind eine Wasserfläche westlich vor dem Hörsaalgebäude und eine Skulptur mit versetzten Stahlringen des Künstlers James Reineking auf der Ostseite, am Rand dieses Platzes.

Die Freiräume wurden mit Einzelbäumen in Reihen oder im Raster bepflanzt, so dass Bäume, Rasen- und Wiesenflächen ein heiteres Freiraumensemble bilden. Zurückhaltung wurde bei den Baumarten geübt, sie beschränken sich auf Platanen (*Platanus acerifolia*) im Süden, Schnurbaum (*Sophora japonica*) entlang der Magistrale und Ahorn (*Acer platanoides*) in linearer und freier Gruppierung.

Mit einem einfachen, durchgängigen Materialkonzept für Wege und Plätze, bestehend aus hellen sandgestrahlten Betonplatten, mittelgrauem Granitpflaster und feinen weißen Pflasterzeilen aus Carrara-Marmor, entstand ein prägnantes Erscheinungsbild.

Projektbeteiligte
Bachmann Marx Brechenbauer, Architekten, München

Chemistry, Pharmacy, Molecular Biology – a scientific mile

An architectural complex was developed on a narrow plot with a sequence of spaces consisting of narrow sections and piazza-like areas which provided a good structure for the design of the open spaces. A main thoroughfare leads from Molecular Biology past the Institutes of Pharmacy and Chemistry to the centre by the lecture theatre building – an open space for spending time, for encounters and communication.

The campus is practically linked by paths with the access areas from the public space and the underground system. Notable accents are set on the campus by an expanse of water to the west of the lecture theatre building and a sculpture with staggered steel rings by the artist James Reineking on the eastern side, on the edge of the square.

The open spaces were planted with single trees in rows or arranged along a grid, so that the trees, lawn and grass areas form a casual open-air ensemble. The choice of tree species was conservative; they are limited to plane trees (*Platanus acerifolia*) in the south, Japanese pagoda trees (*Sophora japonica*) along the main street and maple (*Acer platanoides*) in linear and random groupings.

With a simple and universal material concept for the paths and squares, consisting of light sand-blasted concrete slabs, medium grey granite paving stones and fine white plaster strips of Carrara marble, the result was a distinctive appearance.

Project Team
Bachmann Marx Brechenbauer, architects, Munich

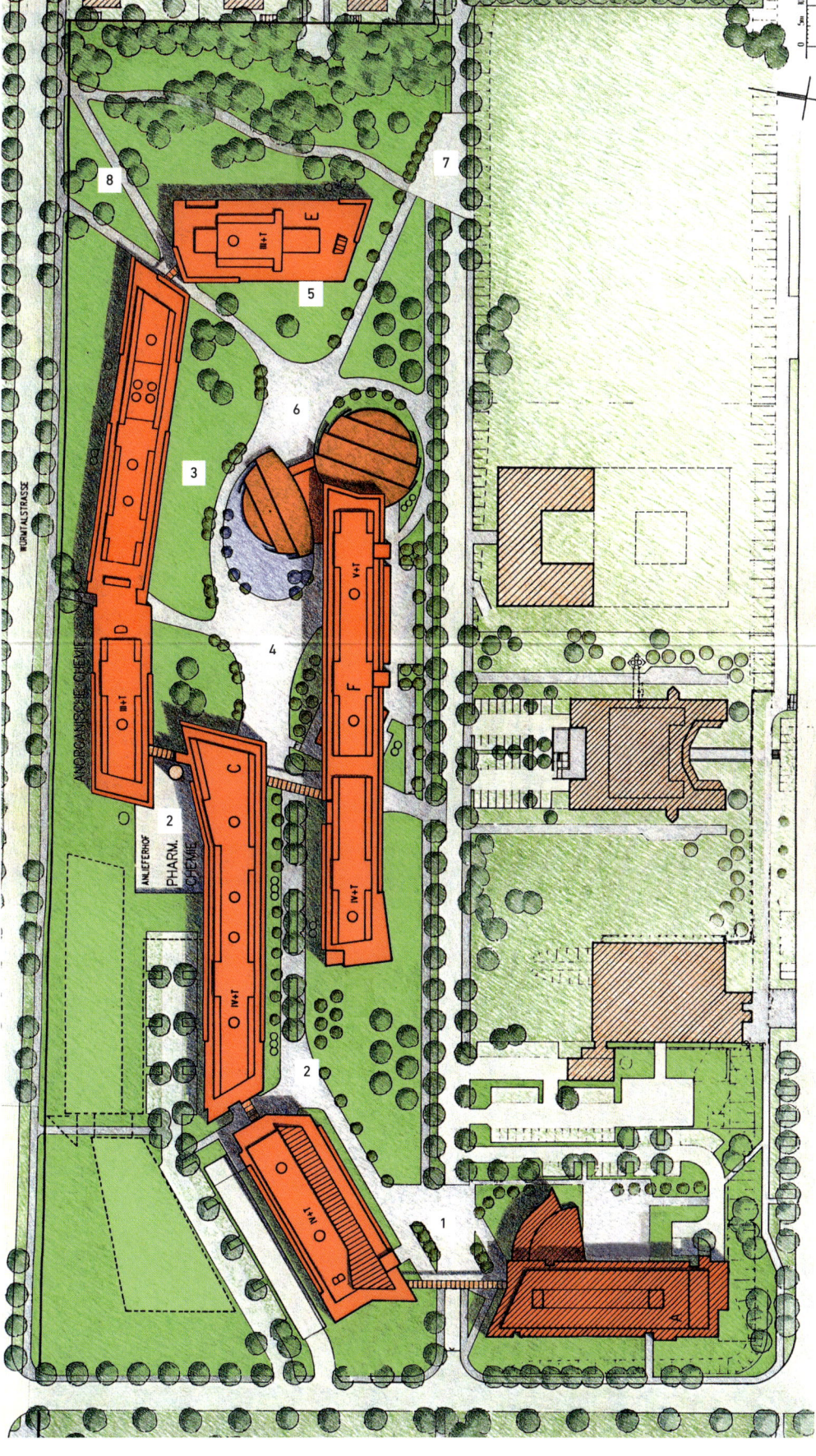

Lageplan Freiraumgestaltung

1 Molekulare Biologie
2 Institut Pharmazie
3 Anorganische Chemie
4 Organische Chemie
5 Physikalische Chemie
6 Hörsäle
7 Fußweg zum Klinikum
8 Fußweg zur U-Bahn

Overview, open-space design

1 Molecular Biology
2 Institute of Pharmacy
3 Anorganic Chemistry
4 Organic Chemistry
5 Physical Chemistry
6 Lecture theatres
7 Footpath to the hospital
8 Footpath to the underground railway

Linke Seite oben:
Die Campus-Achse Richtung Osten, zu den Hörsälen
Linke Seite unten:
Die Campus-Achse Richtung Westen

Left top: The main campus axis looking east towards the lecture halls
Left bottom: The main campus axis looking west

Campus-Achse
mit Durchgang zum
Parkplatz

Campus axis with path
through to car park

Der Campus-Weg nach Westen, Richtung Wissenschaftszentrum Martinsried

The campus path heading west towards the Science Centre in Martinsried

Einrichtungshaus Theresienhöhe
Dachbegrünung
München

Furniture store on Theresienhöhe
Rooftop greening
Munich

»Eine Dachwiese über der Oktoberfest-Wiesn«

»Eine Dachwiese über der Oktoberfest-Wiesn«, mit diesen Worten bezeichnete der Münchner Oberbürgermeister Christian Ude das Planungsprojekt.
Unter der Bedingung einer intensiven Dachbegrünung wurde dem damaligen Eigentümer des Gebäudeensembles, der Firma Karstadt, die Aufstockung ihres Möbelhauses um ein Geschoss genehmigt. Die statischen Gegebenheiten waren äußerst ungünstig, die Aufbauhöhen über der neuen Decke sehr gering. Dementsprechend war nur punktuell eine höhere Gewichtsbelastung möglich, weshalb für die Standorte von Einzelbäumen erhöhte Tröge aus Betonfertigteilen mit einem Wurzelraumvolumen von ca. 7 Kubikmeter Erdsubstrat gebildet wurden. Zwischen dem Raster dieser Bäume wurde eine Rasenfläche angelegt. Von diesem Baumhain aus (*Gleditsia triakanthos* 'Skyline') kann man bei Föhn das Alpenpanorama und während der Oktoberfestzeit die großen Bierzelte und Fahrgeschäfte zu sehen. Urbanität und weiträumige Landschaft fließen dann zusammen.

Projektbeteiligte
Fred Angerer und Gerald Hadler, Architekten, München

"A rooftop meadow overlooking the Oktoberfest site"

"A rooftop meadow overlooking the Oktoberfest site", was how Munich's Lord Mayor Christian Ude described the planning project.
The owner of the property at the time, the company Karstadt, was granted permission to build an additional floor on top of their furniture store on condition that the rooftop was intensively landscaped. The static conditions were highly unfavourable, and the height available for building up above the new roof was minimal. Correspondingly it was only possible to apply an increased load in places, so that deeper tubs made of precast concrete with a root volume of about seven cubic metres of potting soil were selected to hold the individual trees. An area of lawn was planted between the grid-like grove of trees. When the Föhn wind is blowing, you can see the panorama of the Alps from the trees (*Gleditsia triacanthos* 'Skyline'), and during the Oktoberfest the vast beer tents and fairground rides can be observed. On such occasions, the urban setting and expansive landscape merge together.

Project Team
Fred Angerer and Gerald Hadler, architects, Munich

Neue Fassade des Einrichtungshauses von Fred Angerer

New façade of the furniture store by Fred Angerer

Extensive Dachbegrünung auf einem Nebengebäude, im Hintergrund die Paulskirche

Extensive rooftop greening on a neighbouring building; in the background is St. Paul's Church

Das neue, erhöhte Dach, mit Wiese und Baumhain (*Gleditsia triacanthos* 'Skyline')

The new raised roof with grass and grove of trees (*Gleditsia triacanthos* 'Skyline')

Rechte Seite: Bäume und extensive Dachbegrünung. Einzelbäume, die zu einem Hain wurden (*Gleditsia triacanthos* 'Skyline')

Right: Trees and extensive rooftop greening. Individual trees which together form a grove (*Gleditsia triacanthos* 'Skyline')

155

Postbank Paul-Heyse-Straße
Innenhöfe und Dachbegrünung
München

Postbank Paul-Heyse-Strasse
Courtyards and rooftop greening
Munich

Dachgärten – blühende Innenhöfe inmitten der Stadt

Die Idee der Architekten Koch, Benedek + Partner war es, die hohe Lärm- und Abgasbelastung aus den umliegenden Straßen in Bahnhofsnähe durch eine fünfgeschossige Randbebauung auszugrenzen und das Innere des Gevierts mit terrassenartig absteigenden Baukörpern zu gestalten.
Die Idee der Landschaftsarchitekten war es dagegen, die horizontalen Dächer intensiv zu begrünen und daraus eine Gartenkomposition zu entwickeln. Mit Kletterpflanzen wurden die verschiedenen Ebenen »verbunden« und die Fassaden in die Begrünung miteinbezogen. Es entstand eine ruhige, grüne Oase im Innenraum, die Büros öffnen hier ihre Fenster und freuen sich an diesen Gärten, während außerhalb der Verkehr unentwegt lärmt.
Die »hängenden Gärten« wurden möglich, weil Architektur, Statik und Freiraumplanung eng zusammenarbeiteten. Es wurden bei einem Erdsubstrataufbau von 30 bis 60 Zentimeter Intensivpflanzungen mit blühenden Stauden, Gehölzen und Kletterpflanzen vorgenommen, so dass eine terrassierte Oase der Ruhe und der Gartenkultur entstehen konnte.

Projektbeteiligte
Koch Benedek + Partner, Architekten, München

Roof gardens – blossoming courtyards in the heart of the city

The idea of the architects Koch, Benedek + Partners was to block out the high levels of noise and exhaust-fume pollution from the streets surrounding the station by erecting a five-storey building around the perimeter of the site and then designing the inner part of the quadrangle with a building descending in steps like terraces.
The idea of the landscape architects was to green the horizontal roofs intensively and to develop thereby a garden composition. The various levels were "linked" with climbing plants and the façades were also integrated into the greening scheme. The result was a tranquil, green oasis inside the complex. The people in the offices open their windows and take pleasure in the gardens, while the traffic continues to roar away outside.
The "hanging gardens" were possible because of the close cooperation between architecture, statics and open-space planning. By building up the potting soil to a depth of 30–60 centimetres it was possible to carry out intensive planting with flowering plants, groups of shrubs and climbing plants, so that a terraced oasis of tranquillity and horticulture could be created.

Project Team
Koch Benedek + Partners, architects, Munich

Lageplan, Dachaufsicht. Intensive Begrünung in den terrassierten Höfen, extensive Begrünung auf den obersten Dächern

Site plan, view of the roof. Intensive greening of the terraced courtyards, extensive greening on the rooftops

Fassadenbegrünung in den Innenhöfen (*Clematis montana* 'Rubens')

Greening of the façades in the inner courtyards (*Clematis montana* 'Rubens')

Cafeteria im Erdgeschoss mit Anschluss an die öffentlichen Straßen rund um den Hauptbahnhof

Cafeteria on the ground floor with access to the public streets around the railway station

Dachterrasse über der Baumallee auf der Paul-Heyse-Straße

Roof terrace above the avenue of trees on Paul-Heyse-Strasse

Rechte Seite: Außen Straßen- und Verkehrslärm, innen ruhige Gartenatmosphäre in den terrassierten Höfen

Right: Outside, street and traffic noise; inside, a quiet garden atmosphere in the terraced courtyards

Bürogebäude der Swiss Re Germany
Unterföhring

Office building for Swiss Re Germany
Unterföhring

Architektur und Natur – »schwebende Hecke«

Mit der Idee einer schwebenden Hecke, die das Bauwerkensemble umläuft und damit zum kennzeichnenden Erscheinungsbild wird, gewannen die Architekten BRT Bothe Richter Teherani aus Hamburg den Wettbewerb.

Es war eine exzellente fachliche Planungsaufgabe und eine Herausforderung, die architektonische Absicht zuverlässig zu erfüllen. Die konstruktiven Vorgaben für die Begrünung bildeten die in jedem Geschoss umlaufenden Stege mit vorgespannten Stahlnetzen, die zugleich Fluchtwege sind. Zunächst musste geprüft werden, ob eine flächige Fassadenbegrünung, die es in dieser Dimension noch nicht gegeben hatte, möglich ist, da sie nur unter optimalen Wachstumsbedingungen erreicht werden kann. Dazu muss in erster Linie ein ausreichender Wurzelraum gegeben sein. Mit Containern, ohne Bodenanschluss, wie es sich die Architekten vorstellten, wäre eine flächendeckende Begrünung nicht möglich gewesen. Das zweite Kriterium war die richtige Auswahl der Pflanzen, sie orientierte sich vor allem an der Wuchskraft, dem Höhenwachstum, der Vitalität, der Alterungsfähigkeit und der Klimaverträglichkeit. Hierfür waren nur Glycinien (*Wisteria sinensis*) und Wilder Wein (*Parthenocissus quinquefolia*) geeignet. Dies sind die einzigen Pflanzen, die die Anforderungen einer Begrünung von der Unterkante 6,50 Meter bis zur Oberkante 17 Meter dauerhaft erfüllen.

Eine weitere Voraussetzung für den Erfolg der Pflanzung war die optimale Bodenvorbereitung und eine frühzeitige Auswahl der Pflanzen. Im Frühjahr 1999 wurden nach einer Ausschreibung unter den größten Baumschulen über 200 Pflanzen mit einer Wuchshöhe von 5 Metern in der Baumschule Carobbi in Pistoia (Mittelitalien) bestellt. Sie wurden einzeln ausgesucht und dort bis zu einer Höhe von 9 Metern weiter kultiviert. Im Mai 2001 wurden die Pflanzen in belaubtem Zustand in Kühltransportern von Pistoia direkt an die Baustelle transportiert, sofort eingepflanzt und an die dünnen Seilabspannungen der Netzkonstruktion gebunden.

Dank der guten Bodenvorbereitung sind alle Pflanzen angewachsen und es fiel keine aus. Die »schwebende Hecke« hat nach vier Jahren das Ziel eines flächendeckenden Bewuchses erreicht. Dazu war eine optimale Betreuung mit jährlicher Bodenuntersuchung und Düngeangaben sowie eine intensive Pflege durch Schnittmaßnahmen und Einflechtung der Triebe in die Stahlnetze erforderlich. Das Experiment ist gelungen und die architektonischen Computer-Simulationen der Entwurfsplanung sind Wirklichkeit geworden.

Projektbeteiligte
Planung und Ausführung Peter Kluska
BRT Bothe Richter Teherani, Architekten, Hamburg
Martha Schwartz, Landschaftsarchitektin, New York (Entwurf innerer Bereich)

Architecture and nature – "floating hedges"

The architects BRT Bothe Richter Teherani from Hamburg won the competition for their idea of a floating hedge surrounding the perimeter of the group of buildings, and it has in the meantime become a dominant visual feature.

It was an excellent professional planning task and a challenge to fulfil the architectural purpose reliably. The constructional conditions for the greening were provided by the platforms running round each floor with pre-stressed steel nets which serve simultaneously as escape routes. First we had to examine whether it would actually be possible to create a greening of the façade across the entire area. Such a solution had not been attempted on this scale before, and it could only be achieved under optimal growth conditions. First and foremost, there had to be sufficient space for the roots. Using containers but without ground contact, as the architects had imagined it, it would not be possible to achieve an overall greening effect. The second criterion was the correct choice of plants, which was based primarily on vigorous growth, height, vitality, longevity and climate compatibility. The only suitable plants were wisteria (*Wisteria sinensis*) and Virginia creeper (*Parthenocissus quinquefolia*). These are the only plants which can fulfil in the long term the requirements of providing greening from the lower level of 6.50 metres to the upper edge at 17 metres.

A further precondition for the success of the planting was optimal soil preparation and an early selection of plants. In the spring of 1999, following an invitation to tender issued to the biggest nurseries, over 200 plants of five metres in height were ordered from the Carobbi nursery in Pistoia (Central Italy). They were selected individually and continued to be grown there until they reached a height of nine metres. In May 2001, the plants, which had already sprouted leaves, were transported in refrigerated lorries from Pistoia directly to the building site, where they were planted immediately and tied to the thin cables of the netting construction.

Thanks to the careful preparation of the soil, all the plants took and none of them died. After four years the "floating hedge" achieved the target of providing continuous growth across the entire surface. To achieve this, it was necessary to look after the plants very carefully; this entailed annual soil examination and a fertilising programme as well as intensive maintenance by pruning and weaving the shoots into the steel netting. The experiment has succeeded and the architectural computer simulation of the original plans have become reality.

Project Team
Planning and execution Peter Kluska
BRT Bothe, Richter Teherani, architects, Hamburg
Martha Schwartz, landscape architect, New York (design of interior area)

Die »schwebende Hecke« in Vorbereitung mit ausgewählten Pflanzen in der Baumschule Carobbi in Pistoia, Italien

Preparations for the "floating hedge" with selected plants from the nursery Carobbi in Pistoia, Italy

Linke Seite: Die
»schwebende Hecke«
im zeitigen Frühjahr,
kurz vor dem Austrieb

Left: The "floating
hedge" in early spring,
just before sprouting

200 Pflanzen haben den
Weg von Pistoia nach
München-Unterföhring
im Kühlwagen gut
überstanden. Sie waren
im vollen Laub, alle sind
angewachsen, keine ist
ausgefallen.

200 plants survived the
journey from Pistoia to
Munich-Unterföhring in
the refrigerated lorry.
They are in full leaf; all
have continued to grow,
and not a single one
has died.

Die »schwebende Hecke« vier Jahre nach der Pflanzung

The "floating hedge" four years after planting

**Zentraler Bereich –
Farbe, Kunst und Natur**

Für die Entwurfsgestaltung des zentralen Bereichs innerhalb der »schwebenden Hecke« wurde die Landschaftsarchitektin Martha Schwartz beauftragt. Sie hatte die Idee, die trapezförmige Grundfläche in vier Farbquadranten in Rot, Gelb, Grün und Blau zu gliedern und darin farbige Materialien und Pflanzungen, jeweils in der Grundfarbe der Quadranten, zu integrieren. Ferner sollte bei Dunkelheit farbiges Licht aus den Belichtungsschlitzen der darunterliegenden Tiefgarage strahlen.

Diese Planunsideen wurden konsequent umgesetzt, die Pflanzen nach Blütenfarbe zusammengestellt und innerhalb der Quadranten eingesetzt sowie durch farbigen Glassplit in Streifenstruktur ergänzt. Somit wurde die Farbintensität der vier Quadranten deutlich verstärkt

Für die Flächen unterhalb der auf Stützen stehenden Bürotrakte, die für Pflanzen nicht genügend Licht haben, verwendete Martha Schwartz artifizielle Elemente von besonderer Ausdruckskraft, darunter verspiegelte Glaskugeln und rote Holzstämme. Auch die flachen Wasserflächen im Innenhofbereich erhielten entsprechende farbige Materialien: mit grünem und blauem Glassplitt gefüllte Metallkuben, mit roten Holzstämmen und gelben Natursteinquadern und mit flächigen, farbigen Glastropfen-Strukturen.

Diese Entwurfsideen in eine Pflanz- und eine technische Ausführungsplanung umzusetzen, war Aufgabe meines Büros. An dieser Stelle möchte ich meinen langjährigen Mitarbeiter Jürgen Hertlein anerkennend für seine Verdienste bei diesem Projekt erwähnen.

Mit diesem Projekt ist es gelungen, für ein Gewerbegebiet auf ehemaligem Ackergelände eine neue überzeugende Freiraumkultur zu entwickeln. Selten hat eine Gartenanlage so viel Aufmerksamkeit erregt und sie wird weiterhin mit unverminderter Intensität gepflegt und gärtnerisch betreut.

**Central Area –
Colour, art and nature**

The landscape architect Martha Schwartz was commissioned with the design of the central area inside the "floating hedge". She had the idea of dividing the trapezium-shaped area into four coloured quadrants in red, yellow, green and blue and of integrating coloured materials and plants to match the basic colour of the quadrant. After dark, coloured light was to shine out of the lighting slits from the underground garage below.

These planning ideas were carried out in detail; the plants were assembled according to the colour of the flowers and were then planted inside the quadrants and complemented by strips of coloured glass chippings. This considerably increased the intensity of the colour in the four quadrants. The areas beneath the office wing, which was positioned on pillars, did not have enough light for plants. Here Martha Schwartz used highly expressive artificial elements including reflective glass balls and red tree trunks.

The shallow water areas within the inner courtyard were also given corresponding coloured materials: metal cubes filled with green and blue glass chippings, red tree trunks and yellow natural stone blocks as well as flat coloured glass bead structures. It was the task of my office to translate these designs into a plan for the planting and technical implementation. I should like to take this opportunity of expressing my thanks to Jürgen Hertlein, a long-standing colleague, for his contribution to this project.

In this project, we succeeded in developing a new and convincing open-space culture for an industrial area on a former agricultural site. Seldom has a garden aroused so much attention, and it continues to be cared for and looked after by the gardeners with equal commitment.

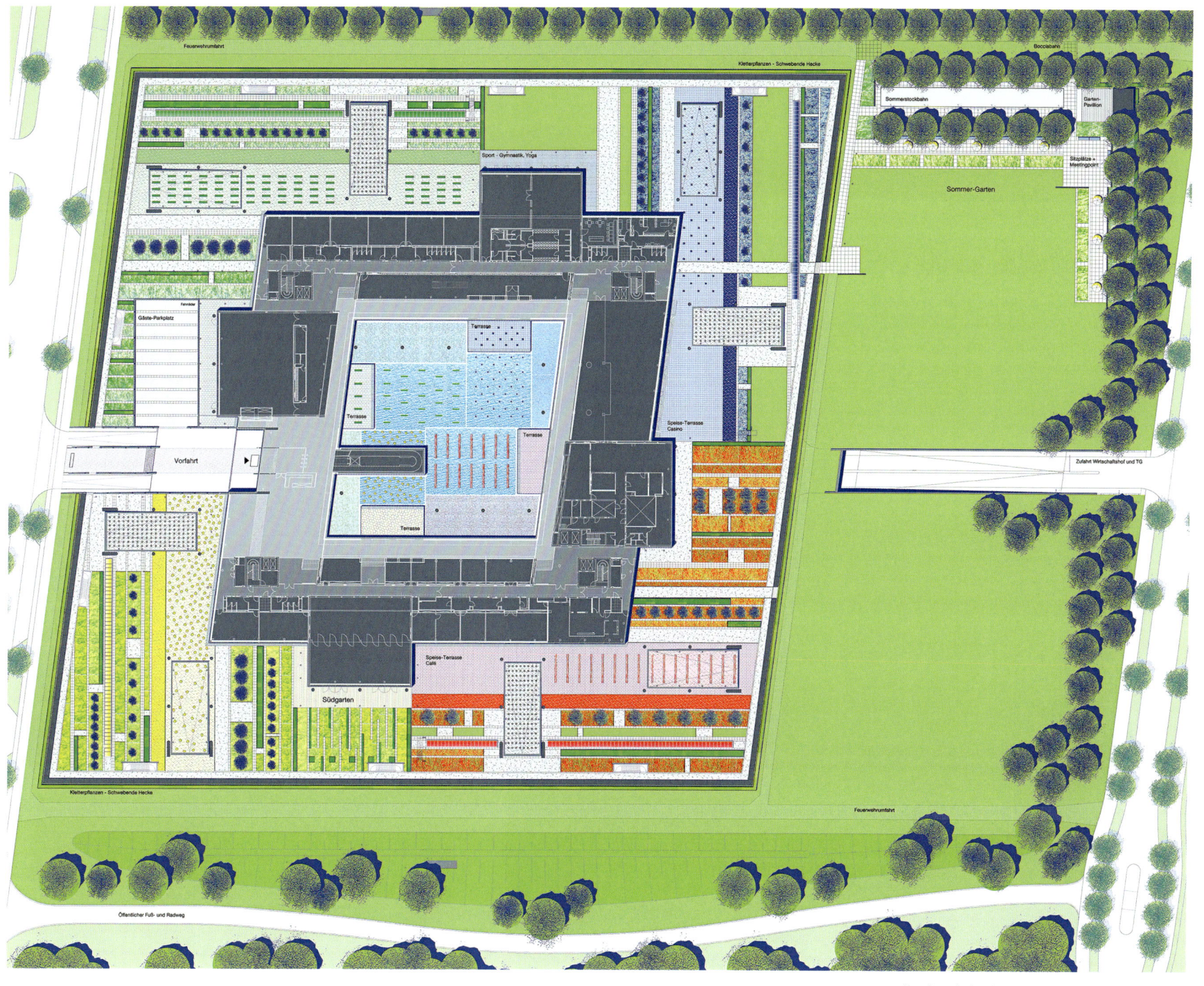

| Der Gestaltplan des inneren Bereichs ist von Martha Schwartz in vier Farbsegmente mit farbigem Glassplitt, mit Blütenfarbe und farbigen Lichtschlitzen der Tiefgarage gegliedert worden. Im Innenhof flache Wasserbecken mit farbigen Installationen | The design plan for the inner area was subdivided into four colour segments by Martha Schwartz, using coloured glass chippings to match the colour of the flowers and coloured strips of light from the underground garage. In the inner courtyard there are shallow areas of water with coloured installations. |

Linke Seite oben:
Ausschnitte aus dem roten und dem gelben Segmentteil
Linke Seite unten: Der Innenhof mit den farbigen Segmenten gelber Natursteinplatten, roten Baumstämmen sowie grünen Glassplittkuben im Flachwasser, darin die »eingehauste« Aufgangsrampe ins erste Obergeschoss

Left top: Details from the red and yellow sections
Left bottom: The inner courtyard with the coloured pieces of yellow natural stone slabs, red tree trunks and cubes full of green glass chippings in shallow water, as well as the "built-in" ramp leading up to the first floor

Ausschnitte aus dem blauen Segmentteil. Unter den aufgeständerten Bürotrakten silbern glitzernde Kugeln

Details from the blue segment section. There are shiny silver balls under the supported office wings.

Robert-Bosch-Haus
Parksanierung
Stuttgart

Robert Bosch House
Park renovation
Stuttgart

Der Garten zur Villa – ein Park

Als Robert Bosch das ehemalige Sommerdomizil des Hofrats Friedrich Wilhelm Hackländer erwarb, um dort seine Villa zu errichten und einen Garten anzulegen, waren bereits landschaftliche Parkstrukturen vorhanden. Umgeben von schmal parzellierten Nutzgärten war der »Hackländer-Park« bereits mit großen Bäumen bestanden. Die Einbeziehung und Schonung der Bäume waren ein maßgebliches Ziel für Planung und Bau der Villa. Diese Grundhaltung der behutsamen Integration seines Neubaus in die Natur setzte sich in allen weiteren Entwicklungsschritten fort. Mit der Beauftragung des Künstlers Franz Boeres, der ab 1910 auch die »Möblierung« des Parks und die Integration architektonisch-künstlerischer Bauelemente übernahm, war die Parkgestaltung abgeschlossen. Das Konzept des Gartens entsprach offenbar ganz der Lebensphilosophie von Robert Bosch, nämlich Klarheit und Genauigkeit im Inneren zu pflegen, gepaart mit Weitblick und Offenheit nach außen. Auch lassen sich aus der Gartenanlage ein ausgeprägter Sinn für künstlerische Qualitäten, ein großes Schönheitsempfinden und ein Sinn für Gartenkultur ablesen.

Die zu Lebzeiten von Robert Bosch liebevoll gepflegte Naturoase wurde in den wechselvollen Jahren der Nachkriegszeit zwar betreut, jedoch nicht im Sinne einer Erhaltung der wesentlichen Grundmerkmale des Parks, was bedeutet hätte, die großzügige Offenheit nach außen in die Weite der Landschaft und des Neckartals zu erhalten. Mit der Zeit gingen die Ausblicke verloren, vor allem durch den stetigen freien Wuchs der Gehölze, durch Naturaussaat oder durch die immer dichter werdenden wintergrünen Eiben. Das hatte auch zur Folge, dass die räumliche Großzügigkeit im Inneren des Parks mehr und mehr verschwand.

Intensive, ausführliche Begehungen im Park und Spurensuche durch Beobachtung ergaben das Konzept für die Restaurierung mit dem Ziel, überflüssigen Zuwachs der letzten Jahrzehnte zu entfernen, das zu dichte Gehölzpotential zu roden sowie die Gartenräume und Ausblicke wieder freizustellen.

Es ergaben sich dabei auch Erkenntnisse, die dazu führten, verlorengegangene Wege, kleine Plätze sowie die defekte Brunnentechnik wiederherzustellen. Auch die alten Bäume und deren Wurzelraum waren fachkundig zu sanieren. Der Teich wurde von den einengenden Rand- und Uferbepflanzungen befreit, neu abgedichtet und zur Villa hin um ein Drittel vergrößert, damit Bauwerk, Park und Wasserfläche in eine ausgeglichene Beziehung zueinander gebracht werden konnten.

Die am Ostrand des Parks verlaufende historische Stützmauer, die einen Höhenunterschied von 4 bis 5 Metern markiert, war notwendig, um das ebene Plateau der Anlage zu schaffen. Die Verbindung zu der unteren Ebene führte ursprünglich nur über eine kleine, in eine Bastion eingebaute Treppe direkt in den Nutzgarten.

Der Neubau des Bosch-Hauses Heidehof mit dem neuen Garten erforderte, zwischen den beiden Ebenen neue Verbindungselemente herzustellen, die den veränderten Nutzungsanforderungen entsprechen sollten. Durch eine großzügige, in die historische Stützmauer eingeschnittene Treppenanlage und durch einen weitläufigen Rundweg zwischen Park und neuem Garten konnte das Ziel einer angemessenen Verbindung beider Gartenteile erreicht werden. Zu dem als Naturdenkmal geschützten alten Baumbestand im Bereich der Villa zählen zwei mächtige Platanen, eine Linde, eine Schwarznuss, eine Zerreiche und eine Stieleiche. Ein weiteres markantes Baumensemble bilden die im Kreis stehenden Schwarzkiefern auf der Südwestseite der Villa.

Die große Aussichtsterrasse im nördlichen Bereich, die sich durch eine der zwei geschützten Platanen besonders markant darstellt, ist ein wesentlicher Teil des Gartenensembles. Erneuert, erweitert und von Wildwuchs befreit, wurde diese Aussichtsplattform in ihrer Axialität wieder an die Terrasse der Villa angebunden.

Das Römerbad mit Felsenbächlein wurde restauriert, so dass das Wasser wieder bis zum See fließen kann. Der See gehört zu den besonders wertvollen Elementen im Park. Die freie Uferlinie wurde zu den offenen Rasenflächen erweitert, damit die Wasserfläche jetzt von der Villa aus wahrgenommen werden kann.

Dieser Park von Robert Bosch ist ein Zeugnis schwäbischer Gartenkunst, ein einzigartiger Beitrag zur Freiraumkultur Stuttgarts. Mittlerweile erfreuen sich die Ensembles von Villa mit Park und Neubau mit Garten bei Mitarbeitern und Gästen größter Beliebtheit.

Auch für mich als Planer war es eine Begegnung mit dem Geist von Robert Bosch, die anregte und mir eine wertvolle Erfahrung war.

Projektbeteiligte
Christian Deplewski, Leiter der Bauabteilung, Stuttgart

Robert Bosch und seine Frau im Gespräch mit einem Besucher

Robert Bosch and his wife talking with a visitor

»Meine Absicht geht dahin, neben der Linderung von allerhand Not, vor allem auf die Hebung der sittlichen, gesundheitlichen und geistigen Kräfte des Volkes hinzuwirken.«
Robert Bosch, 1935

"Apart from helping to alleviate all kinds of hardship, my main intention is to contribute to the improvement of the moral strength, health and intellectual powers of the people."
Robert Bosch, 1935

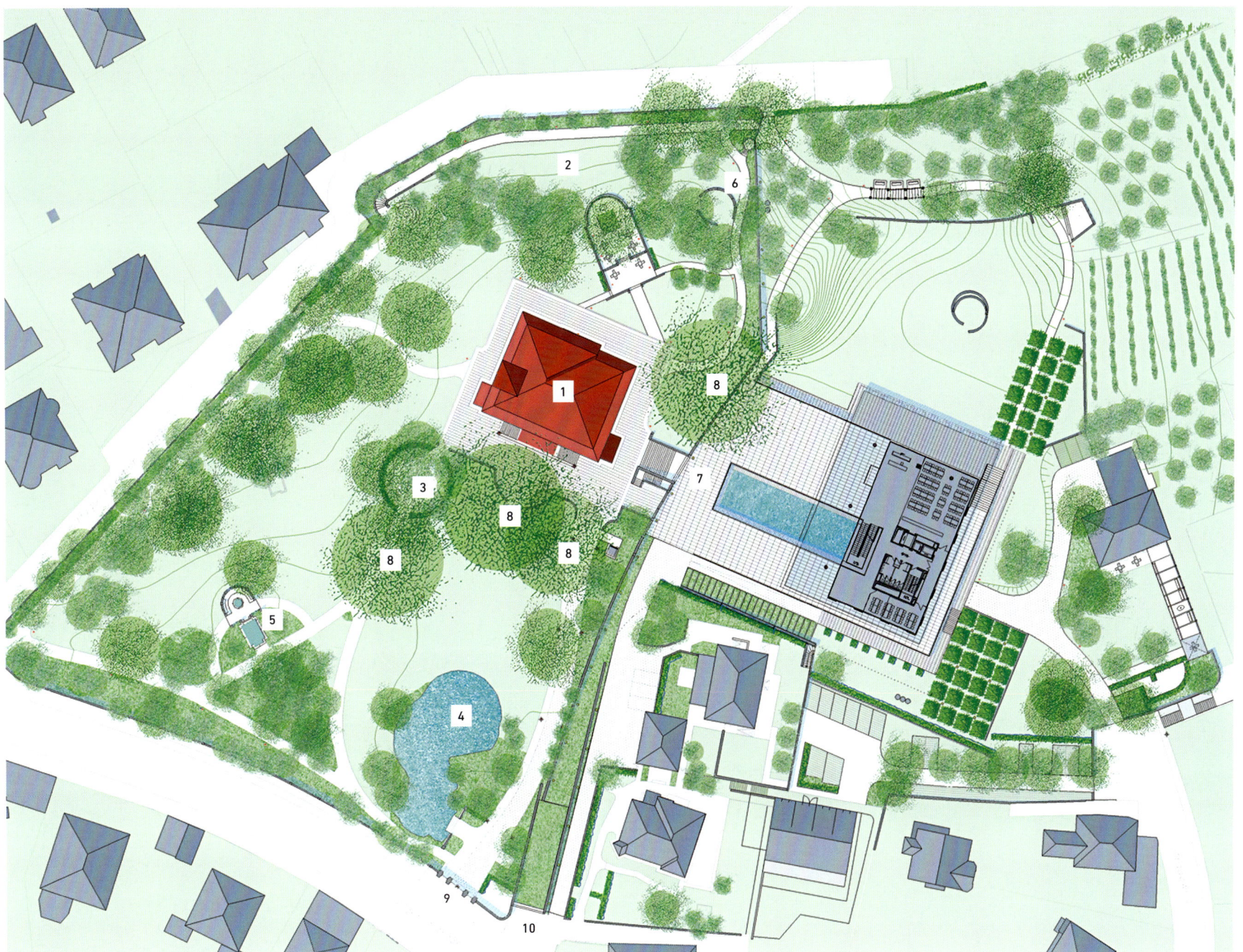

Lageplan Robert-Bosch-Haus

1. Robert-Bosch-Haus, historische Villa, 1906
2. Aussichtsterrasse mit alter Platane
3. Kiefernrondell
4. Erweiterter Teich
5. Römisches Bad
6. Bastion
7. Neuer Treppenabgang zum Vorplatz, Neubau
8. Unter Schutz stehende alte Bäume
9. Portal, Zugang zur Villa
10. Tiefgaragenabfahrt

Site plan for the Robert Bosch House

1. Robert Bosch House, historic villa, 1906
2. Observation terrace with old plane tree
3. Round bed with pine trees
4. Extended lake
5. Roman bath
6. Buttress
7. New stairs leading to the forecourt in front of the new building
8. Protected old trees
9. Entrance to the villa
10. Entrance to the underground garage

The garden surrounding the villa – a park

When Robert Bosch purchased the former summer residence of Privy Councillor Friedrich Wilhelm Hackländer with the intention of building his villa on the site and creating a garden, it already included a number of landscaped park features. Surrounded by narrow strips of kitchen garden, the "Hackländer Park" was already planted with mature trees. The incorporation and retention of the trees was one of the main considerations in the planning and construction of the villa. This basic approach entailing careful integration of his new building into the natural setting was continued through all the further phases of the development. The park design was completed after the commissioning of the artist Franz Boeres, who from 1910 assumed responsibility for the "furnishing" of the park and the integration of architectural and artistic building elements.

The concept of the garden apparently corresponded with the philosophy of Robert Bosch: the cultivation of clarity and precision in domestic affairs and far-sightedness and openness towards the outside world. The garden layout also reveals a marked sensitivity towards artistic qualities, a great sense of beauty and a sense of garden culture.

The natural oasis, lovingly cared for during Robert Bosch's lifetime, was looked after in the turbulent post-war years, but not with a view to maintaining the important basic features of the park, which would have meant retaining the expansive openness towards the outside, incorporating the wide-open spaces of the landscape and the Neckar valley. Over the years, the views were lost, especially through the unhindered growth of the copses, through natural sowing and the evergreen yews, which became progressively denser. The result was that the generous proportions of the park itself increasingly disappeared. Intensive and extensive surveys of the park resulted in the concept for the restoration. It was decided to remove the superfluous growth of the last decades, clear the potentially over-dense copses and once again reveal the spaces and vistas of the garden. The insight gained led to the restoration of paths and little open spaces which had been lost and to the repair of the faulty fountain technology. The old trees and the areas around their roots were also to be professionally restored. The artificial lake was freed from the restricting planting around the edge and along the shore. It was re-sealed and extended by about a third on the villa side, so that the relationship between the building, the park and the area of water could be properly balanced.

The historic retaining wall running along the east side of the park, marking a height difference of four to five metres, was necessary in order to create a flat site for the park. The link to the lower level originally led directly only into the kitchen garden via a small set of stairs built into a buttress. The new building of the Bosch house at Heidehof with its new garden required new links to be established between the two levels in line with the requirements brought about by its changed purpose. Through a generous staircase cut into the historic retaining wall, and an expansive curving route between the park and the new garden it was possible to achieve the aim of establishing an appropriate link between the two sections of the garden.

Among the old trees in the vicinity of the villa which are protected by a preservation order there are two mighty plane trees, a lime tree, a black walnut, a turkey oak and a common oak. Another prominent group of trees is the circular bed of black pines on the south-western side of the villa.

The large observation terrace on the northern side forms an important part of the garden ensemble. It is particularly prominent because of one of the two protected plane trees. Renewed, extended and freed of rank growth, this observation platform was linked again in its axiality to the villa terrace.

The Roman bath and the rock stream were restored, so that the water can flow to the lake once more. The lake is one of the main highlights in the park. Its open shoreline was extended towards the open lawn areas, so that the water can now be seen from the villa.

This park by Robert Bosch bears witness to Swabian garden art and makes a unique contribution to the open-space culture of Stuttgart. Today the ensemble of the villa in its park and the new building with its garden are very popular with staff and visitors alike.

For me, as a planner, it represented an encounter with the spirit of Robert Bosch, which inspired me and proved a valuable experience.

Project Team
Christian Deplewski, Head of the Construction Division, Stuttgart

Rechte Seite:
Bosch-Areal an der Heidehofstraße mit alter Villa und Neubau

Right: The Bosch site on Heidehofstrasse with the historic villa and new building

Linke Seite: Villa Robert-Bosch-Haus mit erweiterter Wasserfläche und den geschützten Bäumen

Left: Robert Bosch House: The villa with the extended lake and the protected trees

Freigelegtes Kiefernrondell mit Taxus-Hecke vor der Terrasse

Round bed with pine trees and taxus hedge in front of the terrace

Das neue Ensemble: alte Villa mit Sockelmauer, Neubau mit offenem Untergeschoss, geschützte Bäume (Platane und Flügelnuss)

The new ensemble: The old villa with retaining wall, new building with open lower storey, protected trees (plane and wingnut)

Rechte Seite: Das neue Ensemble: alte Villa mit Sockelmauer, Neubau mit offenem Untergeschoss, geschützte Bäume (Platane und Flügelnuss)

Right: The new ensemble: The old villa with retaining wall, new building with open lower storey, protected trees (plane and wingnut)

Bilder aus dem
historischen Park

Pictures of the historic
park

Rechte Seite: Erweiterte
Wasserfläche,
römisches Bad im
Hintergrund

Right: The extended
lake with the Roman
bath in the background

Bosch-Haus Heidehof
Der neue Park
Stuttgart

Bosch House Heidehof
The New Park
Stuttgart

Der neue Garten zwischen Architektur und Landschaft

1964 wurde ganz im Sinne der Philosophie von Robert Bosch eine gemeinnützige Stiftung gegründet. Diese benötigte für ihre Aufgaben eine Erweiterung der Nutzflächen. Gleichzeitig wollte die Robert Bosch GmbH die Weiterbildung ihrer Führungskräfte mit Seminaren und Tagungen weiter ausbauen. Dazu wurde ein Neubau immer dringlicher, so dass sich der Bauherr entschloss, im Jahr 2000 einen Architekturwettbewerb für das ehemalige Gärtnereigelände von Robert Bosch auszuloben. Den Zuschlag erhielt Peter Kulka, er nahm in seiner Arbeit den Dialog mit dem Altbau auf. Beide Bauwerke sollten ihre eigene Identität haben und durch die Freiraumgestaltung zu einer Einheit werden. Eine markante Stützmauer trennte die beiden unterschiedlich hoch liegenden Standorte von Villa und Neubau. Dieser Höhenunterschied von 4 bis 5 Meter wurde mit einer Freitreppe überwunden, die Öffnung der Stützmauer war die Voraussetzung für das Ineinandergreifen und Verbinden beider Projekte. Aus dem Park der Villa kommt man hinabsteigend auf den großen Vorplatz des Neubaus. Von hier aus öffnet sich ein ungehinderter Blick auf die Stadtstruktur und in die Ferne des Neckartals. Von der Terrasse der Kantine steigt man hinunter auf die Ebene des Untergeschosses. Hier beginnt ein Rundweg, der den neuen Garten mit dem alten Park der Villa verbindet. Die Vegetationsstrukturen im Umfeld des Neubaus sind zwei Baumhaine mit geschnittenen Platanen, die die kubische Form des Neubaus aufnehmen.

Aus der Distanz des Rundwegs betrachtet wirken Villa und Neubau trotz größter Verschiedenheit als einheitliches Ensemble. Die Freiraumplanung leistete dazu einen wesentlichen Beitrag.

Nördlich des Neubaus entstand eine frei modellierte Wiese, die in den erhalten gebliebenen Obstbaumgarten aus der alten Bosch-Gärtnerei übergeht. Auf dem Rundweg begegnet man auch einem Versatzstück aus dem Altgelände, einer Pergola, die vor der Obstbaumkulisse neu aufgebaut und mit Sitzplätzen ausgestattet wurde. An den Rundweg anschließend wurde eine Aussichtsterrasse angelegt, die gleichsam ein Pendant zu der Terrasse im Villenpark ist.

Im Zentrum der großen Wiese hat der Künstler Bernar Venet seine Bodenskulptur sehr sensibel in der leicht geneigten Wiesenfläche positioniert. Damit zeigt sich auch, dass Kunst am richtigen Ort Verbindungskräfte erzeugt.

Projektbeteiligte
Kulka und Partner, Architekten, Köln/Dresden

The new garden between architecture and landscape

In 1964, a charitable foundation was set up in line with the philosophy of Robert Bosch. More office space was required for this work. Robert Bosch GmbH also wanted to expand its management training programmes to include seminars and conferences. This made the need for a new building increasingly urgent, so that the client decided in 2000 to stage an architecture competition for the former site of Robert Bosch's market garden.
The winner was Peter Kulka, who included dialogue with the old building in his design. Each building was to have its own identity, but to fuse together through the design of the open spaces. A prominent retaining wall separated the sites of the villa and the new building, which are on different levels. The difference in height of between four and five metres was bridged by a flight of stairs; the opening in the retaining wall was the prerequisite for the interaction and interlinking of the two projects. From the park surrounding the villa, the visitor climbs down to the expansive forecourt in front of the new building. From here there is an unimpeded view of the layout of the city with the Neckar valley in the background. From the canteen terrace, you can climb down to the level of the lower floor. This marks the start of a circular path which links the new garden with the old park surrounding the villa. The vegetation structures in the vicinity of the new building are two groves of trimmed plane trees which are a fair match for the cuboid shape of the new building.
As you follow the circular path, from a distance the villa and new building form a unified ensemble despite their differences of style. The planning of the open space plays an important role in this respect.
A freeform meadow was created to the north of the new building. It gives way to the orchard of the old Bosch market garden, which has been preserved. On the circular path you will also come across a piece of scenery from the old site, a pergola which was repositioned in front of the backdrop of fruit trees and provided with seats. An observation terrace was also constructed next to the circular path, which acts as a counterpart to the terrace in the park of the villa.

The artist Bernar Venet positioned his floor sculpture very astutely on the gently sloping expanse of grass in the centre of the large meadow, and it is another example of the way that art in the right location can help to establish connections.

Project Team
Kulka and Partners, architects, Cologne/Dresden

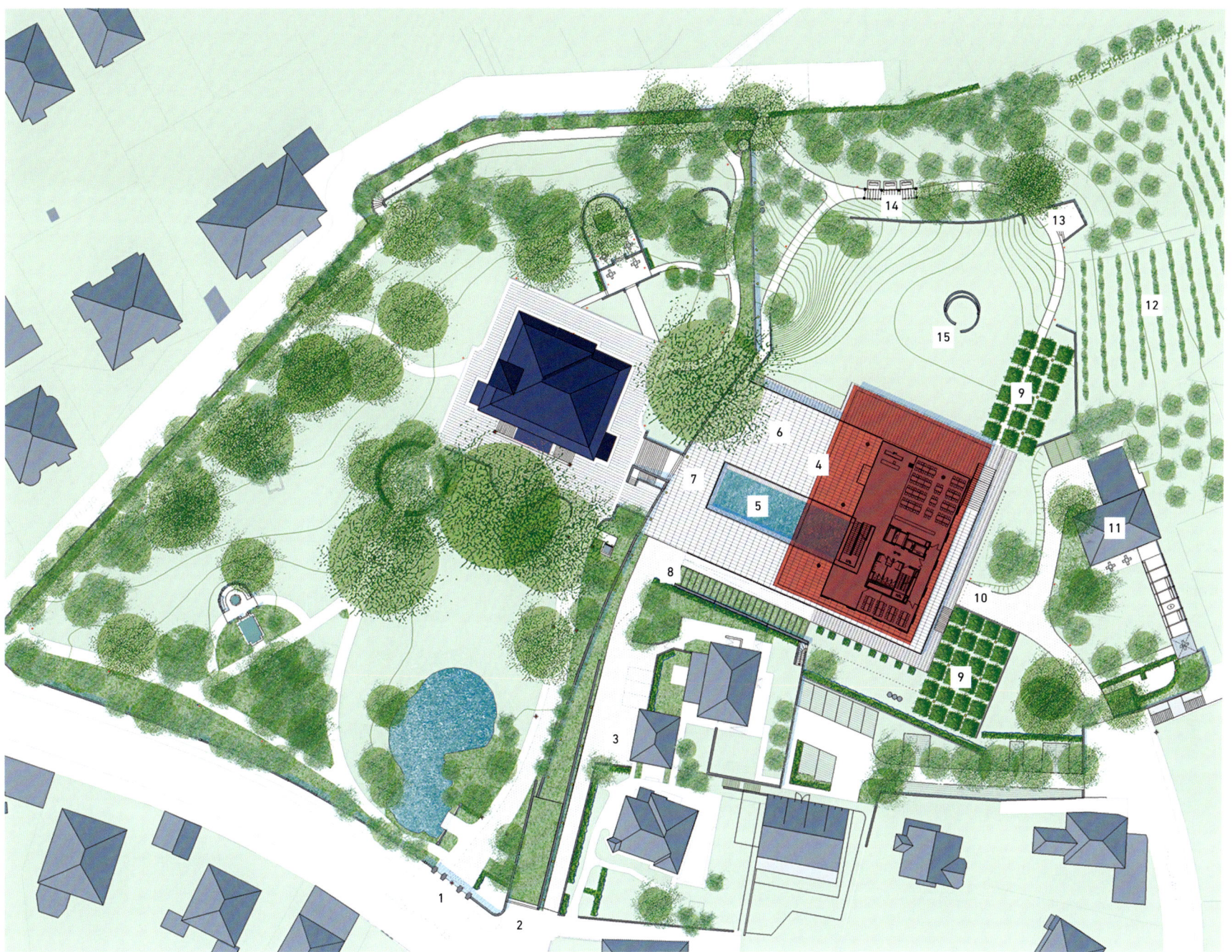

Lageplan Neubau
Bosch-Haus Heidehof

1 Portal der Villa
2 Zufahrt der Tiefgarage
3 Zugang zum Neubau Bosch-Haus
4 Eingang zum Neubau
5 Tiefhof des Untergeschosses
6 Vorplatz
7 Treppenaufgang zur Villa
8 Rampe, Abgang zum Untergeschoss mit Pflanzterrassen
9 Geschnittene Platanen
10 Anlieferung
11 Sammlung Homöopathie
12 Spalierobst-Quartier, ehemaliger Nutzgarten
13 Neue Aussichtsterrasse am Rundweg
14 Sitzplatz und neuer Standort der alten Gartenpergola
15 Bodenskulptur, Bernar Venet

Site plan of the new building for the Bosch House Heidehof

1 Villa entrance
2 Entrance to the underground garage
3 Entrance to the new building of the Bosch House
4 Entrance to the new building
5 Sunken courtyard of the lower ground floor
6 Forecourt
7 Stairs leading up to the villa
8 Ramp leading down to the lower level with planted terraces
9 Pruned plane trees
10 The tradesman's entrance
11 Homeopathic collection
12 The espalier fruit tree area, formerly the kitchen garden
13 New observation terrace by the circular path
14 Seating area and new location of the old garden pergola
15 Floor sculpture, Bernar Venet

Linke Seite: Robert-
Bosch-Haus und
Bosch-Haus Heidehof,
ein neues Ensemble
der Baukultur und
Freiraumkultur

Left: Robert Bosch
House and Bosch
House Heidehof, a new
ensemble of buildings
and gardens

Rechte Seite:
Neubau Bosch-Haus
Heidehof, Architekt
Peter Kulka, ausge-
zeichnet mit dem
Hugo-Häring-Preis,
2006

Right: Bosch House
Heidehof, the new
building. Architect Peter
Kulka, awarded the
Hugo Häring Prize, 2006

Linke Seite: Die Platanenallee führt zur neuen Terrasse am Rundweg

Left: The avenue of plane trees leads to the new terrace by the circular path

Die neue Aussichtsterrasse am Parkrundweg

The new observation terrace by the circular path through the park

Natur und Kunst
Johann Wolfgang Goethe

Natur und Kunst, sie scheinen sich zu fliehen
Und haben sich, eh' man es denkt, gefunden.
Der Widerwille ist auch mir verschwunden,
Und beide scheinen gleich mich anzuziehen.

Es gilt wohl nur ein redliches Bemühen!
Und wenn wir erst in abgemessnen Stunden
Mit Geist und Fleiß uns an die Kunst gebunden,
Mag frei Natur im Herzen wieder glühn.

So ist's mit aller Bildung auch beschaffen.
Vergebens werden ungebundne Geister
Nach der Vollendung reiner Höhe streben.

Wer Großes will, muss sich zusammenraffen.
In der Beschränkung zeigt sich erst der Meister,
Und das Gesetz nur kann uns Freiheit geben.

Nature and Art
Johann Wolfgang Goethe

Nature and art seem ofttimes to be foes,
But, ere we know it, join in making peace;
My own repugnance, too, has come to cease,
And each an equal power attractive shows.

Let us but make an end to dull repose:
When art we serve in toil without release,
Through stated hours, absolved from vain caprice,
Nature once more within us freely glows.

All culture, as I hold, must take this course:
Unbridled spirits ever strive in vain
Perfection's radiant summit to attain.

Who seeks great ends must straitly curb his force;
In narrow bounds the master's skill shall show,
And only law true freedom can bestow.

Translation: Prof. James Taft Hatfield

Rechte Seite: Skulptur, Bernar Venet

Right: Sculpture, Bernar Venet

Pionierkaserne Auf der Schanz
Ingolstadt

Pionierkaserne Auf der Schanz
Ingolstadt

Soldaten-Campus – die Neuordnung einer Kaserne

Die traditionsreiche Kaserne Auf der Schanz wurde im Zuge der Strukturreform der Bundeswehr zum Ausbildungszentrum. Die Gerätschaften der Kampftruppenausbildung wurden entfernt, die Unterstellhallen für Panzer und Großfahrzeuge abgebrochen.

Ein mit einem Realisierungsteil kombinierter städtebaulicher Wettbewerb wurde ausgelobt, und von dem Team der Architekten gmp von Gerkan, Marg und Partner Hamburg gemeinsam mit Peter Kluska gewonnen. Vorgesehen waren zunächst der Abbruch aller Gebäude und eine vollständige Neubebauung. Es folgte ein zweijähriger Abwägungsprozess mit dem Ergebnis, bestehende Bauten umzuwidmen und zu erhalten sowie ein neues Gesamtkonzept zu entwickeln.

Das Programm für die Neuordnung wurde zur Grundlage der realisierten Konzeption mit Lehrgebäude, »Bauhof« zur praktischen Schulung, einer Doppelsporthalle und Antretplatz. Ferner mit Wohnungen für die Schulungsteilnehmer, Verwaltung, Kasino und einer Hindernisbahn. Planungsaufgabe war vor allem die innere Erschließung, Parkplätze und Zufahrtspforte sowie die Integration aller verbleibenden Bauten in ein umfassendes Freiraumkonzept.

Die neue Konzeption wurde zu einer schlüssigen Raumkomposition mit einer großzügigen weiträumigen freien Mitte und einer Wasserachse vom Schulungsgebäude im Westen bis zum Antretplatz vor der Sporthalle im Osten.

Eine Platanenallee flankiert in linearer Anordnung diese Mittelzone. Im Kontrast dazu sind die Randzonen unter Einbeziehung vorhandener Baumbestände parkartig gestaltet.

Projektbeteiligte

gmp von Gerkan, Marg und Partner, Architekten, Hamburg

Military campus – The reordering of a barracks

The renowned Auf der Schanz barracks was transformed into a training centre during the course of the structural reforms within the German armed forces. The equipment used for training the strike forces was removed and the shelters for the tanks and other large vehicles were demolished.

A town-planning competition combined with an implementation component was organised; the winners were the team of architects gmp von Gerkan, Marg and Partners, Hamburg, together with Peter Kluska. It was initially planned to demolish all the buildings and replace them with new ones. However, during the course of a two-year assessment process it was agreed to retain and convert the existing buildings and to develop a new overall concept.

The programme for the reorganisation became the basis for the design which was subsequently carried out, including a lecture complex, a "construction yard" for practical training, a dual sports hall and a parade ground. There were also living quarters for those attending the training courses, administration buildings, a mess and an obstacle course. The task of the planners was the internal infrastructure, parking spaces and entrance gate as well as integrating all remaining buildings into an integral open space concept.

The new design became a harmonious spatial layout with a generous and spacious open central area and a water axis from the training complex in the west to the parade ground in front of the sports hall in the east.

An avenue of plane trees arranged in a line borders this central area. The side zones form a contrast and include existing trees to create a park-like setting.

Project Team

gmp von Gerkan, Marg and Partners, architects, Hamburg

Kasernengelände vor der Umgestaltung. Hallen für Panzer und Schwerlastfahrzeuge im zentralen Bereich

The military campus before its transformation. The shelters for tanks and heavy vehicles are in the central area.

Wettbewerbsplan vor der Neuordnung der Bundeswehrstandorte

Competition plan before the reorganisation of armed forces locations

Nördlicher Teil: Übernahme des Geländes durch die Stadt Ingolstadt für Büro- und Wohnungsbau sowie für städtisches Grün

Northern section: Acquisition of the site by the city of Ingolstadt for office buildings and residential accommodation and for urban green areas

Südlicher Teil: Pionierkaserne

Southern section: Pionierkaserne (military barracks)

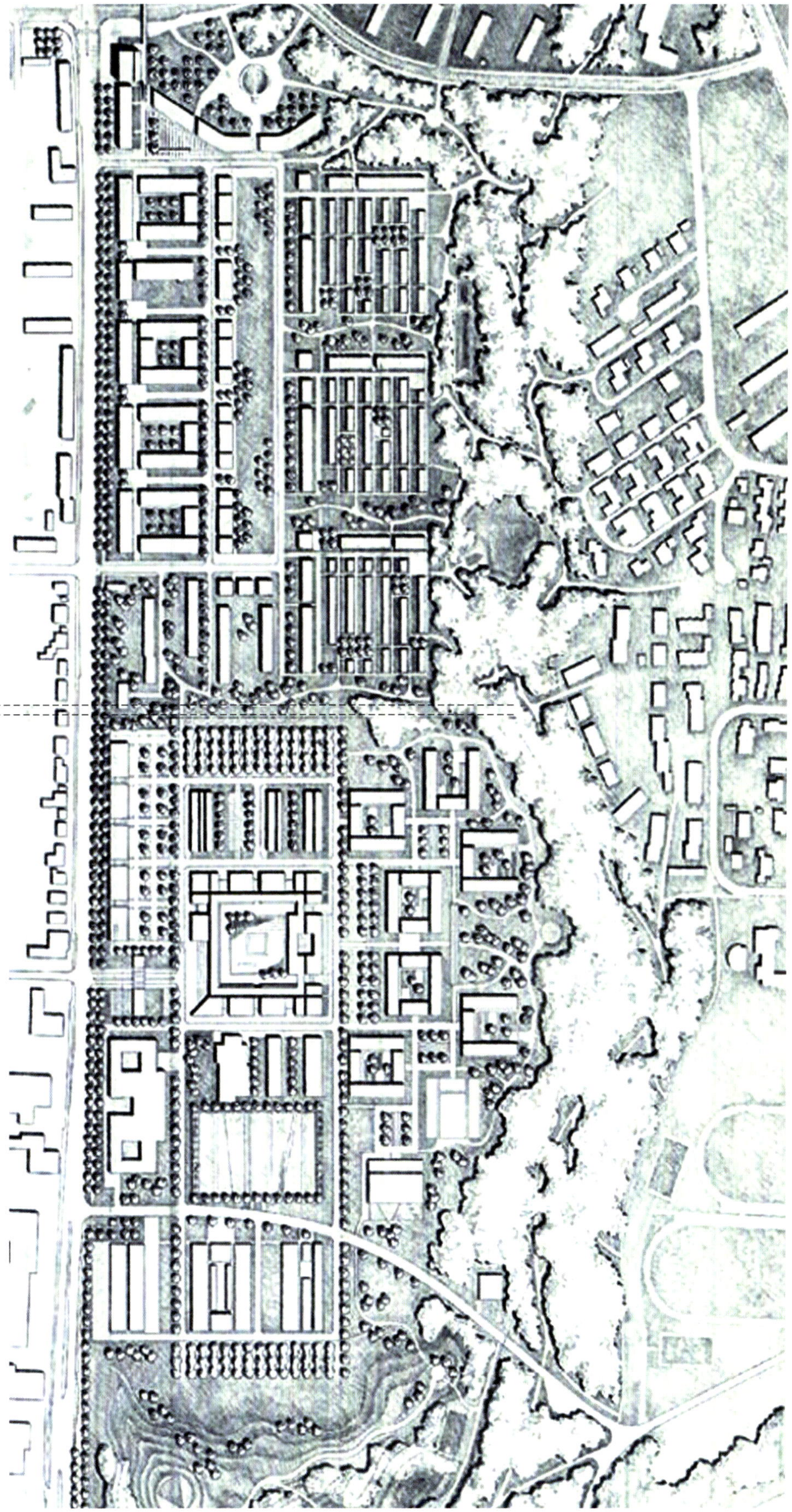

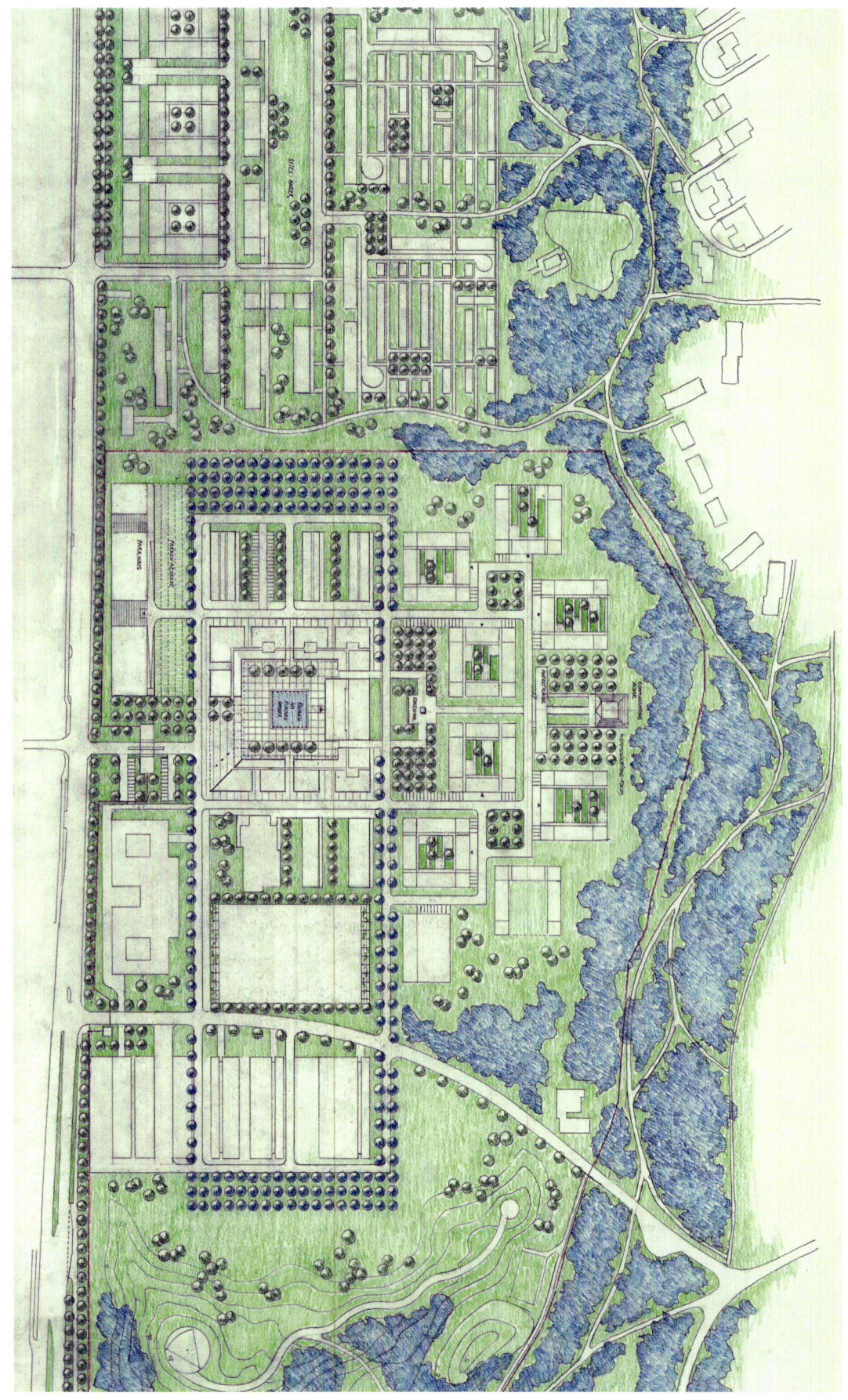

Überarbeitete zweite Entwurfsfassung vor der Standortneuordnung

Revised second draft before reordering of the location

Lageplan 3, Grundlage der Realisierung

1. Pforte
2. Kantine
3. Lehrgebäude
4. Wohnungen
5. Bauhof
6. Antretplatz
7. Sporthallen
8. Hindernisbahn
9. Lagerhalle
10. Gebirgsjäger
11. Dienste
12. Sozialgebäude
13. Fahrzeuge
14. Parkplätze
15. Großer innerer Freiraum, Wasserachse, Allee, Soldaten-Campus

Site plan 3, Basis for implementation

1. Gate
2. Canteen
3. Teaching building
4. Living quarters
5. Construction yard
6. Parade ground
7. Sports halls
8. Obstacle course
9. Storage depot
10. Mountain troops
11. Services
12. Employee facilities
13. Vehicles
14. Parking spaces
15. Large open space, water axis, avenue, military campus

Gesamtareal westlich der Autobahn München-Nürnberg. Ein neuer städtebaulicher Akzent ist entstanden: Baukultur und Freiraumkultur.

Complete site west of the Munich-Nuremberg motorway. A new urban accent has been set by combining buildings with open spaces.

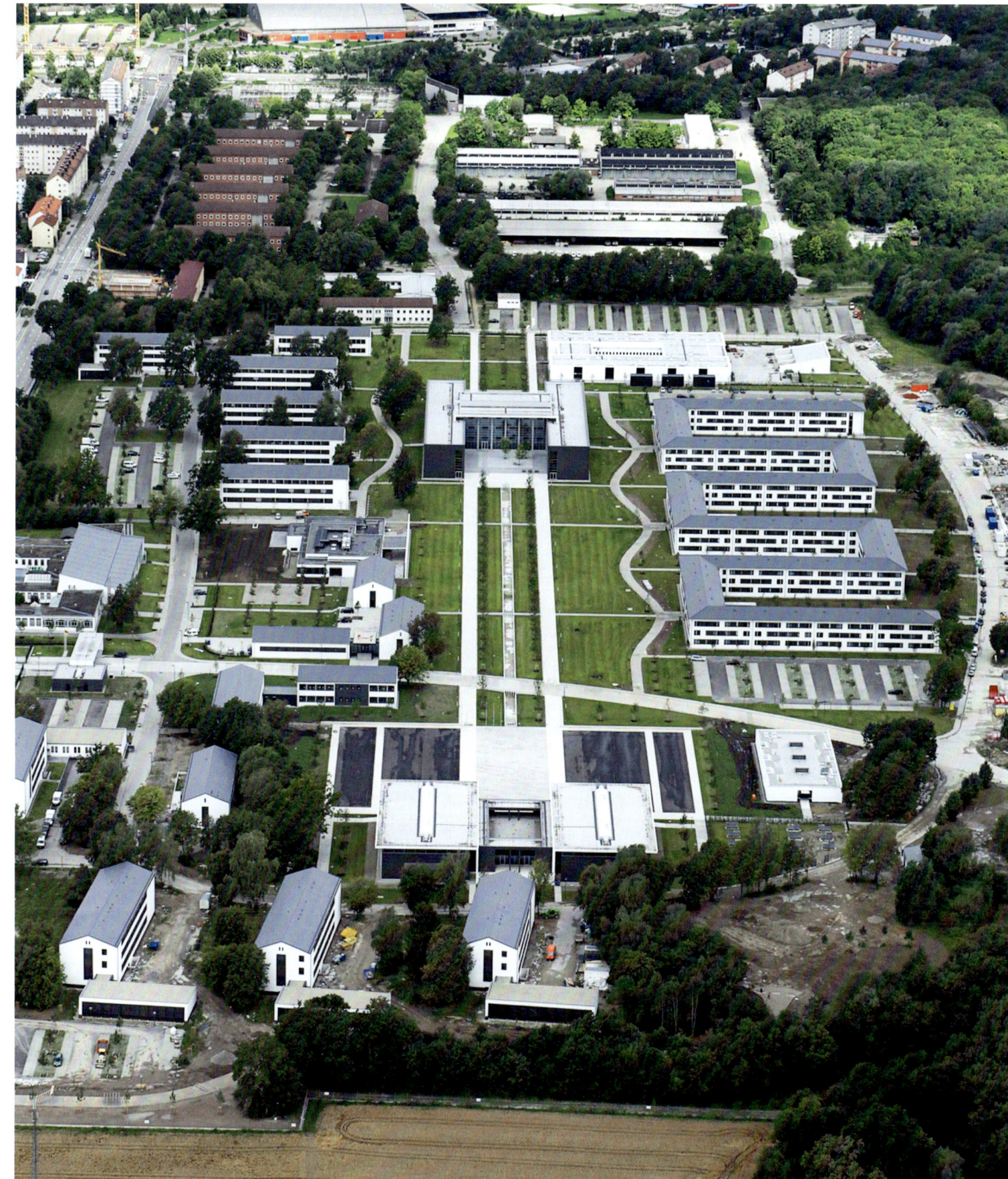

Soldaten-Campus kurz vor der Fertigstellung

The military campus shortly before completion

Vorplatz Lehrgebäude

Forecourt, teaching building

Rechte Seite:
Soldaten-Campus
Wasserachse und
Mittelallee

Right: Military campus
Water axis and central avenue

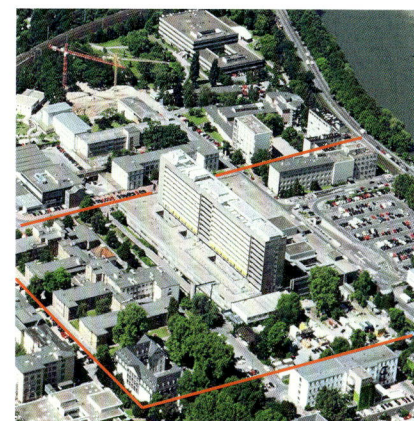

Klinikum der Goethe-Universität

Medizinische Einrichtungen und städtebauliche Verdichtung
Frankfurt am Main

Goethe University Clinic

Consolidation of medical facilities in an urban setting
Frankfurt am Main

Medizin, Lehre und Forschung am Mainufer

Die Sanierung und Erweiterung des Klinikums bei laufendem Betrieb ist ein langer Planungs- und Bauprozess, der zu einer baulichen Verdichtung führte. Nach einem Planungswettbewerb 1999 wurden zunächst die Erschließungsstruktur geändert, der Hauptzugang neu positioniert und die Straßenbahnhaltestelle verlegt. Auf dem bestehenden Parkplatz soll ein offenes, grünes Forum entstehen, das sich zum Main hin öffnet. Der erste Bauabschnitt und der neue Hauptzugang sind bereits realisiert, ebenso das Hörsaal- und zwei Forschungsgebäude.

Jenseits der Hochhausscheibe war ein großzügiger Patientenpark beabsichtigt, der aufgrund einer zusätzlichen Erweiterung und Verdichtung der Bausubstanz entfallen musste. Stattdessen ist nun eine Gartenachse geplant, eine Art Promenade mit intensiver Bepflanzung, Wasserflächen und Sitzplätzen. Die Tiefhöfe der Untergeschosse werden in dieses System eingebunden. Sie werden nicht bepflanzt, sondern aus Gründen der Hygiene und des Unterhalts flächig mit farbigem Glassplitt und senkrechten farbigen Glasstelen ausgestattet. Dem erweiterten Bauvolumen sollen markante raumgliedernde Baumgruppen und -reihen entgegengesetzt werden, die eine wirksame Durchgrünung für Patienten und Personal gleichermaßen bewirken. Wenn es um Gesundwerden und Regeneration geht, ist jeder Baum wichtig.

Projektbeteiligte
Nickl + Partner, Architekten, München

Medicine, teaching and research on the banks of the Main

The renovation and extension of the clinic while maintaining day-to-day operations involved a lengthy planning and building process. Following a planning competition in 1999, the first thing that was changed was the access to the building. The main entrance was repositioned and the tram stop moved. It was decided that an open green forum looking out onto the Main should be created on the site of the existing car park. The first building phase and the new main entrance have already been implemented, as have the lecture hall and two research buildings.

A large patients' car park was initially planned beyond the flat high-rise building. As the result of an additional expansion and consolidation of the buildings, this had to be abandoned. A garden axis is now planned instead, a sort of promenade with lots of plants, small pools of water and benches. The courtyards of the lower floors were incorporated into this scheme. They are not to be planted for reasons of hygiene and ease of maintenance, but will be covered instead with coloured glass chippings and vertical coloured glass steles. The additional building volume is to be set off against rows of trees to create an effective green environment for patients and staff alike. When it is a question of restoring health and regenerating strength, every tree helps.

Project Team
Nickl + Partners, architects, Munich

Rhythmisierter Patientengarten – Regenerationsboulevard mit Sitzplätzen, Blütenbäumen, Wasserflächen, Rosen und Stauden

Rhythm in the patients' garden – a regeneration boulevard with seats, flowering trees, pools of water, roses and shrubs.

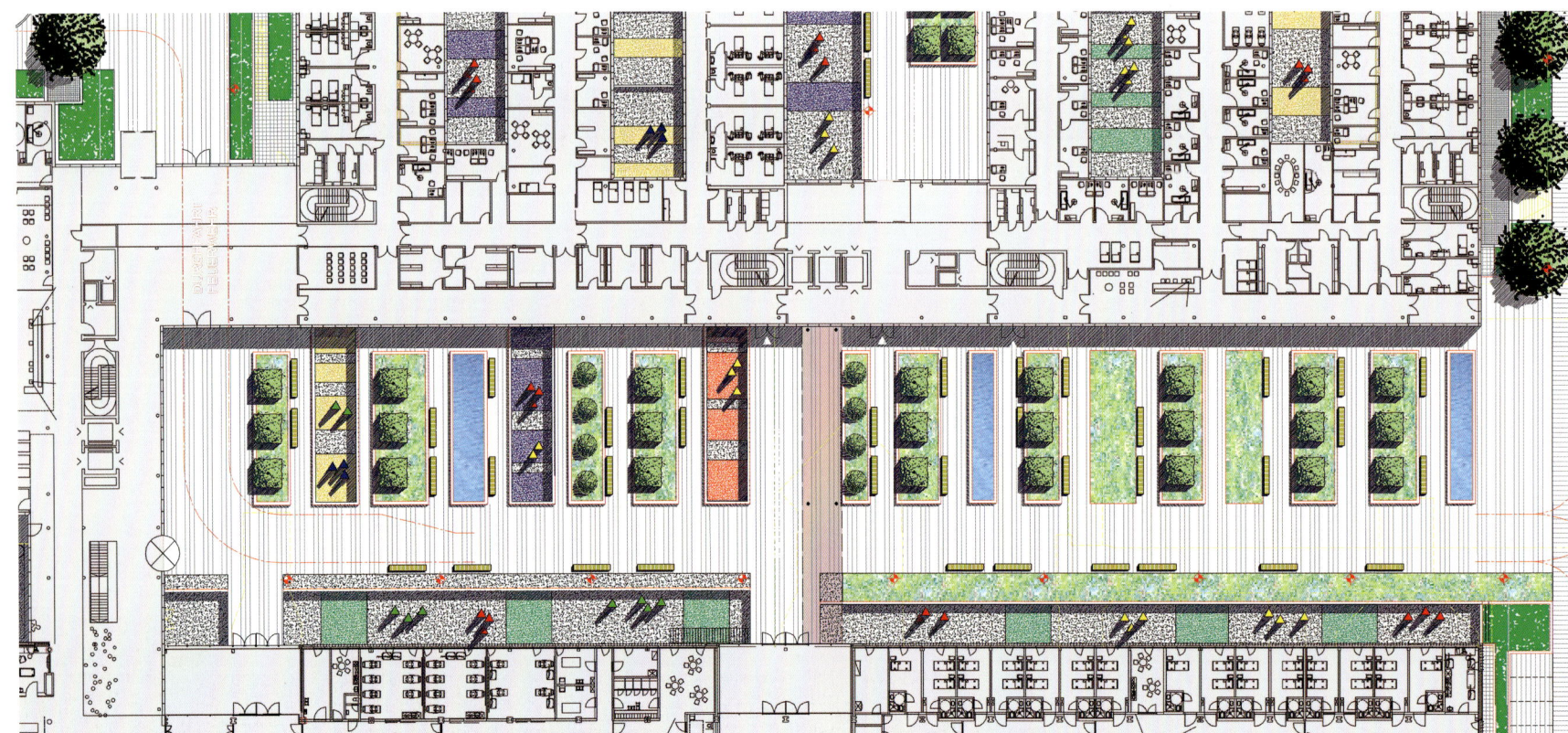

Lageplan

Site plan

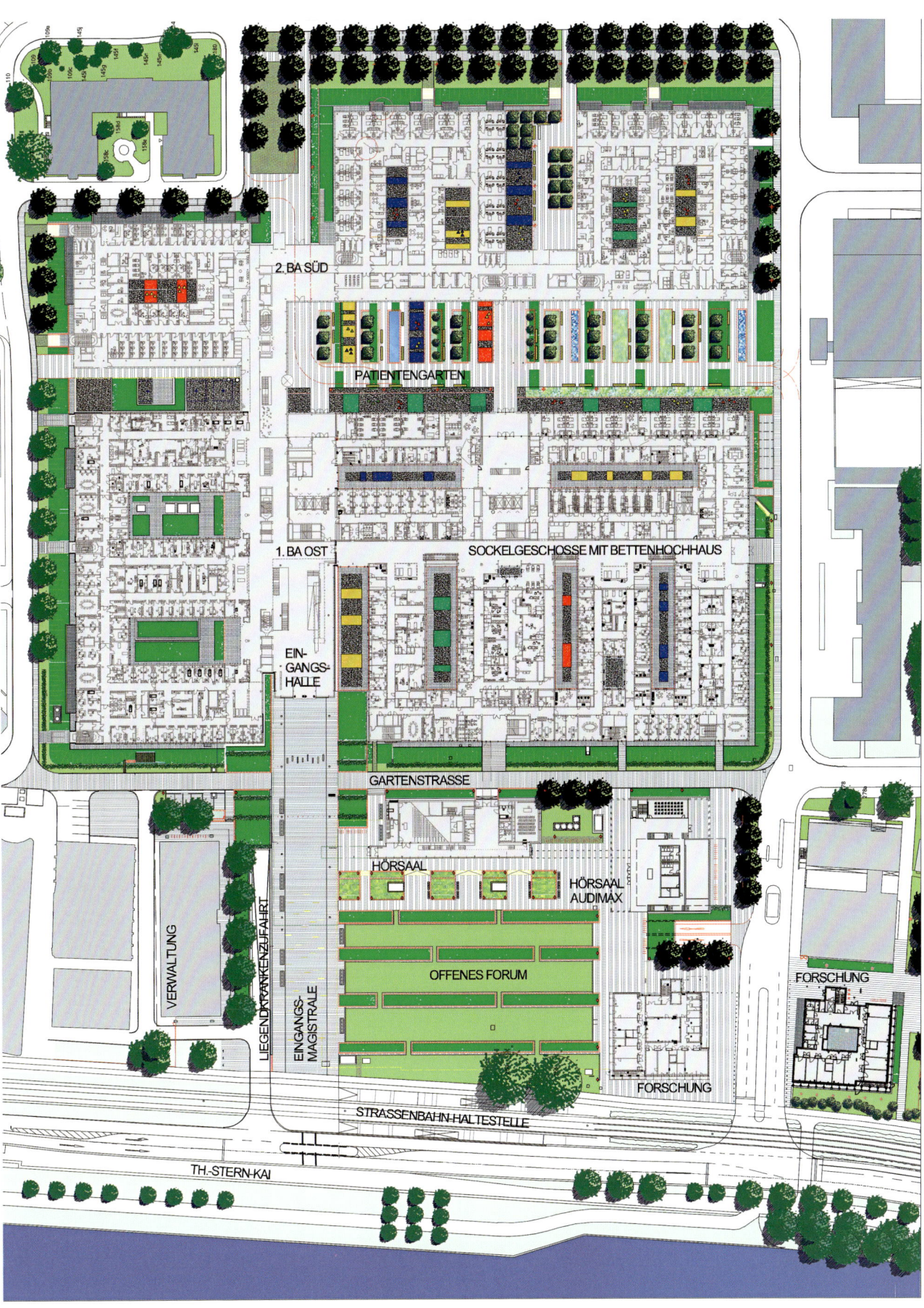

Kabinettsgarten der Residenz
München

Kabinettsgarten of the Residenz
Munich

Kabinettsgarten – ein Garten inmitten königlicher Baukultur

Der Kabinettsgarten ist der neueste und vielleicht der kleinste öffentliche Garten der Münchner Innenstadt. Innerhalb der Residenz gelegen, wurde er jahrzehntelang vernachlässigt und erst mit der Wiederherstellung der Allerheiligen-Hofkirche 2003 zu einem neuen Garten ausgebaut. Historische Pläne waren nicht erhalten.

Aus einem Gutachterverfahren erfolgreich hervorgegangen, konnte mit Unterstützung des Bauherrn ein ganzheitliches Planungskonzept erarbeitet werden. Dazu gehörten die Gestaltungsanforderungen innerhalb dieses neu erschlossenen Architekturraums: der neue Treppenabgang aus der Allerheiligen-Hofkirche in den Garten, die Wasser- und Brunnengestaltung einschließlich ihrer Technik sowie die Lichtplanung. Eine besondere Anforderung an die Planung war es, den Garten so zu gestalten, dass er sowohl für Einzelbesucher als auch für die Gäste des Cuvilliés-Theaters und der Allerheiligen-Hofkirche mit bis zu 400 Personen als Foyer benutzt werden kann und attraktiv ist.

Das besondere Merkmal des Gartens sind die flachen Wasserbecken beiderseits des Mittelwegs, die durch die grünen, roten und weißen Glasmuster auf dunkelgrünen Natursteinuntergrund bei Tageslicht wie zwei Blumenrabatten leuchten. Bei Dunkelheit entsteht dagegen eine stille Festlichkeit durch das indirekte Reflexionslicht der Fassaden und der kleinen Lichtstelen, die sich mittels Spiegelung im Wasser scheinbar vermehren.

Die Atmosphäre des Gartens wird durch den runden Brunnen unter den vier geschnittenen Platanen geprägt sowie durch zwei Linden, sechs Magnolien, niedrige Buchshecken, einige Stauden, Rosen und Kübelpflanzen (Agapanthus) am Wasser bestimmt.

Der Garten entwickelte sich zu einer beliebten Stadtoase. Die Menschen kommen gerne, vielleicht weil er eine Art von kontemplativer Ausstrahlung hat, vielleicht aber auch nur deshalb, weil mit ihm eine neue Freiraumkultur in der Stadt entstanden ist.

Projektbeteiligte
Staatliches Bauamt München 1

Kabinettsgarten – a garden framed by royal architecture

The Kabinettsgarten (Cabinet Garden) is the newest and possibly the smallest public garden in Munich city centre. It lies within the Residenz palace complex and was neglected for many years. It was only transformed into a new garden in 2003 as part of the restoration of the Allerheiligen-Hofkirche (Court Church of All Saints). None of the original plans still exist.

As the result of a successful review process, and with the support of the client, it was possible to develop an integral planning concept. This embraced the design requirements for the recently developed architectural space: the new stairs leading from the Allerheiligen-Hofkirche down into the garden, the design of water features and fountains including the relevant technology, and light planning. One of the special requirements for the planning was to design the garden in such a way that it was attractive and could be used as a reception area by individual visitors as well as by up to 400 guests from the Cuvilliés Theatre and the Allerheiligen-Hofkirche.

The shallow pools of water on both sides of the central path are a highlight feature. As a result of the green, red and white glass patterns on the dark green natural stone base, they glow like flower beds by day. At night, by contrast, a tranquilly festive air is produced by the indirect reflection of the light from the façades and the little light pillars which seem to be multiplied by the reflection in the water.

The atmosphere in the garden is accentuated by the circular fountain beneath the four trimmed plane trees as well as by two lime trees, six magnolias, low box hedges, and a few shrubs, roses and plants in tubs (Agapanthus) beside the water.

The garden soon became a popular city oasis. People like to come here, perhaps because the garden radiates a contemplative mood, or perhaps simply because it marks the creation of a new culture of open spaces in the city.

Project Team
State Construction Authority, Munich 1

1 Neue Freitreppe von der Allerheiligen-Hofkirche in den Garten
2 Residenz, Charlottenzimmertrakt
3 Notausgang Cuvilliés-Theater
4 Allerheiligen-Hofkirche
5 Skulptur »Flora« von Fritz König
6 Apothekenstock
7 Zugang

1 New stairs leading from the Allerheiligen-Hofkirche into the garden
2 Residenz Palace rooms
3 Emergency exit Cuvilliés theatre
4 Allerheiligen-Hofkirche
5 Sculpture Flora Fritz König
6 "Apothekenstock"
7 Entrance

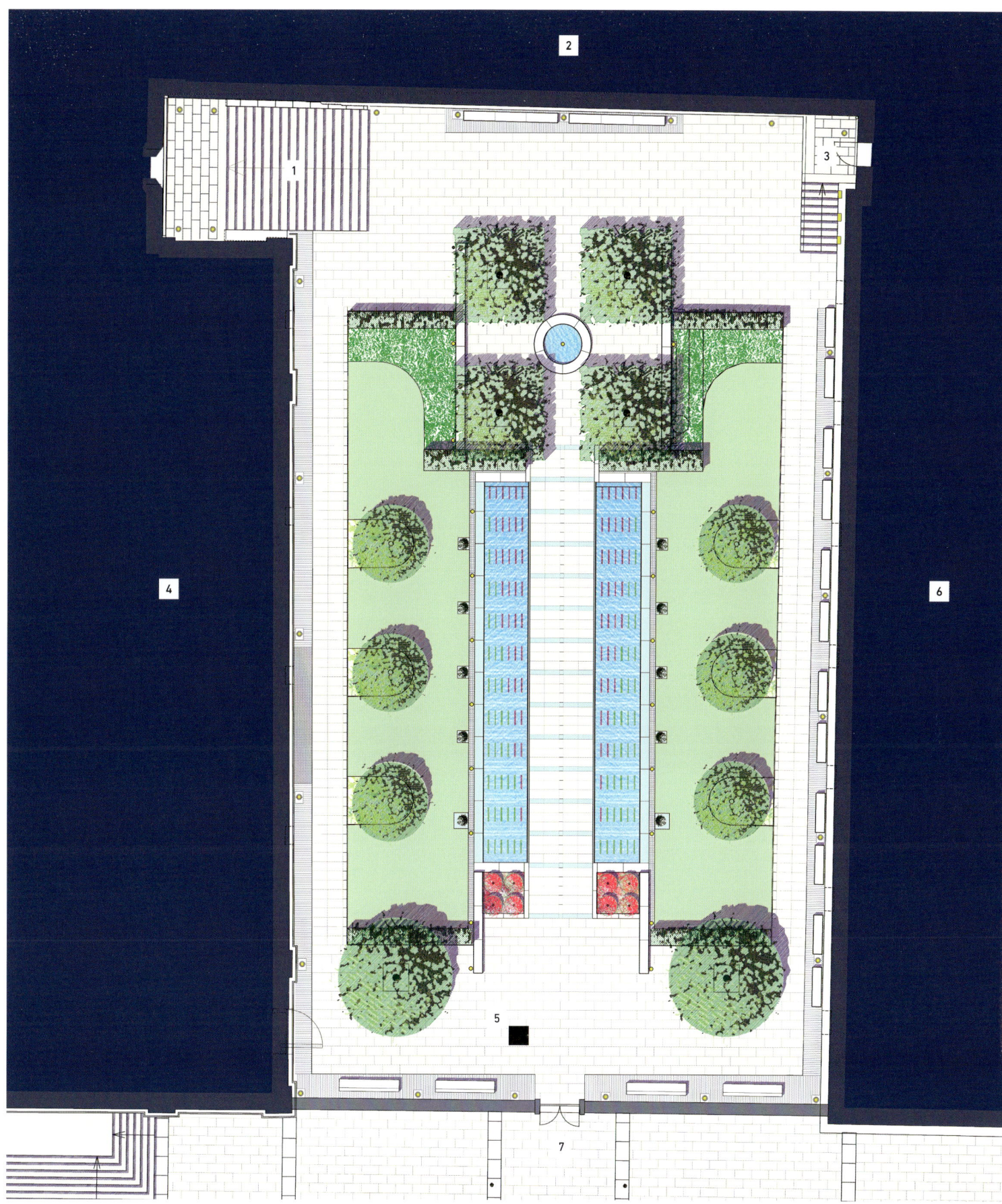

Neuer Gartenzugang aus der Allerheiligen-Hofkirche mit Freitreppe am Tag der Eröffnung

New stairs leading from the Allerheiligen-Hofkirche down into the garden – on opening day

215

Sommerfest des spanischen Kulturinstituts

Summer party of the Spanish Cultural Institute

Rechte Seite: Abendatmosphäre mit Licht und Wasser

Right: Evening atmosphere with light and water

Artifizielle Blumenrabatten: Wasserflächen mit Strukturen aus farbigem Glas

Artificial flower beds: expanses of water with structures of coloured glass

Linke Seite: Geschnittene Platanen, ein grüner Baldachin über dem Brunnen

Left: Pruned plane trees form a green canopy above the fountain

Eingang zum Garten, »Flora«, Skulptur von Fritz König

Entrance to the garden, *Flora*, sculpture by Fritz König

Stadtteilpark Haidenau
München

Haidenau District Park
Munich

Ein kleiner Park für viele

A small park for many visitors

Grundlage der Planung war ein städtebauliches Gutachten für einen alten Gewerbestandort an der Kirchenstraße, dem sogenannten alten Postviertel in Au-Haidhausen. Dieser kleine Quartierpark wird im Osten und Westen von neuen Wohnbauten flankiert, im Norden und Süden von vorhandener urbaner Wohnbebauung.
Die Schüler einer nahe gelegenen Schule wurden in die Bürgerbeteiligung miteinbezogen. Ein großer Spielplatz mit hohem Turm, ein Forum für Musik und Theater und ein Ort der Begegnung waren die Wünsche, die umgesetzt wurden. Darüber hinaus gibt es Sitzplätze zwischen den Bäumen, farbige Rosenpflanzungen an Sitzplätzen und große Wiesenflächen für freies Spiel.
Der erhaltenswerte alte Baumbestand wurde in die Konzeption einbezogen und durch neue Baumreihen hainartig ergänzt. Der Meeting Point wird durch sechs in Kastenform geschnittene Platanen zu einem Baumbaldachin mit Sitzplätzen im Halbschatten. Die Randzonen des Parks sind mit geschnittenen Hecken umgeben, die den Zaun unsichtbar machen, denn Hunde müssen draußen bleiben.
Die Dichte der umgebenden Bebauung und die soziale Vielschichtigkeit in diesem Stadtviertel erzeugen einen starken Nutzungsdruck auf den kleinen Park, der sich zwischen die vier- und fünfstöckige Bebauung schiebt. Unter den Besuchern sind alle Altersschichten vertreten, womit der kleine Park eine wichtige soziale Einrichtung ist.

Projektbeteiligte
München, Baureferat, Abt. Gartenbau

The basis of the scheme was a town planning survey carried out for an old industrial site on Kirchenstrasse, in what was referred to as the old Post Office district in Au-Haidhausen. This little district park is flanked to the east and west by new residential buildings, and to the north and south by existing residential buildings. The pupils of a nearby school were included in the participation of the local citizens. The requests that were fulfilled included a large playground with a high tower, a forum for music and drama and a meeting place. There are also seats between the trees, colourful rose beds beside the benches, and large grass play areas. The old trees that were worth preserving were incorporated into the design and enhanced by new avenues of trees planted in a grove-like manner. The meeting point has been transformed by six box-shaped trimmed plane trees which form a tree canopy with seats in the semi-shade. The fringes of the park are surrounded by trimmed hedges which hide the fence preventing dogs from entering.
The density of the surrounding buildings and the broad social mix in this district place considerable pressure on the little park tucked away between the four- and five-storey buildings. The visitors include people of all ages, so that the little park also fulfils an important social function.

Project Team
Munich Building Division, landscaping department

Lageplan: Spielplatz, Bühne, Meetingpoint, Baumhain mit Sitzplätzen

Site Plan
Playground, stage, meeting point, grove with seats

Rechte Seite: Raumbildende Modellierung, Liegewiese im Sommer, kleiner Rodelhügel im Winter

Right: Space-defining elements, lawn for sunbathing in summer, small sleigh hill in winter

Palais Holnstein
Neugestaltung von Innenhof und Dachgarten
München

Palais Holnstein
Redesign of inner courtyard and roof garden
Munich

Das erzbischöfliche Palais Holnstein

Das Palais Holnstein, 1733–1737 von François Cuvilliés d. Ä. erbaut, ist in eine Bebauungszeile der Münchner Innenstadt integriert, in die sich auch andere historische Bauwerke dieser Qualität und Epoche einreihen. Die Fassaden sind sehr anspruchsvoll gegliedert: eindrucksvolle Portale, große Innenhallen und Innenhöfe charakterisieren diese Gebäude. Eine leichte Krümmung der Straße gibt den Blick auf die Türme des Münchner Doms frei.

Im Innenhof des Palais musste der Unterbau im Zusammenhang mit der Trockenlegung der Fundamente vollständig erneuert und die Hoffläche neu gestaltet werden. In Übereinstimmung mit der Helligkeit der Fassaden und mit Bezug auf deren Rhythmisierung wurden die Hofflächen mit hellen Plattenbändern gegliedert (Auerkalk, 60 x 40 cm) und die Flächen dazwischen mit gesägtem hellen Muschelkalkpflaster (6 x 6 cm) fein strukturiert.

Der Dachgarten auf dem nördlichen Flügel des Bauwerks musste wegen der undichten Decke im vierten Obergeschoss vollständig erneuert und neu aufgebaut werden. Die Pflanzflächen wurden wegen der geringen Aufbauhöhen auf 40 Zentimeter angehoben, um mehr Wurzelraum und eine größere Vielfalt der Pflanzungen zu ermöglichen.

Eine mit Glycinien begrünt Pergola bildet den südlichen Rand des Gartens mit freiem Blick auf die umgebende Dachlandschaft. Den nördlichen Abschluss begrenzt eine vorhandene Mauer mit 3 Metern Höhe, die den Garten zu einem Raum macht. Am Sitzplatzbereich wurde eine Öffnung eingeschnitten, die wie ein Fenster mit Schiebelamellen geöffnet oder geschlossen werden kann. Von hier aus bietet sich ein herrlicher Ausblick auf die Türme und Kuppeln der nördlichen Innenstadt.

Projektbeteiligte
Innenhof und Dachgarten 2009
Klaus und Forster, Architekten, München
Staatliches Bauamt München 1

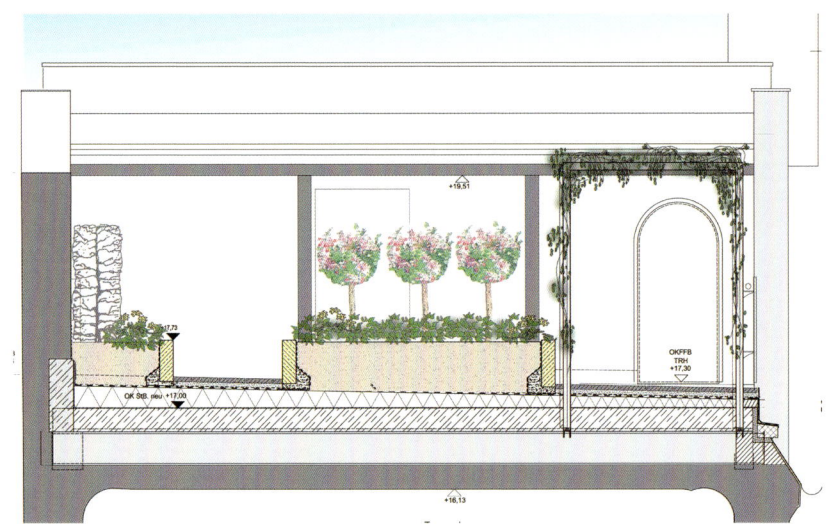

Querschnitte Dachgarten

Cross section of the roof garden

Längsschnitt mit Blick aus dem geöffneten Schiebefenster

Plan showing view from sliding window

Palais Holnstein, the residence of the archbishop

Palais Holnstein, built between 1733–1737 by François Cuvilliés the Elder, is integrated into a row of buildings in Munich city centre, and is flanked by other equally prestigious residences from the same period. The façades are very elaborate and the impressive doorways lead into large entrance halls and inner courtyards. A gentle bend in the road affords a view of the towers of Munich Cathedral.

It was necessary to completely renew the substance in the inner courtyard of the palace as a result of the draining and drying of the foundations, after which the courtyard area was redesigned. In line with the lightness of the façades and in order to create the desired rhythm, the courtyard area was subdivided by means of light stripes of paving stones (Kehlheim limestone, 60 x 40 centimetres), and the areas between were finely structured with sawn light shell limestone slabs (6 x 6 centimetres).

The roof garden on the north wing of the building had to be completely renewed and recreated because of the leaking ceiling on the fourth floor. The planting areas were raised to 40 centimetres because of the shallow depth of the previous structures, in order to provide more space for roots and a greater variety of plants.

A pergola covered with wisteria forms the southern edge of the garden and provides an unobstructed view of the surrounding rooftops. The northern boundary consists of an existing wall which is three metres high and which transforms the garden into a room. An opening was cut near the sitting area. It can be opened or closed with sliding slats like a window. From here, there is a magnificent view of the towers and domes of the northern city centre.

Project Team
Inner courtyard and roof garden 2009
Klaus and Forster, architects, Munich
State Building Authority; Munich 1

Lageplan Dachgarten 4. Obergeschoss und Innenhof Erdgeschoss

Site plan: roof garden, fourth floor and inner courtyard, ground floor

Linke Seite: Rokoko-Fassaden und neue lineare Strukturen im Innenhof

Left: Rococo façades and new linear structures in the inner courtyard

Rechts: Innere Halle mit Durchblick in den Hof

Right: Inside hall with view of the courtyard

Der Garten auf dem 4. Obergeschoss

The garden on the fourth floor

Wettbewerbe
Competitions

IBA Emscher Park
Fortbildungsakademie
Herne
IBA Emscher Park
Academy for Further Education
Herne

Augustusplatz
Leipzig
Augustusplatz
Leipzig

Rotteck-, Werder- und Friedrichring
Freiburg
Rotteckring, Werderring and Friedrichring
Freiburg

Platz der alten Synagoge
Freiburg
Platz der alten Synagoge
Freiburg

Landesmesse
Stuttgart
Landesmesse (Trade Fair Centre)
Stuttgart

Würth-Kulturzentrum
Garten und Parklandschaft
Künzelsau
Würth Cultural Centre
Garden and park landscape
Künzelsau

Spreebogen
Berlin
Spreebogen
Berlin

Akropolismuseum
Athen
Acropolis Museum
Athens

Röthelheimpark
Ehemaliges Armeegelände
Erlangen
Röthelheimpark
Former military base
Erlangen

Güterplatz
Frankurt am Main
Güterplatz
Frankurt am Main

BMW-Werk
Neubau
Leipzig
New BMW Factory
Leipzig

Isar-Amper-Klinikum München-Ost
Haar
Isar-Amper Clinic Munich East
Haar

IBA Emscher Park

Fortbildungsakademie Herne

IBA Emscher Park

Academy for Further Education Herne

Die Außenanlagen dieser vielgliedrigen Architektur der Akademie sollten sich aus der umgebenden Landschaft entwickeln und sich mit dieser verklammern.
Das Ziel war eine erlebnisreiche Akademie mit Durchdringung von Architektur und Natur, mit Natur als Fortbildungsfaktor im täglichen Erleben und zu allen Jahreszeiten. Die Gruppierung von Bäumen sollte sowohl eng und waldartig als auch locker und parkartig erfolgen, Einzelbäume sich gartenartig in das raumbildende Gerüst der Freianlagen einfügen, ergänzt um ökologisch wirksame Vegetation. So wurde eine Akademie geplant, die den Gästen ganz nebenbei auch eine Fortbildung im Erleben von Natur ermöglicht.

Planungsbeteiligte:
Krug und Partner, Architekten, München

The outdoor facilities of the academy's multifaceted architecture were designed to grow out of the surrounding countryside, and merge with it.
The aim was to create a stimulating academy with flowing boundaries between architecture and nature, with nature as a factor in further education in everyday experience, and at all times of the year. The groupings of trees were designed to be at once compact and forest-like, but also casual and park-like, with the garden-like integration of individual trees into the space-creating framework of the green area, supplemented by ecologically effective vegetation. In this way, a design was produced for the academy that would at the same time provide visitors with further education in experiencing nature.

Planning Team:
Krug and Partners, architects, Munich

Rechte Seite: Vernetzung des Bauwerks mit den Strukturen der Landschaft

Right: Interplay of the building and the landscape structures

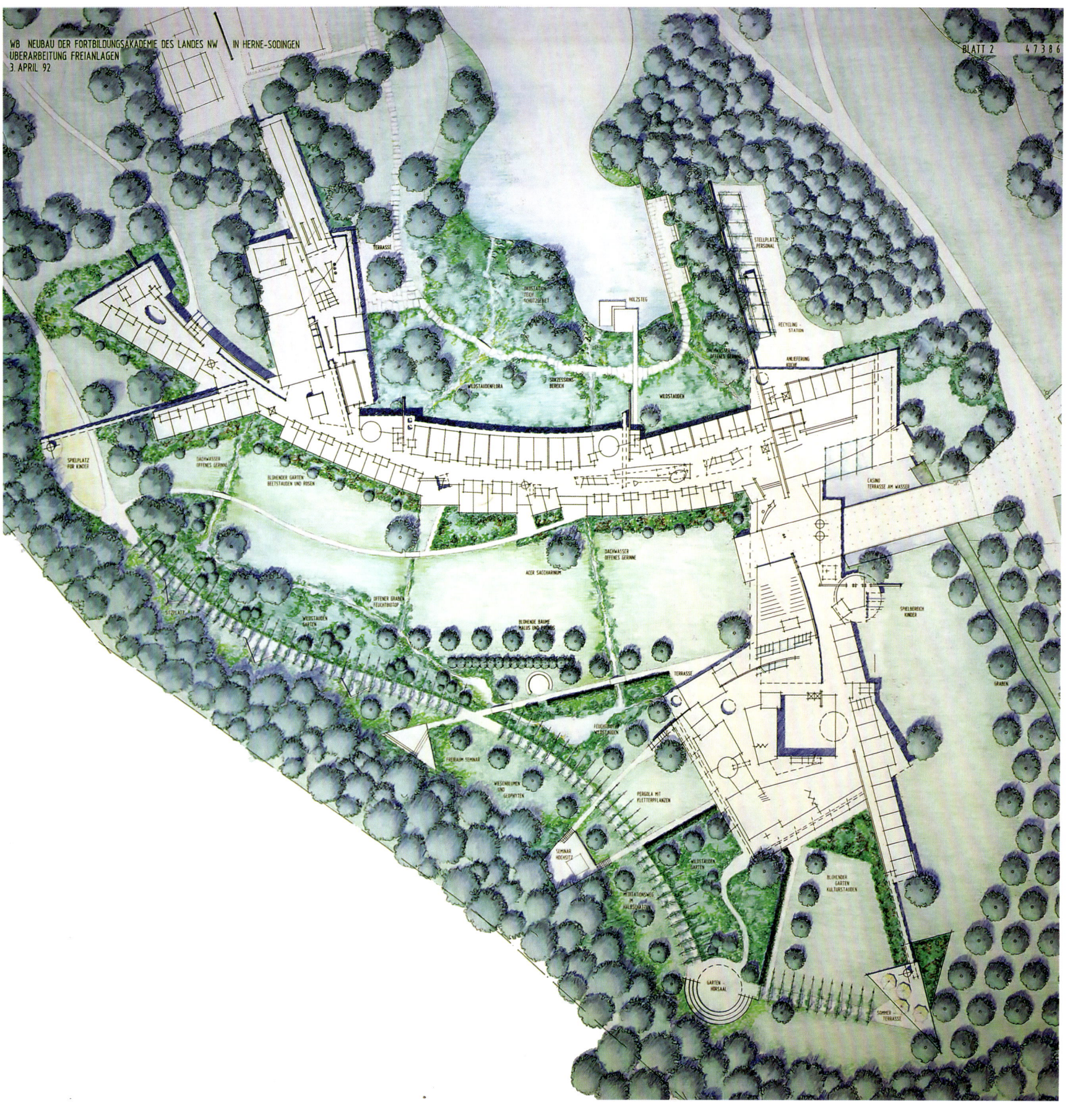

Augustusplatz

Leipzig

Augustusplatz

Leipzig

Am Vormittag des Kolloquiums, an dem die Preisrichter in Leipzig zusammenkamen, um die Sitzung mit den eingeladenen Teilnehmern vorzubereiten, saß ich im Gewandhausfoyer auf der obersten Ebene hinter der großen Glaswand und sah hinunter auf den Platz, sah die Menschen, die diesen Platz querten, sah hinüber zum Opernhaus und dachte über den neuen Charakter dieses Platzes nach. Vor mir tief unten der Platz, hinter mir der große Konzertsaal, aus dem, trotz geschlossenen Türen, das Gewandhausorchester zu hören war. Die Musiker probten mit ihrem Chefdirigenten Kurt Masur. Die Serenade Nr. 48, C-Dur, den zweiten Satz »Valse«, der so klingt wie der jubelnde Flug der sommerlichen Schwalben, der Mauersegler. Masur ließ viele Stellen mehrfach wiederholen, um die Zartheit und den bewegten Schwung dieses Satzes zu optimieren. Für mich waren es die beiden glücklichsten Stunden meiner Planungsarbeit, denn angeregt durch die Musik war ich mit meinen Entwurfsideen schon fertig, als ich mittags zum Kolloquium ging.

Der Platz, so meine Idee, sollte die beiden berühmten Häuser der Musik, das Opern- und das Gewandhaus mit einer Flächenstruktur verbinden, das sich wie ein Notenblatt ausbreitet. Die ständige Bewegung von Menschen auf dem Platz ergibt eine sehr künstlerische Formation, die sich ständig verändert. Durch Bewegungsgeschwindigkeit, Zielrichtung, die Dichte der Nutzung, die Farbe der Kleidung würden ständig neue Bilder entstehen. Da sich alles auf einem artifiziellen Notenblatt bewegt, würde eine immer neue Partitur geschrieben. Die Musikstadt Leipzig sollte eine neue, eindrucksvolle Zeichenhaftigkeit erhalten, die keine andere Stadt der Welt so bieten kann. Musik und Architektur gingen eine neue Verbindung ein – man könnte es auch Baukultur nennen.

Der Anlass des Wettbewerbs war der Bau einer flächendeckenden Tiefgarage unter dem gesamten Platz. Der historische Brunnen vor dem Gewandhaus war für den Rückbau zwingend positioniert. Die Entwurfsidee für den Platz vor dem Opernhaus war eine kreisrunde Wasserfläche, die bei Nacht mit einer Inszenierung mit viel wechselndem Licht symbolhaft für das Operngeschehen stehen sollte. Für die zentrale Straßenbahnhaltestelle konzipierte der Tragwerksplaner Jörg Schlaich ein »Flügeldach« als Ganzglaskonstruktion.

———

Planungsbeteiligte:
Schlaich Bergermann und Partner,
Tragwerksplaner, Stuttgart
Florian Burgstaller, Architekt, München

It was the morning of the symposium when the competition judges gathered in Leipzig to prepare for the meeting with the invited participants. I sat on the highest level behind the big glass wall in the foyer of the Gewandhaus, and looked down at the square. I watched the people crossing the square, and looked across at the opera house, thinking about the new character of the square. In front of me, far below, was the square, and behind me was the great concert hall from which, despite the fact that the doors were closed, one could hear the sounds of the Gewandhaus orchestra. The musicians were rehearsing with the principal conductor, Kurt Masur: Tchaikovsky's Serenade in C Major Op. 48, the second movement "Valse", which sounds like the jubilant flight of summer swallows, or swifts. Masur made the orchestra repeat several sections a couple of times to optimise the delicateness and moving sweep of this movement. These were the happiest two hours of my planning work: stimulated by the music, I had already completed my design ideas by the time I went to the symposium at midday.

The square, as I saw it, should connect the two famous houses of music, the opera house and the Gewandhaus, with a surface structure that unfolds like a sheet of music. The constant movement of people on the square results in highly artistic formations that are in constant flux. The speed of movement, the direction of travel, the density of users and the colour of clothing would provide ever-changing pictures. As all of this movement would take place on an artificial sheet of music, they would write a constantly changing score. Leipzig, the city of music, was to have a new, impressive symbolism unrivalled by any other city in the world. Music and architecture would form a new connection, which one could also refer to as architecture culture.

The building of an extensive underground car park below the entire square provided the occasion for the competition. The position of the historic fountain in front of the Gewandhaus was not to be a negotiable factor in the reconstruction of the square. The design idea for the square in front of the opera house featured a round water feature that would symbolise the operatic events with a frequently changing light display at night. Jörg Schlaich, the structural engineer, designed an all-glass "winged roof" construction for the central tram station.

———

Planning Team:
Schlaich Bergermann and Partners,
structural engineers, Stuttgart
Florian Burgstaller, architect, Munich

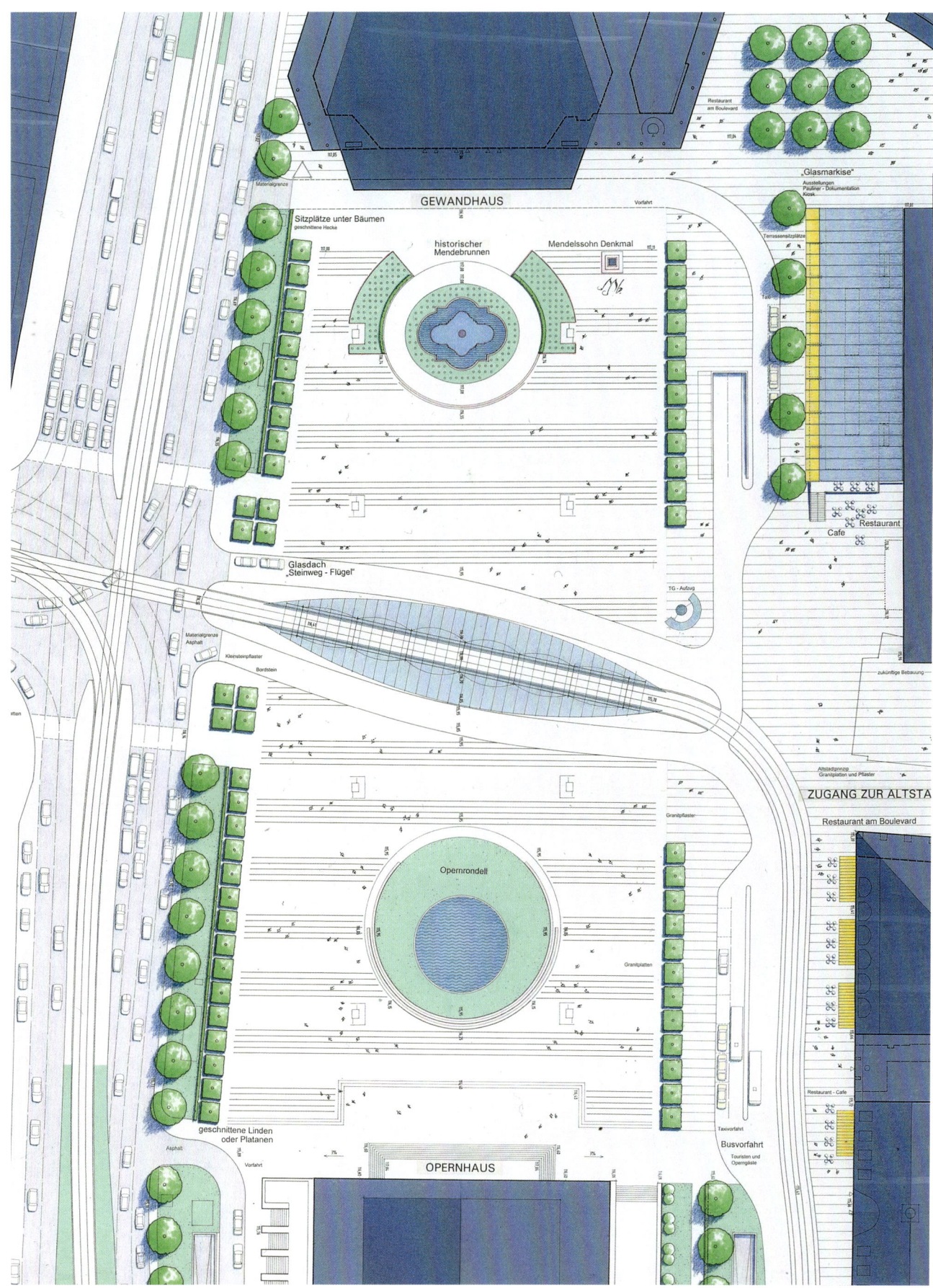

Der Platz als Notenblatt zwischen Konzerthaus und Opernhaus

The square as musical score between the concert hall and the opera house

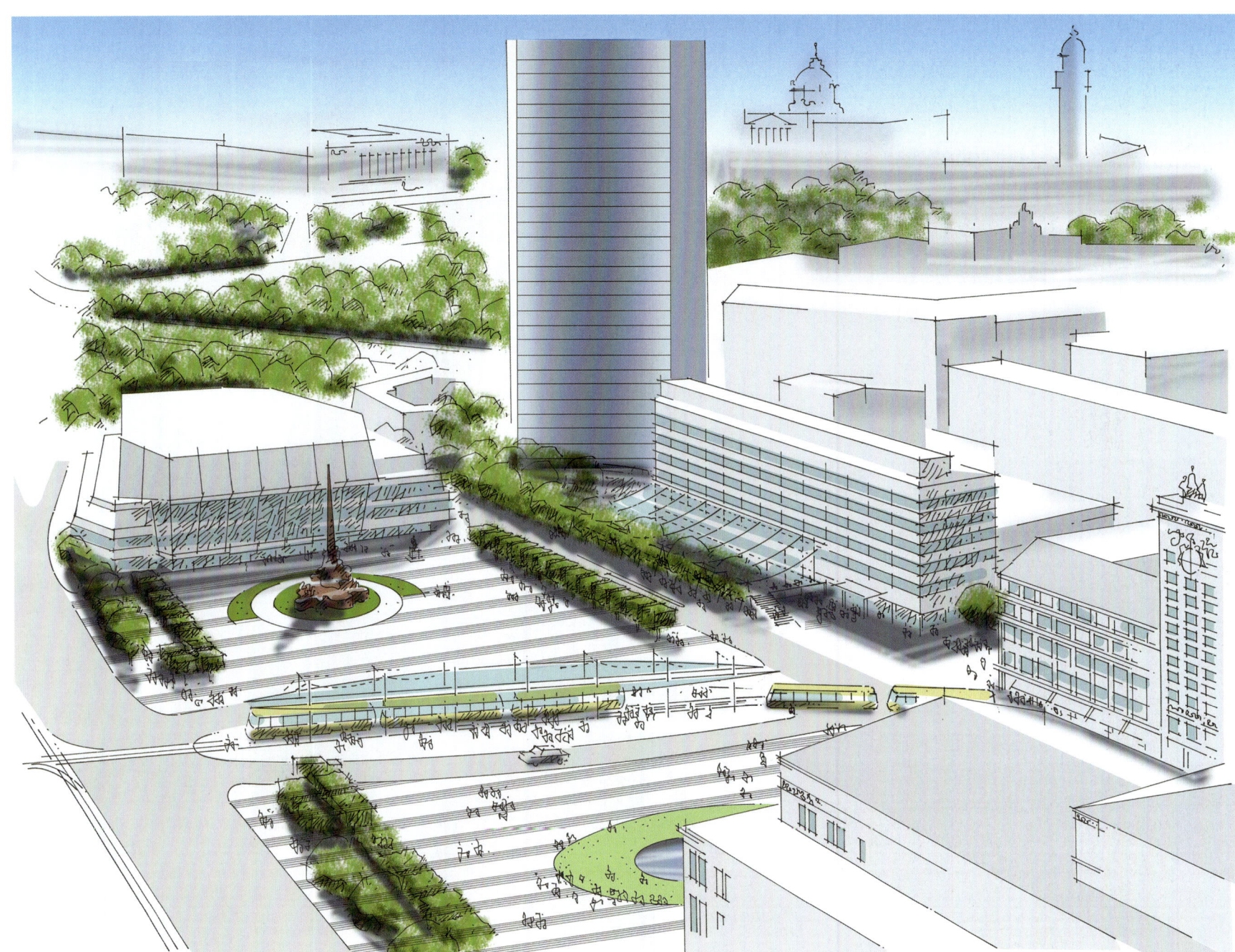

Zeichnung: Florian Burgstaller, München;
Bildbearbeitung: Hao Li, Freising

Drawing: Florian Burgstaller, Munich;
Picture processing: Hao Li, Freising

In der Mitte Straßen-
bahnhaltestelle,
Überdachung in
Ganzglaskonstruktion

In the middle, tram stop,
roofed over with glass
sheeting

Rotteck-, Werder- und Friedrichring

Freiburg

Rotteckring, Werderring and Friedrichring

Freiburg

Preisgerichtsbeurteilung

Leitidee ist eine Allee als Grünraum zwischen mittelalterlicher Stadt und Stadterweiterung mit Unterbrechungen am Universitäts- und am Theaterplatz. Diese Leitidee wird in den unterschiedlichen Ringabschnitten artspezifisch überzeugend umgesetzt. Die Allee ist ergänzt durch Bauten (Mensa, Regierungspräsidium, Café, Colombi, Friedrichseck, »schwebendes Dach«); sie ist überzeugend und in ihrer Ausformung robust.

Der Umgang mit der historischen Substanz ist sensibel und überzeugend selbstverständlich. Der Theaterplatz als ein Hauptanliegen gewinnt durch die Bühne sowie durch den überdachten Bereich als Aktivitätsraum und den benachbarten Baumhain als Ruhebereich ganz neue Nutzungs- und Gestaltqualität. Der dreiteilige Ring beinhaltet ein erhebliches Potential unerschlossener Qualitäten im Lebensgefüge der Stadt. Die bereits vorhandenen Qualitäten (Gärten, alte Bäume, Platzstrukturen, Architektur, Wasser) werden durch eine durchgehende Ringallee und einen großzügigen Ringboulevard verbunden. Darin sind neu formulierte Stadtplätze und die offenen Parkgärten integriert. Tragendes visuelles Gerüst des Rings wäre die durchlaufende Allee mit gleichbleibender Baumart, wodurch eine lebendige, zu allen Jahreszeiten freundliche Atmosphäre gefördert wird.

Die baulichen Ergänzungen sollten städtebauliche und architektonische Akzente sowie neue Belebungsimpulse setzen. Ziel war es, dem Ring ein eigenständiges Stadtbild zu geben, um sich damit deutlich von den Qualitäten der Altstadt zu unterscheiden.

Planungsbeteiligte:
Florian Burgstaller, Architekt, München

The verdict of the jury

The central idea is an avenue as a green space between the mediaeval city and the urban extension, with interruptions at Universitätsplatz and Theaterplatz. This central idea is realised in a convincing, site-specific manner along the various sections of the ring road. The avenue is complemented by buildings (a canteen, the regional-council building, café, Colombi, Friedrichseck, the "floating roof"). It is convincing, and robust in its implementation.

This approach to historical substance is sensitive and convincingly natural. Theaterplatz as a focus of interest gains entirely new qualities of use and form through the stage and the roofed area as an activity space, and the neighbouring cluster of trees as a place to rest. The tripartite ring road has considerable untapped potential within the framework of the city as a living structure. Existing qualities (gardens, old trees, the structures of space, architecture, water) are connected by a continuous ring-shaped avenue and a generous ring-shaped boulevard. Newly formulated city squares and the open park gardens are integrated into this. The continuous avenue with an unchanging tree type would provide the supporting visual structure of the ring, contributing to a lively atmosphere that would remain friendly throughout the seasons.

The built additions should provide urban layout and architectural accents, as well as stimulating impulses. The aim was to give the ring a self-contained cityscape to differentiate it clearly from the qualities of the historic district.

Planning Team:
Florian Burgstaller, architect, Munich

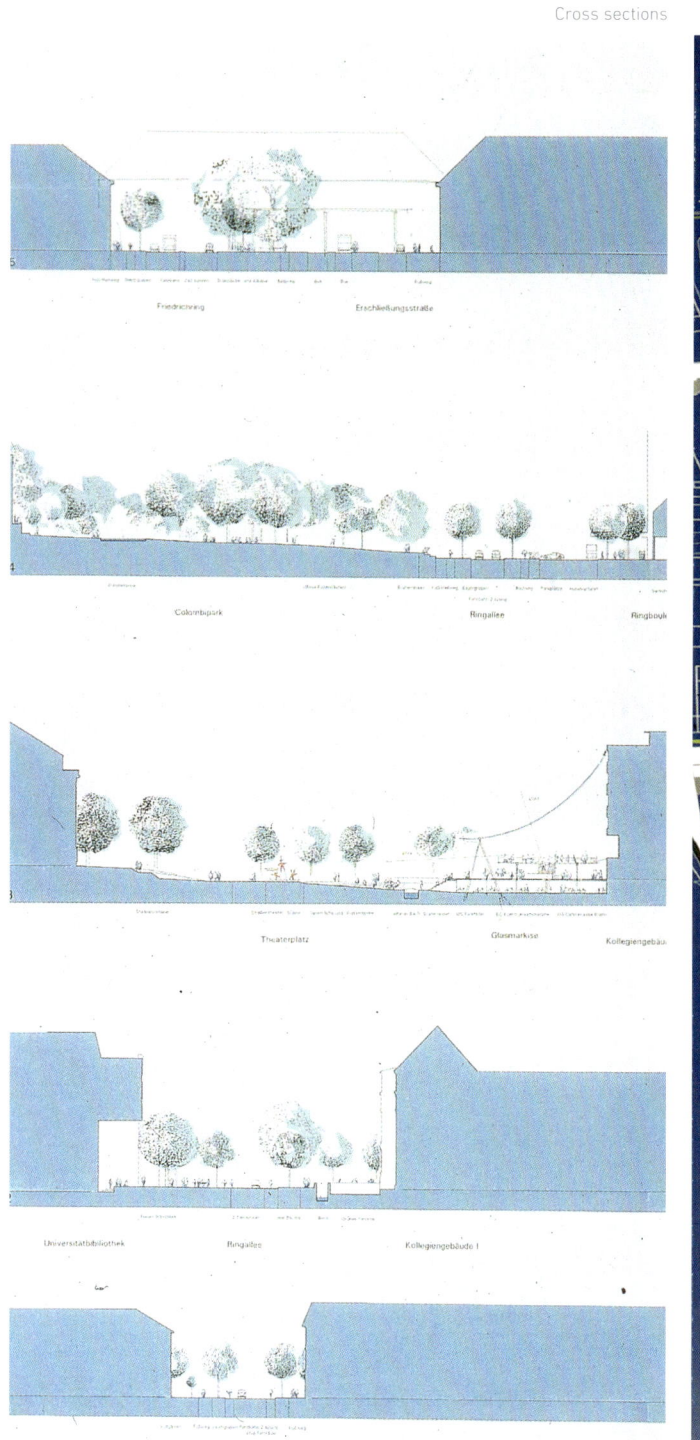

Profilschnitte

Cross sections

Verkehrsfreier grüner Boulevard mit Schnurbaum (*Sophora japonica*)

Vehicle-free green boulevard with Japanese pagoda trees (*Sophora japonica*)

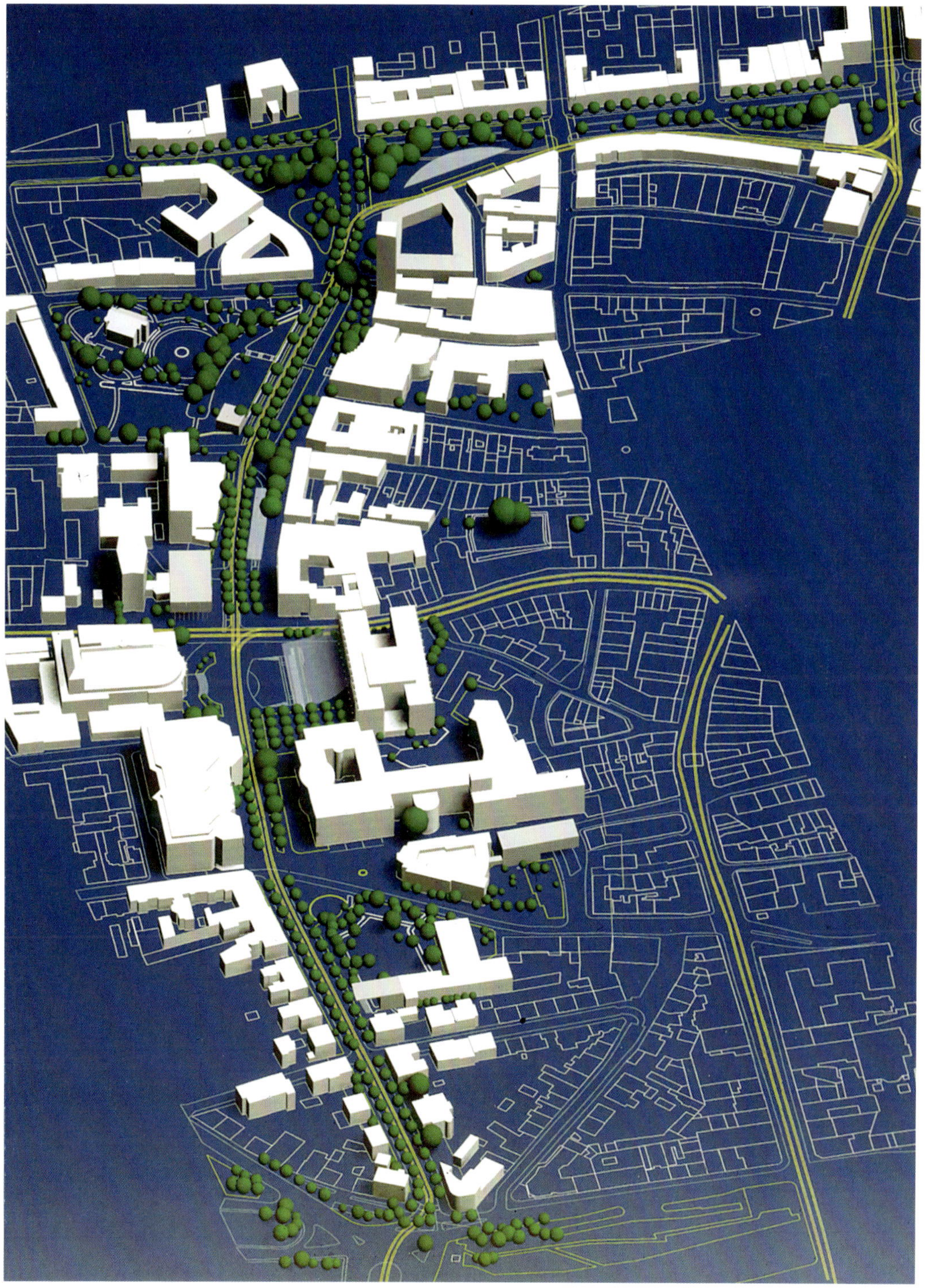

243

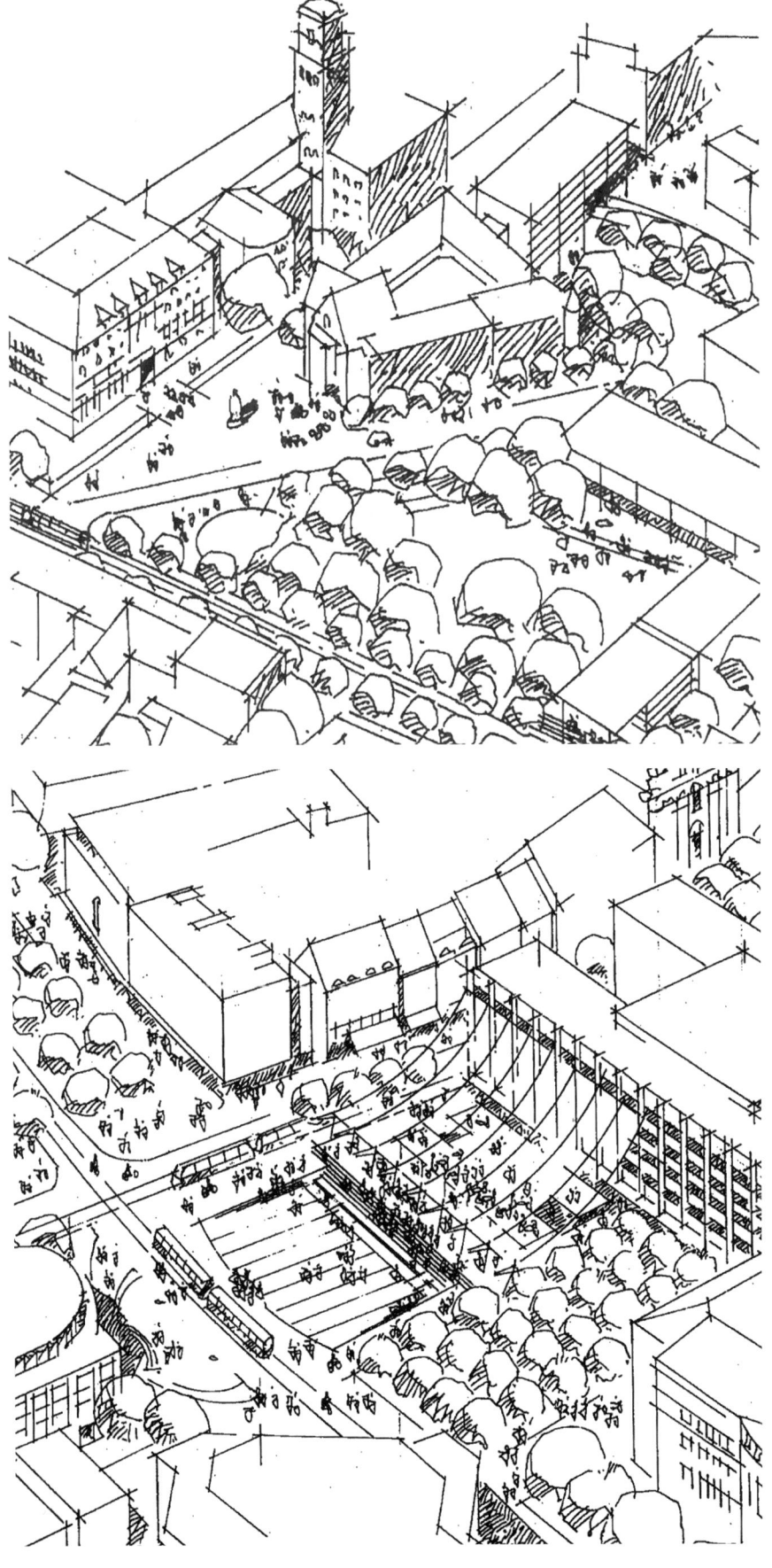

Zeichnungen: Florian Bugstaller, München

Drawings: Florian Bugstaller, Munich

Rechte Seite: Offener Platz mit Platanenhain (ehemaliger Standort der Synagoge), Glasmarkise am Gebäude, Senkplatz mit Tribünenstufen, Wasserband und Spielbühne vor dem Theater (Open Air)

Right: Open space with copse of plane trees (former synagogue site), glass awning, lowered square with terraced steps, channel of water and open-air stage in front of the theatre

Platz der alten Synagoge
Freiburg

Platz der alten Synagoge
Freiburg

Zitat aus dem Auslobungstext

Der »Platz der alten Synagoge« hat in dieser Stadt eine besondere Bedeutung. Er ist in der heute verfügbaren Größe neben dem Münsterplatz der größte Platzraum in der Stadt.
Das Theater, ein Werk des Jugendstils, bestimmt einerseits durch die bauliche Gestalt mit Treppenanlagen und Freirauminszenierung, andererseits durch die temporäre Belebung des Theatervorplatzes vor und nach den Aufführungen das Bild des Platzes.
Die frühere Synagoge wurde in den Jahren 1869 bis 1870 errichtet und bildete bis zu ihrer Zerstörung den Mittelpunkt des jüdischen Gemeindelebens. Ziel ist es, an diesen Standort zu erinnern, zu informieren, auch zu mahnen, vor allem aber einen Ort der Ruhe, der Besinnung und Begegnung zu gestalten.
Die wesentlichen Merkmale zur Neugestaltung des Platzes waren bei dieser Arbeit die Weiträumigkeit des Platzes, ein Hain geschnittener Platanen auf dem Grundriss der alten Synagoge mit Bodenleuchten zu dessen Betonung. Außerdem:
– eine Stadtpergola als regenfreie Nutzungszone,
– ein Turmrestaurant mit Aussichtsplattform,
– viel Licht und bewegtes Wasser auf dem Platz.

Planungsbeteiligte:
Auer + Weber, Architekten, München

Quotation from the design brief

The "Old Synagogue Square", known as "Platz der alten Synagoge" in German, has a special significance in this city. Its present-day size makes it Freiburg's biggest urban space next to Münsterplatz.
The theatre, built in the Jugendstil style, determines the look of the square both through its architectural appearance with the building's distinctive flights of steps and open-space design, and through the lively mulling of people to be found in the square in front of the theatre before and after the performances.
The erstwhile synagogue was built in 1869/70, and formed the heart of Jewish community life until the building was destroyed. The aim is to create a reminder of the significance of this location, to provide information, but also to warn, and, most importantly, to design a place of tranquillity, contemplation and encounters.
The main features of the new design of the square in this project were the square's spaciousness, and a copse of pruned plane trees within the outline of the old synagogue, with uplighting to highlight it. Other features include:
– a city pergola as an area for use, providing shelter from the rain
– a tower restaurant with a viewing platform
– plenty of light and moving water on the square

Planning Team:
Auer + Weber, architects, Munich

Rechte Seite: Nachtbildsimulationen mit Licht- und Nutzungsvarianten

Right: Simulation of night scenes with different lighting and venues

Lageplan mit Schnitt

Site plan with cross section

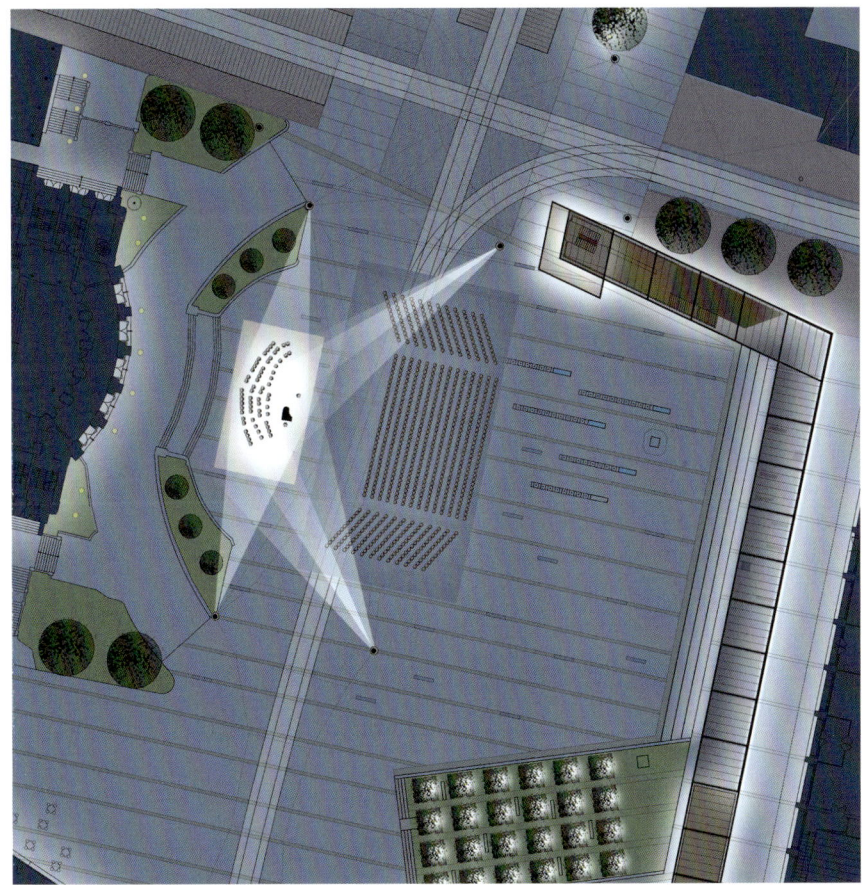
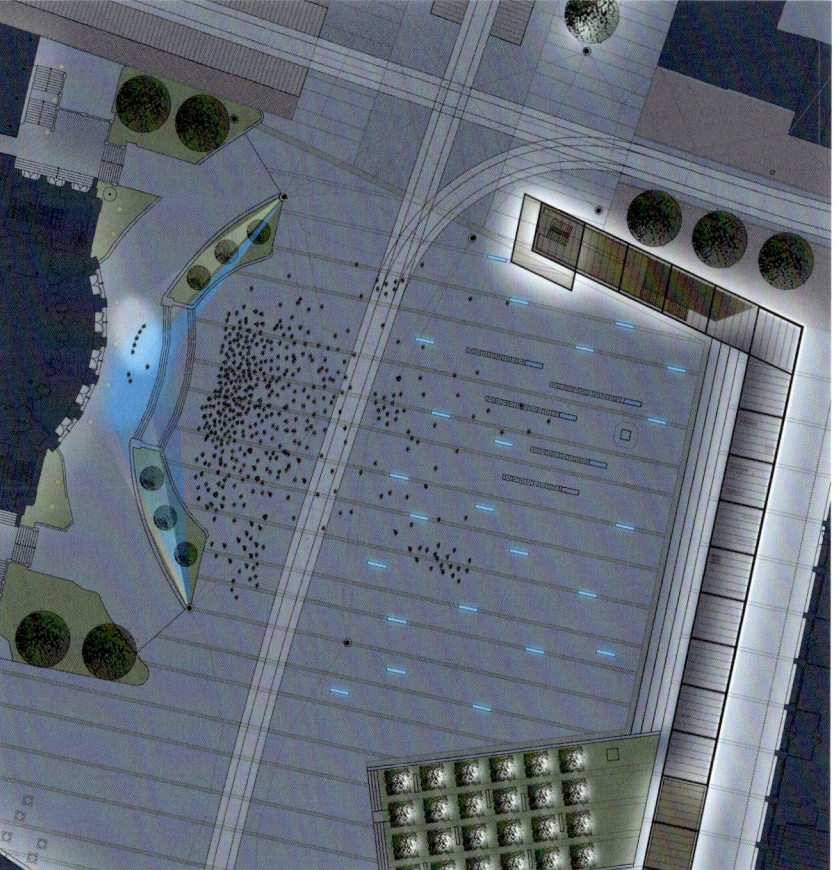

Landesmesse
Stuttgart

Trade Fair Centre
Stuttgart

Im großräumigen Landschaftsumgriff auf der Filderhöhe im Süden Stuttgarts bildet der Standort der Neuen Messe zusammen mit dem Flughafen eine zentrale Position. Die vorhandenen Siedlungsbereiche und Bebauungsstrukturen besetzen einen großen Teil der charakteristischen Landschaft, den Filderraum, der durch den Entwicklungsdruck der Infrastrukturplanungen sowie von Verkehrs- und Baumaßnahmen empfindlich gestört ist.

Als übergeordnetes Planungsziel wurde daher eine städtebaulich und architektonisch kompakte Neue Messe angestrebt, die den Charakter der Landschaft durch neue weitere Baumassen und Infrastruktureinrichtungen nur bedingt stört und sich in das wechselvolle Gesamtbild integriert, da die Kulturlandschaft der landwirtschaftlich genutzten Felder bereits sehr bedrängt und belastet ist.

Dem großen Bauvolumen werden durch Baumreihen und Baumhaine räumlich wirksame neue Vegetationsstrukturen entgegengesetzt, um die Proportionsverhältnisse in der Landschaft auszugleichen. Innerhalb der Neuen Messe ist eine grüne Magistrale vorgesehen, ein Freiraum, der die Hallen verbindet und dabei gleichzeitig Funktions- und Informationsaufgaben übernimmt. Grüne Innenhöfe ergänzen das Leitbild der Messe: »kompakt aber grün«.

Planungsbeteiligte:
Kaup, Scholz, Jesse und Partner, Architekten, München

The location of the Neue Messe (New Trade Fair) and the airport form a central element of the spacious landscape environment at Filderhöhe in the south of Stuttgart.

The existing settlement areas and building structures occupy a large part of the landscape, the Filder area, which is greatly compromised by the pressure of development and infrastructure plans, as well as by transport and construction projects.

The main planning goal was thus to create a new trade fair centre that would be compact in its urban planning and architecture; that would create only limited disruption to the character of the landscape through further construction dimensions and infrastructure facilities; and that would integrate itself into the multifaceted overall picture, as the cultural landscape of the fields put to agricultural use is already subject to considerable pressure and strain.

The large construction volume is counteracted by spatially effective new vegetation structures in the form of rows and copses of trees to balance the landscape's proportional relations.

A green artery is planned within the new trade fair centre, an open space that connects the various halls and simultaneously takes on functional and informational tasks. Green inner courtyards complement the guiding principle of the trade fair centre: "Compact, but green".

Planning Team:
Kaup, Scholz, Jesse and Partners, architects, Munich

Oben: Modell der neuen Messe
Unten: Blick vom Hochhaus am Asemwald auf die Landschaftsstrukturen der Filderebene. Im Hintergrund rot markiert das Wettbewerbsgelände

Above: Model of the new trade fair
Below: View from highrise in Asemwald of the landscape structure of the Filder area. In the background, marked in red, the competition site

Rechte Seite: Die Feldgliederungen waren Vorbild für lineare Messestrukturen.

Right: The arrangement of the fields provided the basis for the linear structure of the trade fair.

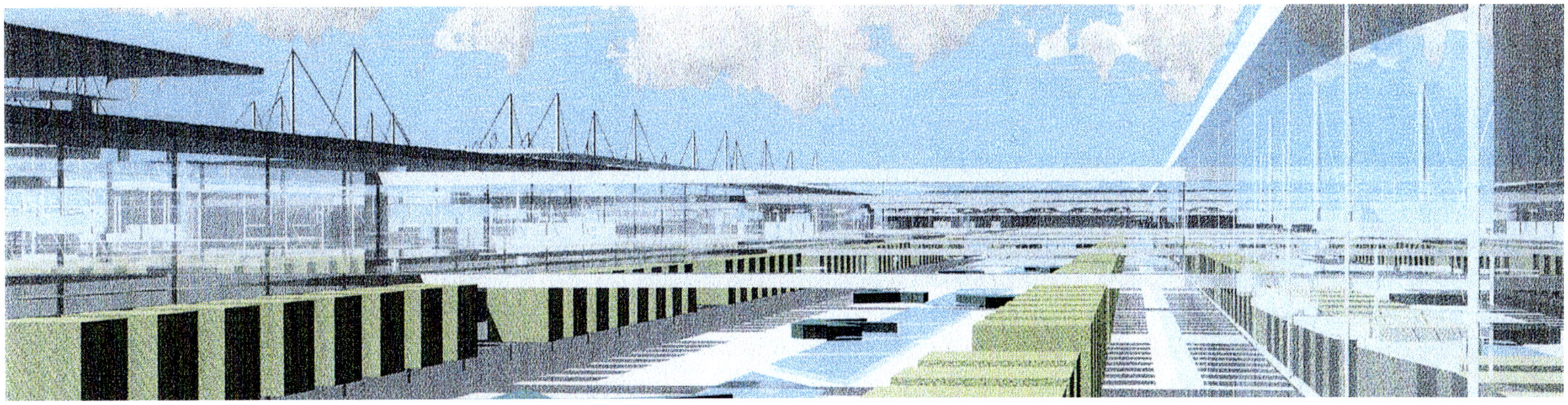

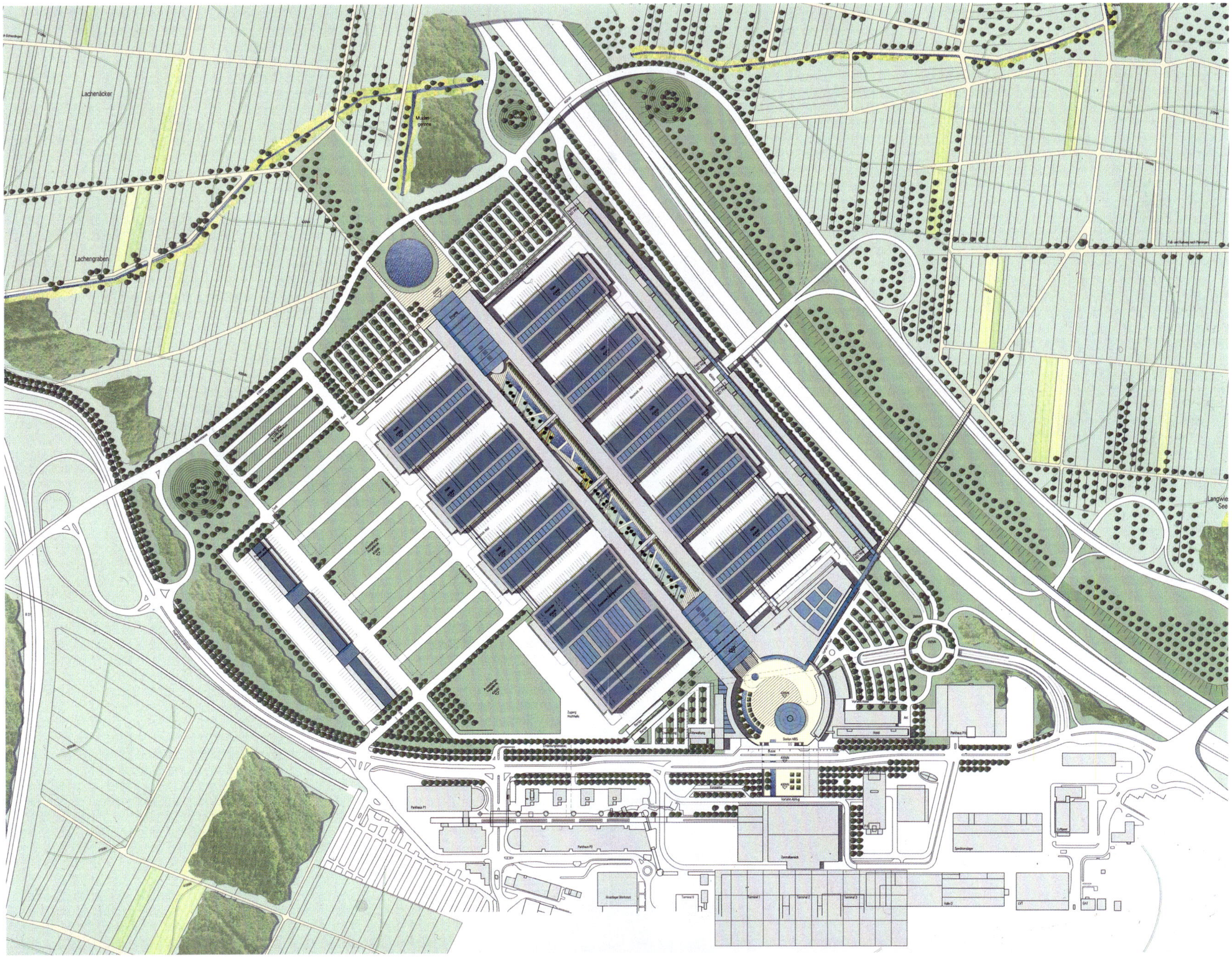
Lachenäcker
Lachengraben

Würth-Kulturzentrum

Garten und Parklandschaft Künzelsau

Würth Cultural Centre

Garden and park landscape Künzelsau

Wettbewerbsentwurf
Lageplan

Competition design
Site plan

Die leicht geschwungene, bewegte Landschaft der Hohenlohe verdichtet sich als Gelände des neuen Kultur- und Kongressareals zu einer von Kunst durchdrungenen Park- und Gartenlandschaft. Es soll ein Ensemble aus Architektur und Landschaft mit klaren Baustrukturen und weich modellierten Geländeformen erzeugt werden. Kunst und Musik werden darin eine bereichernde Dimension entfalten. Es entstehen Räume der Architektur, der Landschaft, des Klangs, Räume der Kunst, der Regeneration, der kontemplativen Erfahrungen. Daraus ergeben sich auch soziale Verflechtungen, die mit den Mitarbeitern über alle gesellschaftlichen Schichten reichen.

Eine Parkgestalt der Weite und Großzügigkeit soll entstehen, räumlich gegliedert durch die inhaltlichen Akzente des Vorplatzes, des Foyergartens, des Skulpturengartens, der Klassikarena und des Open-Air-Festivals.

Der Eingangsplatz wird auf dem Höhenniveau des Parkdecks zu einem Foyergarten mit optimalen Blickbeziehungen vom höchsten Punkt in die offene Landschaft, in den Park, zu dem Werksgelände erweitert.

Am tiefsten Geländebereich liegt ein kleiner See mit gleichbleibender Wasserspiegelhöhe mit Zulauf aus Oberflächen- und Dachwässern sowie Zuspeisung. Ein wertvolles Biotop wird so entstehen und im Gestaltungsensemble des Parks einen Akzent setzen.

Zwischen den beiden Open-Air-Bühnen im Süden soll im Park ein Staudengarten angelegt werden. Er bietet den Mitarbeitern aus dem zukünftigen Betriebsareal ein Entree in den Park und einen Ort der Regeneration.

Die raumbildenden Bepflanzungen werden mit zunehmendem Alter zum räumlichen Gesamtgefüge beitragen.

Planungsbeteiligte:

Kerschbaumer Pichler und Partner, Architekten, Brixen/Südtirol

The gently undulating, lively landscape of Hohenlohe is condensed in the grounds of the new culture and congress area into a park and garden landscape infused with art. The aim is to create an ensemble of architecture and landscape with clear architectural structures and gently shaped terrain, in which art and music can unfold their enriching potential. Architectural, landscape and sound spaces will emerge, spaces for art and regeneration and contemplative experience. This will also lead to the formation of social connections whose reach will extend, through the employees, to all social strata.

A spacious and generous park is to be created, spatially subdivided by the functional accents of the forecourt, the foyer garden, the sculpture garden, the classics arena and the open-air festival.

At the height of the park deck, the entrance will be expanded towards the cultural-centre premises into a foyer garden with ideal views from the highest point of the open landscape, the park and the industrial premises. At the lowest point lies a small lake with a constant water level, fed by surface and roof water, and a water supply. This will create a valuable biotope, setting an accent in the design ensemble of the park.

A shrub garden is to be laid out in the park, between the two open-air stages in the south. It will provide the employees on the planned premises of the cultural centre with an entrance to the park and a place of regeneration.

The space-defining vegetation planted here will, as it matures, add to the overall spatial structure.

Planning Team:

Kerschbaumer Pichler and Partners, architects, Bressanone/South Tyrol

Rechte Seite:
Wettbewerbsmodell

Right:
competition model

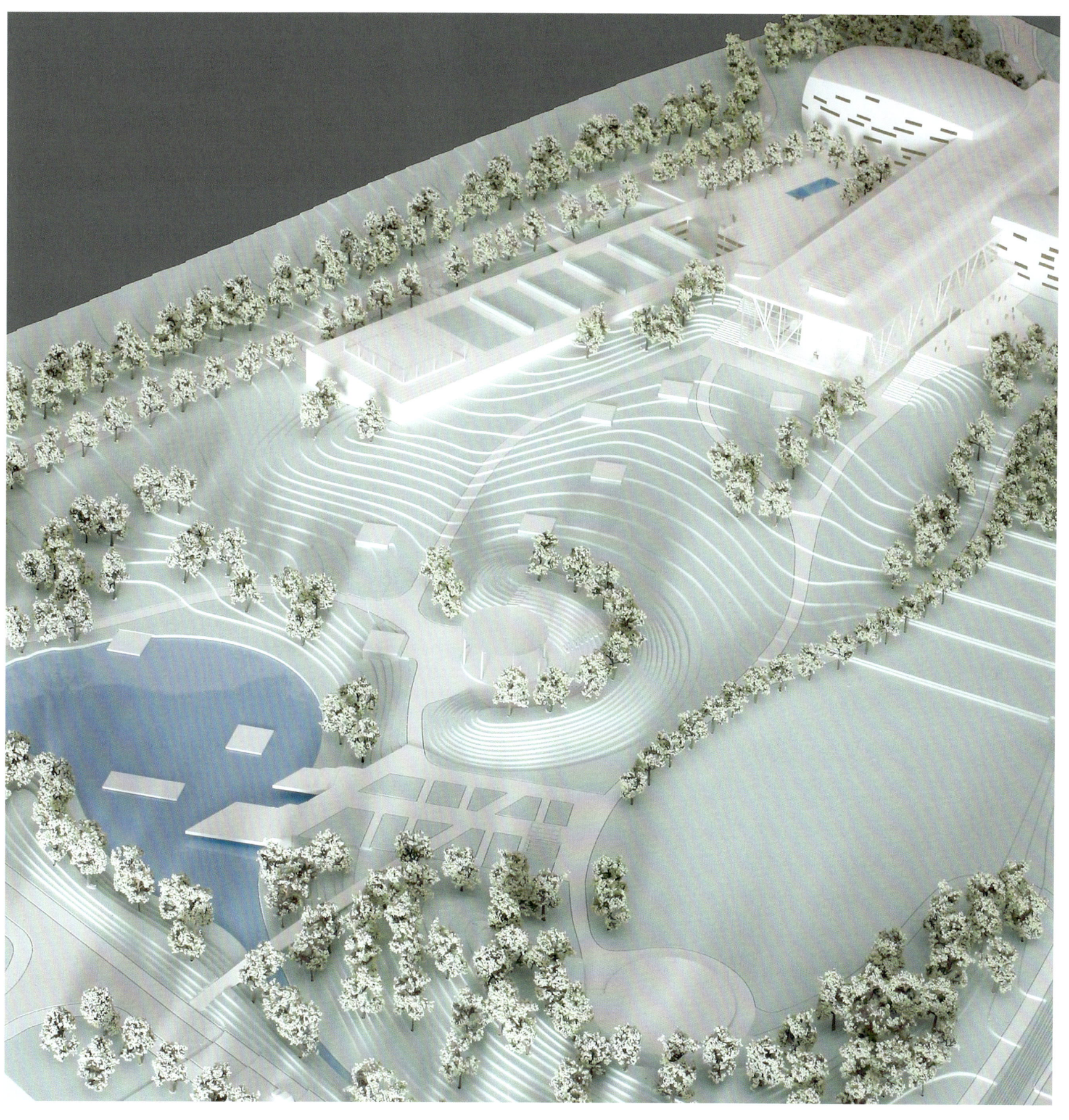

Spreebogen
Berlin

Spreebogen
Berlin

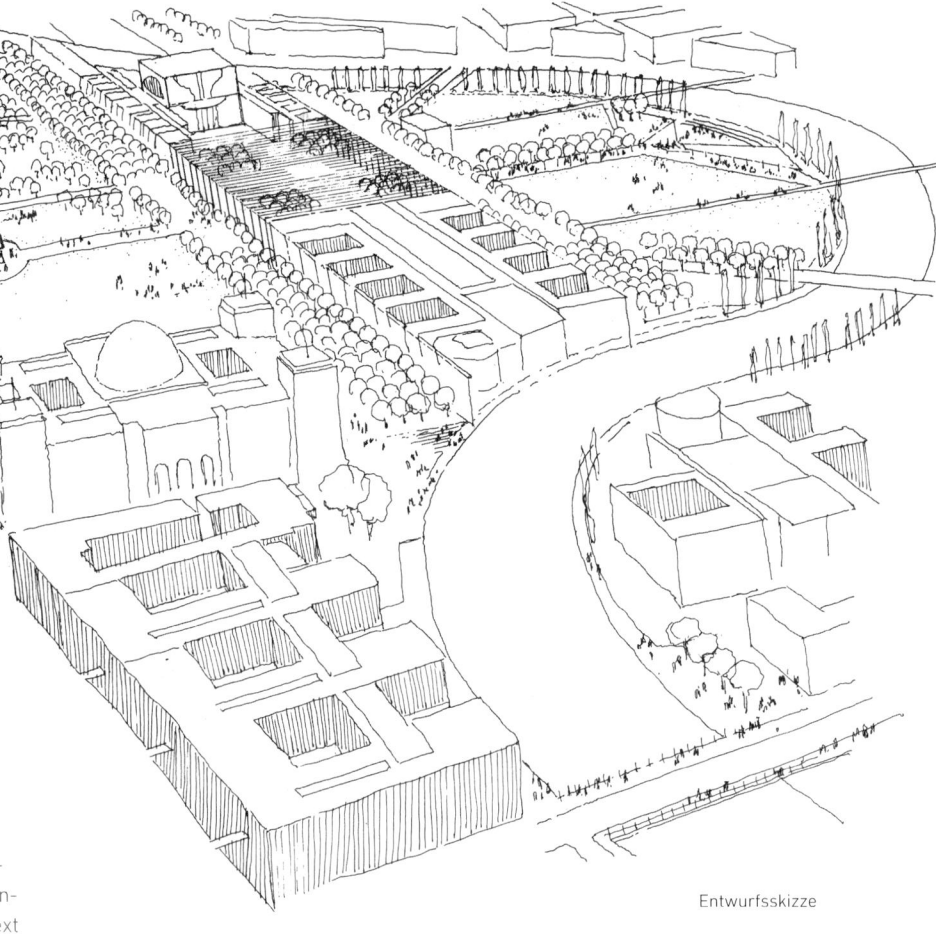

Entwurfsskizze

Design sketch

Einer der bedeutendsten Neubauten der Bundesrepublik, das Regierungsgebäude mit Kanzleramt, das, so könnte man sagen, durch seine lineare Form den Spreebogen wie eine »Klammer« zusammenhält, steht dem parlamentarischen Gebäude, dem Reichstag, in tangierender Position gegenüber. Die Sicht- und Funktionsachsen beider Bauwerke kreuzen sich auf der großen Freifläche vor dem Reichstag. Der Schnittpunkt dieser Achsen ist der Ort, an dem sich symbolisch die Ausstrahlung von Regierungs- und Parlamentsarbeit trifft. Mit einer Großskulptur von Horst Antes, Mitverfasser des Wettbewerbs, sollte ein zeitloses Zeichen gesetzt werden, ein großes Kopfprofil-Segment aus Stahl mit den Chiffren des Denkens und dem Auge des Sehens.

One of the most important new constructions in the Federal Republic is the government building and chancellery located next to the Reichstag. Its linear form appears to hold together both sides of the bend in the river Spree – almost like a paperclip. The visual and functional axes of both structures intersect on the large open area in front of the German parliament. The intersection of these axes is the place where the sphere of government and parliamentary work symbolically meet.
A large-scale sculpture by Horst Antes, a co-presenter of the competition entry, aims to make a timeless statement. The sculpture is of large segment of a head in profile, made of steel, with symbols of thinking and the eye of vision.

Planungsbeteiligte:
Auer + Weber, Architekten, München
Schlaich, Bergermann und Partner, Tragwerksplaner, Stuttgart
Horst Antes: »Kunst im öffentlichen Raum«

Planning Team:
Auer + Weber, architects, Munich
Schlaich, Bergermann and Partners, structural engineers, Stuttgart
Horst Antes: "Art in the Public Space"

Rechte Seite: Ausschnitt aus dem Gesamtlageplan.
Ein Merkmal im Schnittpunkt der Bezugsachsen sollte eine Großskulptur des Künstlers Horst Antes sein: »Der Kopf der Weisen«.

Right: Detail from the general plan. A feature at the intersection of the reference axes was to be a monumental sculpture by the artist Horst Antes: *Der Kopf der Weisen* (The Head of the Wise).

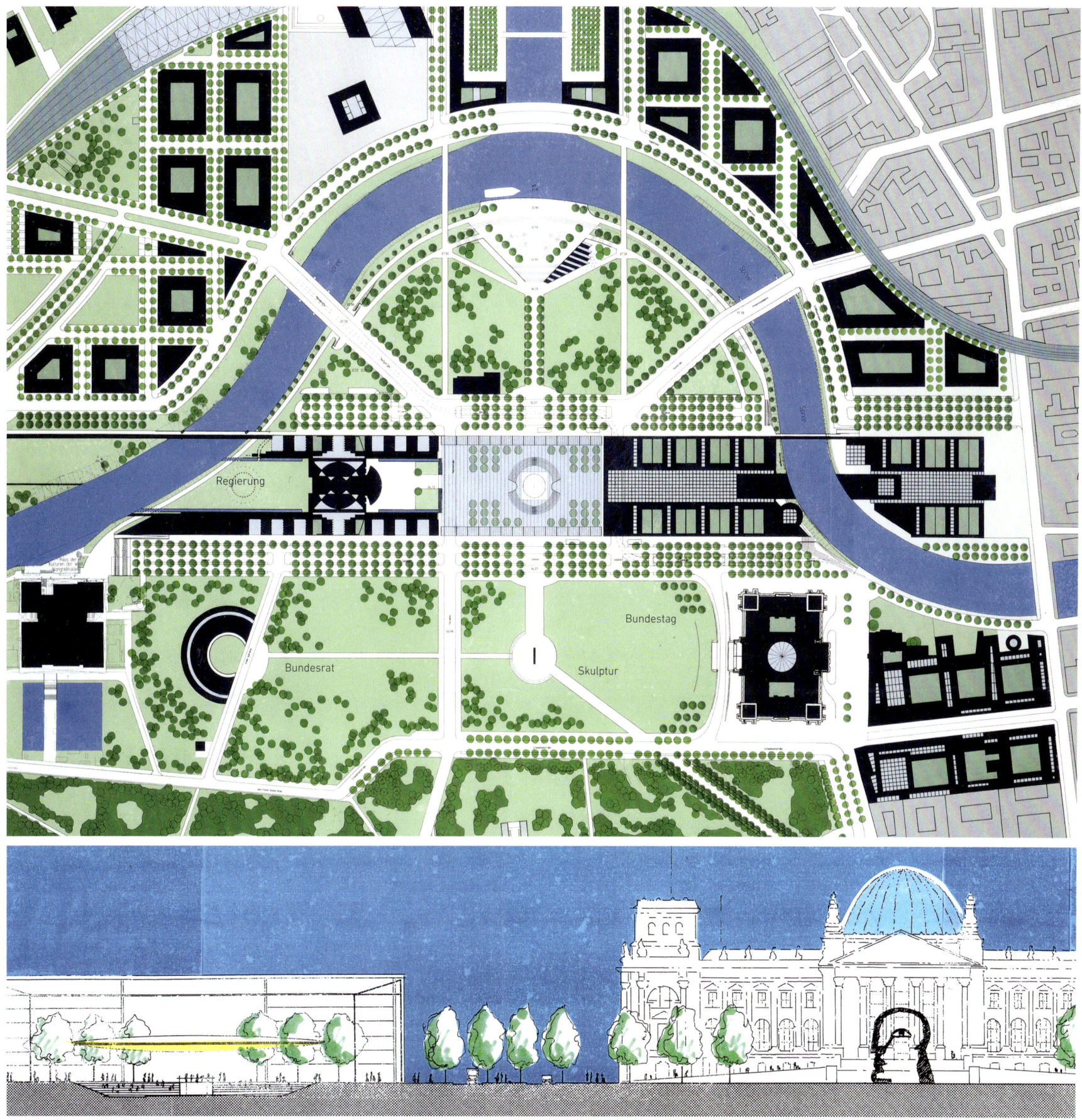

Akropolismuseum
Athen

Acropolis Museum
Athens

Bei dem Wettbewerb für das Akropolismuseum war den Teilnehmern auferlegt, von drei möglichen Standorten einen zu wählen und darauf den Entwurf aufzubauen. Architekt und Landschaftsarchitekt entschieden sich für den dritten Standort, der zwar am weitesten von dem Akropolishügel entfernt ist, aber unerhört schöne, für den Touristen bisher unbekannte Blickbeziehungen über die unbebaute mediterrane Landschaft hinweg direkt zur Akropolis bietet.

Der Standort hätte dazu beigetragen, die Dichte des Autobus- und PKW-Verkehrs am Fuß der Akropolis zu entzerren. Das Preisgericht hat sich allerdings für den ortsnahen Standort entschieden.

Planungsbeteiligte:
Schmidt-Schicketanz + Partner, Architekten, München

In the competition for the Acropolis Museum, the participants were told to select one of three possible sites, and to create a design for it. The architect and landscape architect decided upon the third location. Although it is the farthest from the hill of the Acropolis, it has indescribably beautiful views, previously unknown to tourists, across the undeveloped Mediterranean landscape and directly towards the Acropolis.
The use of this site would have contributed to the easing of bus and car traffic at the foot of the Acropolis. The jury chose the closer site, however.

Planning Team:
Schmidt-Schicketanz + Partner, architects, Munich

Lageplan neues Museum, Landschaft und markierte Blickachse zur Akropolis

Site plan of the new museum, surrounding landscape and marked line of vision to the Acropolis

Rechte Seite: Akropolis aus der Nähe und Ferne mit landschaftlichen Strukturen und Lageplan neues Museum

Right: Close-up and distant shots of the Acropolis with landscape structures and site plan of the new museum

Röthelheimpark

Ehemaliges Armeegelände
Erlangen

Röthelheimpark

Former military base
Erlangen

Auf einem 300 Hektar großen Gelände im Osten der Stadt sollte, das war die Aufgabenstellung im Wettbewerb, ein neuer Stadtteil entstehen.
Es war ein militärisch besetztes Areal: um die Jahrhundertwende für die Deutsche Wehrmacht gebaut, 1945 von der amerikanischen Armee in Besitz genommen und hermetisch abgeschlossen. Den Einzug der Soldaten hat der Verfasser als Kind selbst miterlebt. So entstand über mehrere Jahrzehnte ein Eigenleben militärischer Art mit Kasernen, Wohnen und einem Panzerübungsplatz im Süden, der dann zu einem unmittelbar vor dem Reichswald gelegenen Biotop wurde. Dort hat sich die Universität im Verlauf der Jahre mit ihren naturwissenschaftlichen Fakultäten ausgesiedelt und immer mehr nach Süden entwickelt. Diese städtebauliche Ablösung von der Stadt galt es, nach Freigabe des Geländes, wieder an die Stadtstruktur im Norden anzubinden, und das Vakuum, welches das Armeegelände hinterlassen hatte, durch Wohn- und Gewerbebauten wieder aufzufüllen.

Planungsbeteiligte:
Bachmann Marx Brechensbauer, Architekten, München
Florian Burgstaller, Architekt, München

Preisgerichtsbeurteilung

Der Entwurf baut in seinem städtebaulichen Grundriss auf den Strukturen und Maßstäben der gewachsenen Stadt auf und entwickelt daraus folgerichtig das funktionale System des neuen Stadtteiles. In überzeugender Weise wird Bezug genommen auf den denkmalgeschützten Bereich der Garnisonsgebäude und deren räumliche wie atmosphärische Qualitäten, womit das bauliche Grundmuster der Stadt auf die neuen Quartiere übertragen wird.
Der neue Stadtteil erhält Gliederung und Orientierung durch die Struktur der öffentlichen Räume und Freiflächen. Richtigerweise wird hier in der Verlängerung der Hofmannstraße die Konzentration der zentralen Einrichtungen vorgeschlagen. Vom Stadtplatz ausgehend öffnet sich ein großzügiger Freiraum, der durch abnehmende Nutzungsintensitäten und zunehmende Naturnähe gekennzeichnet ist. Die Randfassung dieses Grünzuges durch öffentliche Einrichtungen bzw. maßvoll hohe Punkthäuser ist funktional und stadträumlich gut. Die Freiräume insgesamt sind in ihren räumlichen Zusammenhängen und insbesondere in der Verbindung zum Reichswald richtig. Ihre Gestaltung reagiert sensibel auf die naturräumliche Situation und bildet abwechslungsreiche Erlebnismöglichkeiten.

According to the competition guidelines, a new district was to be created on a 300-hectare site in the east of the city. This was once a military site: built for the German armed forces around the turn of the nineteenth to the twentieth century, it was occupied and hermetically sealed by the US army in 1945. The author himself experienced as a child the arrival of the soldiers. For several decades, a distinct military life developed, with barracks, accommodation and a training area for tanks in the south. This was then converted into a biotope directly in front of Reichswald forest. Over the years, the university and its science faculties established themselves here, spreading out farther and farther towards the south. Once the site had been released, this development in the urban planning of the city was to be reintegrated into the urban structure in the north, and the vacuum left behind by the military base was to be rebuilt with homes and business spaces.

Planning Team:
Bachmann Marx Brechensbauer, architects, Munich
Florian Burgstaller architect, Munich

The verdict of the jury

In its urban-planning layout, this design builds on the structures and scale of the existing city, from which it accurately develops the functional system of the new district. It makes convincing reference to the listed area of the garrison buildings and their spatial and atmospheric qualities, so that the city's architectural blueprint finds expression in the new quarters.
The structure of the public spaces and open spaces provides the new district with organisation and orientation. It is sensibly suggested that the concentration of central facilities should be along the extension of Hofmannstrasse. A generous open space, characterised by decreasing intensity of use and increasing closeness to nature unfolds from Stadtplatz. The delimitation of this green band by public facilities and multi-storey buildings of moderate height is functional and makes sense from an urban-planning point of view.
The open spaces as a whole are appropriate in their spatial contexts, and in particular in relation to Reichswald forest. Their design reacts in a sensitive manner to the natural environment and provides a choice of different experiential opportunities.

Baumallee, städtebauliches Strukturelement vom Zentrum zum Südgelände der Universität. Lageplan, städtebaulicher Entwurf

Tree-lined avenue, urban planning feature extending from the city centre to the southern site of the university. Site plan, urban-planning design

Städtebauliche Entwicklung auf ehemaligem Armeegelände. Im Vordergrund die Panzerwiese, heute ein Biotop

Urban development on the former military site. In the foreground, the tank ground, today a biotope

Rechte Seite:
Kunst im Park:
Skulptur, Paul Fuchs

Right: Art in the Park:
Sculpture, Paul Fuchs

Güterplatz
Frankfurt am Main

Güterplatz
Frankfurt am Main

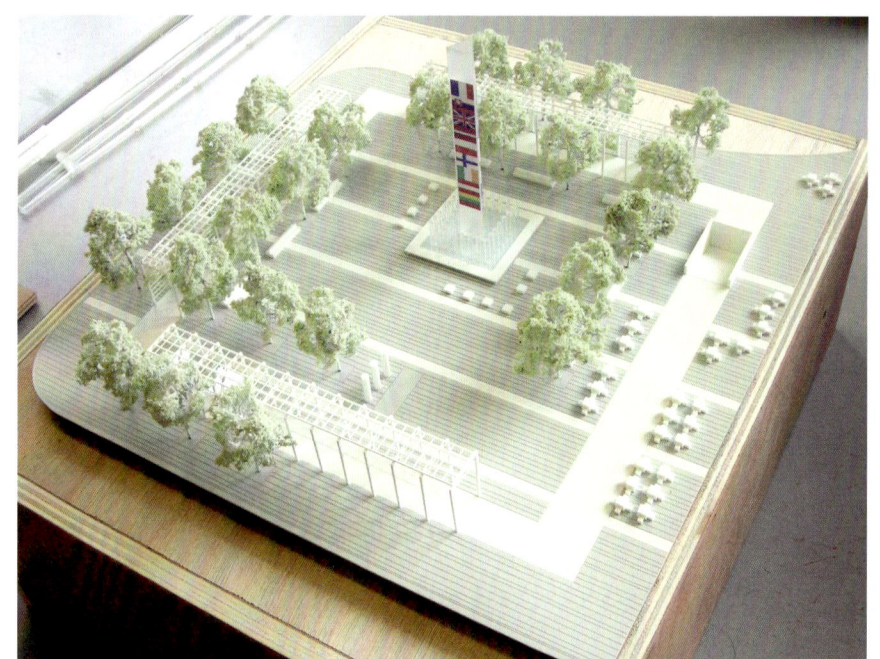

Der Güterplatz im Stadtteil Gallus hat stadträumlich die Funktion eines Gelenks zwischen der bestehenden Bebauung an der Mainzer Landstraße und der Neubebauung an der neuen Europaallee. Er ist auch Bindeglied zwischen der Architektur des 19. Jahrhunderts und der Neuzeit. Das betrifft auch die Verkehrsfunktionen, die hier einen breiten Raum einnehmen. Planungsziel ist ein zeitgemäßer Platz, keine Grünanlage wie bisher, der mit seinen Bäumen auch raumbildend und attraktiv ist. Der Platz im Platz wird von zwanzig Solitärbäumen (Platanen) räumlich gefasst, im Inneren befindet sich ein kleiner Platz mit Brunnen und Fontänen. Der im Wettbewerb noch angedachte Europa-Obelisk, eine räumliche Stele mit den Flaggenfarben der Mitgliederstaaten Europas, wurde zu Gunsten eines Brunnens mit Fontänen fallen gelassen.

Dieser Platz wird eine grüne Oase zwischen den Verkehrsströmen sein und eine räumlich großzügige Atmosphäre besitzen. Die Belagstrukturen sind dem Verlauf des Platzgefälles angepasst, so dass bei allseitig gleichem Gefälle in Richtung Brunnen keine optischen Verzerrungen entstehen können.

From the point of view of urban planning, Güterplatz square in the district of Gallus acts as a link between the existing buildings along Mainzer Landstrasse and the new construction along the new Europaallee. It also forms a connection between the architecture of the nineteenth century and recent times. This applies to the transport functions, too, which occupy a central position here. The goal is to develop a square suited to the needs of the present day, rather than a green space as it has been hitherto. With its trees, it is to have a space-defining and attractive quality.

The square within the square will be defined by twenty individual (plane) trees. A small square with springs and fountains will be in the interior. The Europe Obelisk envisioned during the competition, a solid stele bearing the colours of the European member states' flags, has been replaced by a fountain.

This square will provide a green oasis between the streams of traffic, and be imbued with an atmosphere of space. The surface structures adapt to the course of the slope of the square, so that no optical distortions are present, no matter from which angle the fountain is viewed.

Planungsbeteiligte:
Günther Wagmann und Partner, Architekten, München

Planning Team:
Günther Wagmann and Partners, architects, Munich

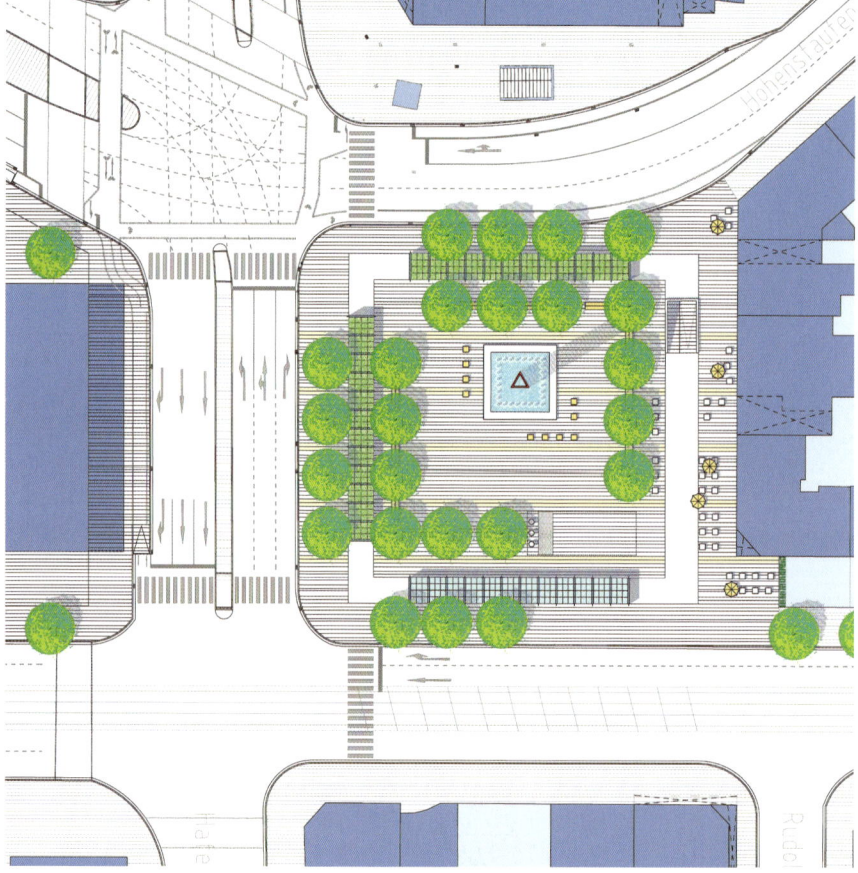

Wettbewerbsmodell und Lageplan

Competition model and general plan

Europäische Flaggen-
Stele im Brunnen –
Wettbewerbsvorschlag

Stele with European
flags in the fountain
competition submission

Nachtbild: Lichtkonzept

Night scene: lighting concept

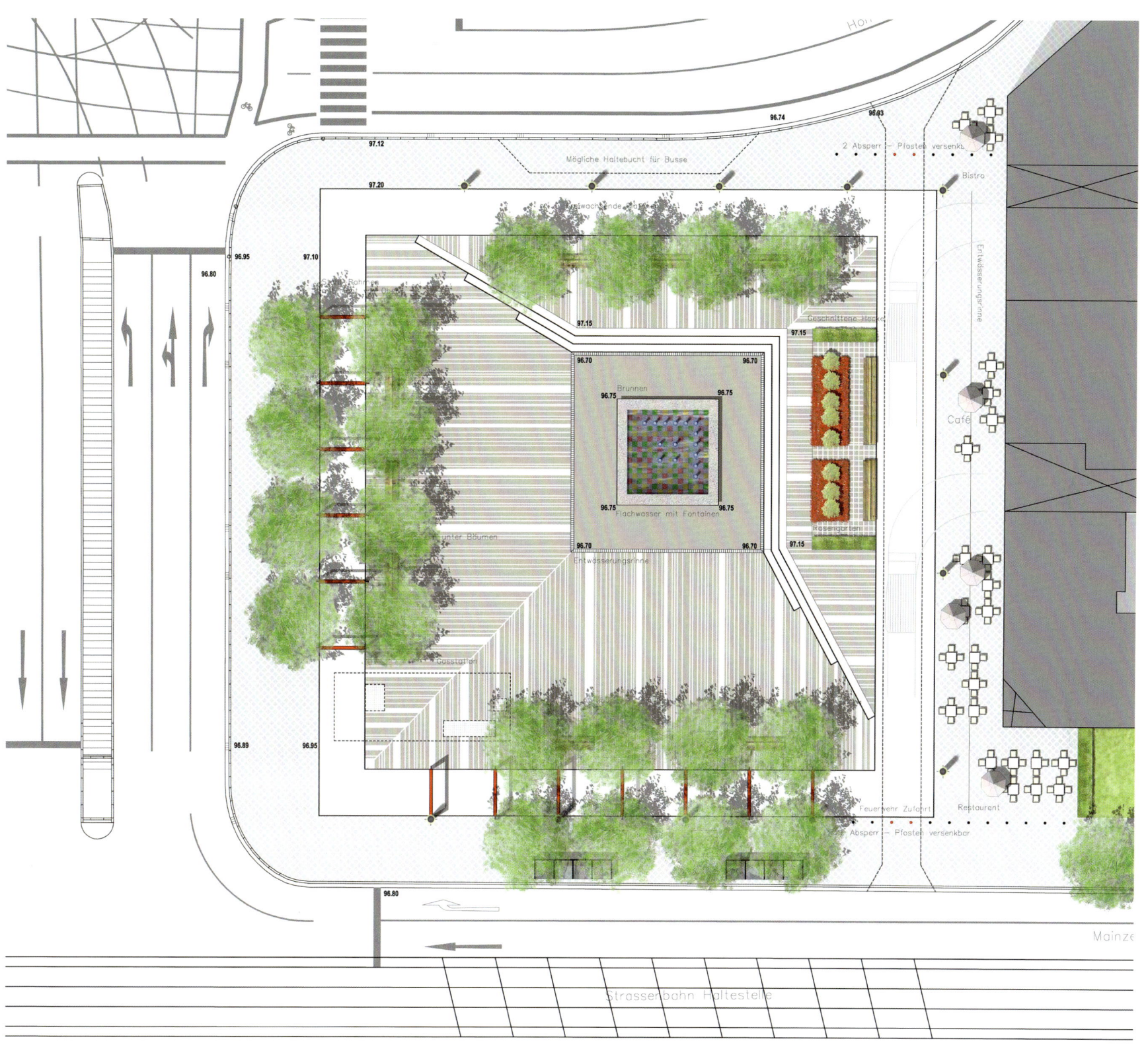

Der Platz mit Platanen,
Stadtpergola, Brunnen

The square with plane
trees, town pergola and
fountain

BMW-Werk Neubau
Leipzig

New BMW Factory
Leipzig

Die erfolgreiche Unternehmensphilosophie des Automobilherstellers BMW beinhaltet, Modelle und die Technik der Fahrzeuge in freien Teams zu entwickeln, die ihre Visionen in einem engen Kontakt verwirklichen. Für diese »Kreativ-Werkstatt« war ein Zentralgebäude zu entwickeln, das diese Aufgabenstellung erfüllt. Das Entwicklungszentrum wurde als »Lichthof-Ensemble« entwickelt, in dem Innen- und Außenraum ineinanderfließen, sich optisch auflösen und eine helle, lichte Arbeitsatmosphäre erzeugen, in die Natur, Vegetation, Tageslicht, Jahreszeiten hineinwirken und wahrgenommen werden. Dieses psychologische Erlebnispotential löst Impulse für Kreativität und Ideenfindung aus.
Funktionsanforderungen der täglichen »Materialeinströmung« und der »Produktausströmung« waren ebenfalls zu erfüllen. Im Außenbereich wurden räumlich wirksame Baumpflanzungen vorgesehen, die nicht nur Begrünung, sondern auch Proportionsausgleich zu den Gebäuden sind. Für die hohe Zahl an ebenerdigen Mitarbeiterparkplätzen wurde ein »Parkierungs-Park« entwickelt, der durch unterschiedlich große raumprägende Haine von hochstämmigen Bäumen ein Ensemble von »Baumhallen« bildet, die grüne Oasen zwischen den parkenden Autos sind.

Planungsbeteiligte:
Kulka und Partner, Architekten, Köln/Dresden

The successful business philosophy of the car manufacturer BMW includes the development of models and vehicle technology in individual teams, which realise their visions in close contact with one another. The brief was to design a central building for this "creative workshop" that would fulfil these requirements. The development centre was designed as a "halo ensemble" in which interior and exterior flow into one another, visually dissolve and create a light, bright working atmosphere in which nature, vegetation, daylight and seasons are absorbed and perceived. This environment is intended to be mentally invigorating and to help stimulate creativity and new ideas. The practical requirements of the daily influx of material and outflow of products also had to be satisfied.
A spatially effective planting of trees was planned for the outside area, not only for the purposes of greening but also to balance the proportions of the buildings. A "parking park" was developed for the large number of ground-level employee parking spaces. Its space-defining copses of high-trunked trees of various sizes form an ensemble of "arboreal halls", constituting green oases between the parked cars.

Planning Team:
Kulka and Partners, architects, Cologne/Dresden

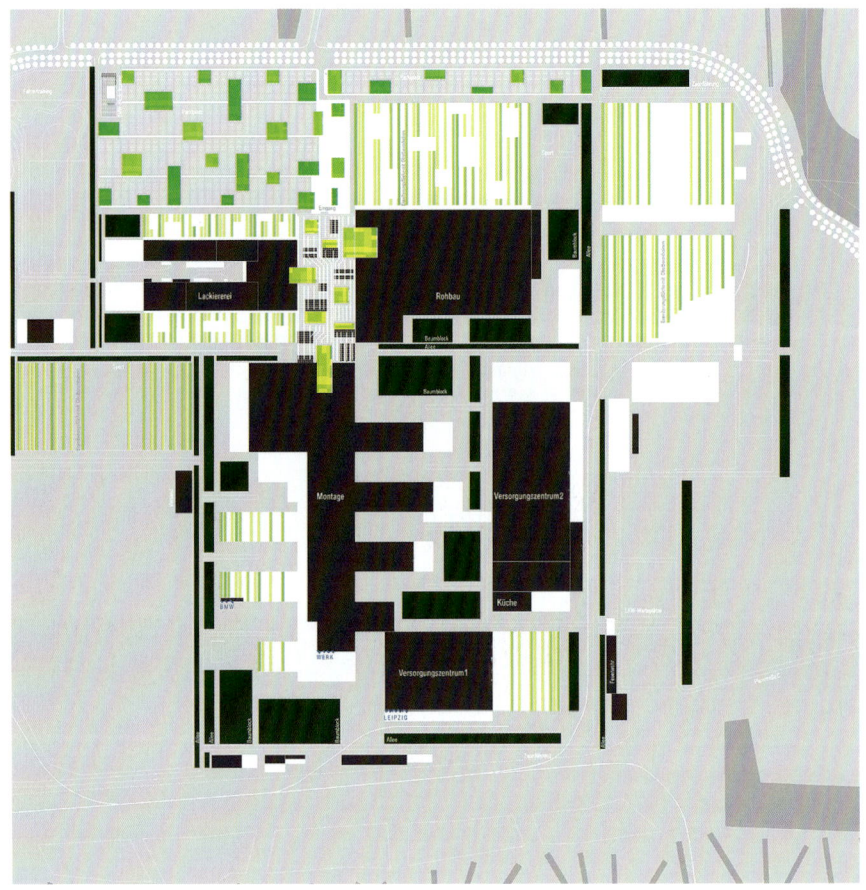

Lageplan

Site plan

Rechte Seite:
Zentraler Bereich mit Innenhöfen, im Norden »Parkierungspark«

Right: Central area with inner courtyards, in the north "Parking park"

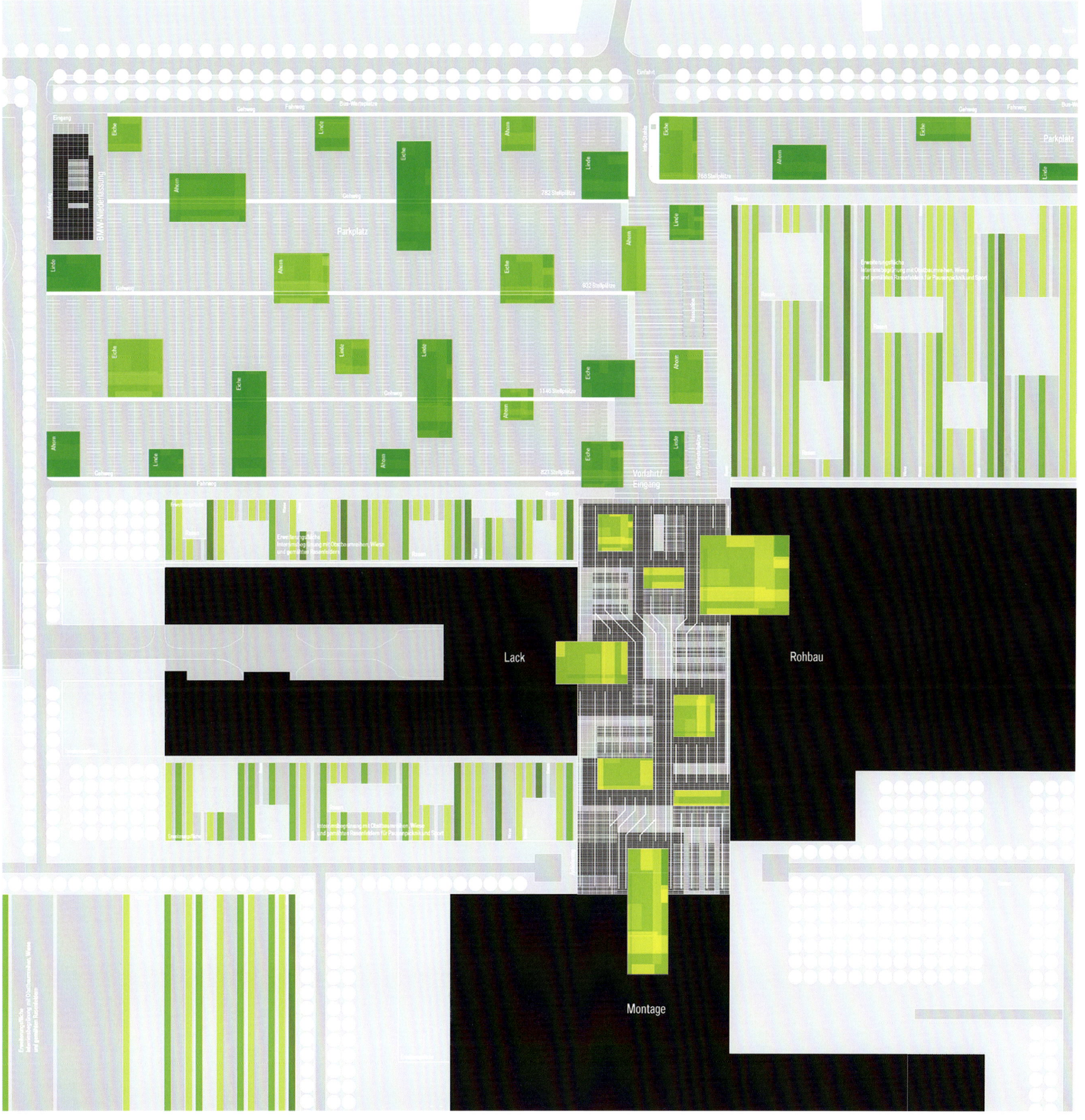

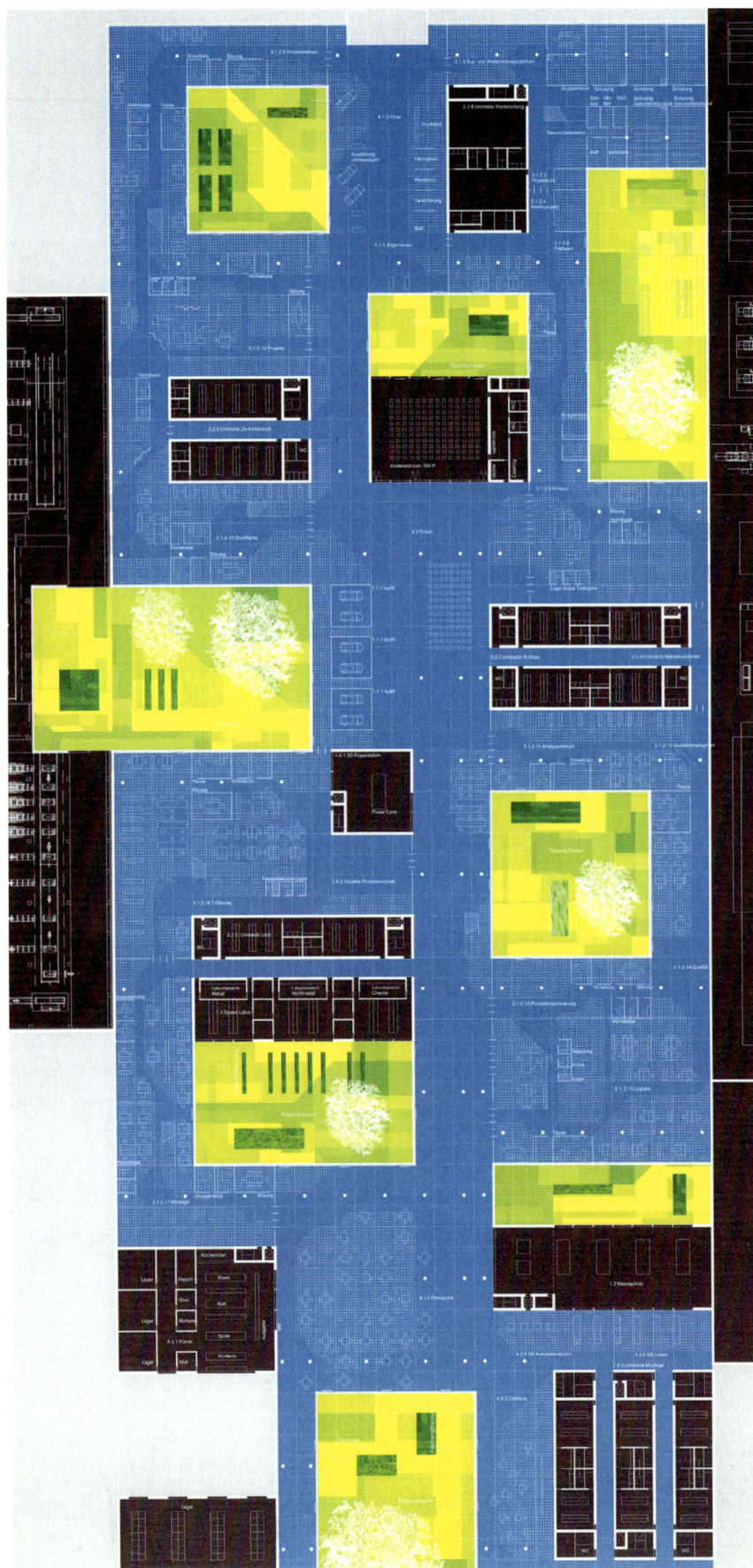

Lichthofensemble im zentralen Gebäude

Atrium ensemble in the central building

Rechte Seite: Modell mit Innenhöfen im zentralen Gebäude

Right: Model with inner courtyards in the central building

Isar-Amper-Klinikum München Ost

Haar

Isar Amper Clinic München Ost

Haar

Die bauliche Neuordnung des Klinikgeländes wurde nötig, da ein im Zentrum stehender mehrgeschossiger Riegelbau abgerissen werden muss. Die Neubauten werden in die vorhandenen Strukturen der Bebauung so integriert, dass dieses Prinzip innerhalb des Gesamtareals mit Einzelhäusern aufgenommen und so verdichtet wird, dass eine neue Mitte entsteht.

Der dichte Bestand großkroniger Einzelbäume innerhalb der Ringstraße ist die Grundlage für ein neu gegliedertes Freiraumkonzept. Darin enthalten:

– Ein Klinikpark, in dem alle Erschließungs-, Fahr- und Spazierwege einheitlich ausgestaltet werden und ein Rundwegsystem entsteht.
– Ein zentraler Klinikgarten in der Mitte der Neubauten, der Begegnungen und Kommunikation ermöglicht; mit Solitärbäumen, farbigen Pflanzungen, vielen Sitzplätzen und Wasserflächen.
– Stationsgärten als Hausgärten, die den Innenhöfen der Neubauten zugeordnet sind und den Patienten für ihren Aufenthalt eine Gartenatmosphäre mit Obstbäumen, Blumen und Gartenterrasse und eine Eigenbetätigung im Garten bieten.

Planungsbeteiligte:

Beeg, Geiselbrecht und Partner, Architekten, München

Linke Seite: Wettbewerbslageplan mit Tiefhof im Zentrum
Rechts: Die historische Gesamtanlage mit neuer Mitte

Left: Competition site plan with lower courtyard in the centre
Right: The historic site with the new central focus

The structural redevelopment of the clinic compound became necessary as a multi-storey timbered building at its centre has to be demolished. The new buildings will be integrated into the existing architectural structures in such a way that this principle is absorbed and consolidated within the compound with its individual houses, creating a new centre.

The dense population of large-crowned individual trees within the ring road is the basis of a newly structured open-space concept. This includes:
- a clinic park, in which all access paths, roads and footpaths are uniformly laid out, forming a circular system of paths.
- a central clinic garden in the middle of the new buildings, which facilitates encounters and communication; with solitary trees, colourful landscaping, many seats and water features.
- ward gardens as house gardens, which are attached to the new buildings' inner courtyards, providing a garden-like atmosphere with fruit trees, flowers and a garden terrace, as well as personal involvement, for the patients during their stay.

Planning Team:
Beeg, Geiselbrecht and Partners, architects, Munich

Weitere
Projekte und
Wettbewerbe
1970–2012

Further
projects and
competitions
1970–2012

Weingarten
Pädagogische Hochschule und Hof der Basilika 1970
Antero Markelin, Architekt, Stuttgart

Weingarten
Teaching College and Basilica Courtyard 1970
Antero Markelin, architect, Stuttgart

Heidelberg-Emmertsgrund
Wohnstift 1971
Von Branca und Mutschler, Architekten

Heidelberg-Emmertsgrund
Residential home 1971
Von Branca and Mutschler, architects

Erlangen
Universitätsklinikum, Kopfklinik 1972
Köhler Kässens, Architekten, Frankfurt am Main

Erlangen
University Hospital, Head Clinic 1972
Köhler Kässens, architects, Frankfurt am Main

München
Kindertagesstätte 1973
Fröttmaninger Straße

Munich
Day care centre 1973
Fröttmaninger Strasse

Pegnitz
Kath. Kirchenstiftung, Kindergarten, Pfarrgarten 1973
Werner Wirsing, Architekt, München

Pegnitz
Catholic Church Foundation, kindergarten, parish garden 1973
Werner Wirsing, architect, Munich

Rom
Deutsche Botschaft
Wettbewerb 1973, 3. Preis
Maurer und Mauder, Architekten, München

Rome
German Embassy
Competition 1973, Third Prize
Maurer and Mauder, architects, Munich

Tübingen
Unibauamt 1973

Tübingen
University Building Department 1973

Bad Honnef
Führungsakademie der Post
Wettbewerb 1974, 1. Preis
Maurer und Mauder, Architekten, München

Bad Honnef
Post Office Management Academy
Competition 1974, First Prize
Maurer and Mauder, architects, Munich

Gessertshausen
Volksschule 1974
Degle, Architekten, Königsbrunn

Gessertshausen
Primary school 1974
Degle, architects, Königsbrunn

Roth
Stiftung Collegium Augustinum 1974

Roth
Stiftung Collegium Augustinum 1974

Thannhausen
Marktplatz und Raiffeisenkasse
Wettbewerb 1975, 1. Preis
Degle, Architekt, Königsbrunn

Thannhausen
Market Square and Raiffeisenkasse
Competition 1975, First Prize
Degle, architect, Königsbrunn

Rosenthal-Studio-Preis
Wettbewerb 1976, 1. Preis
»Die Integration des Menschen in seine Stadt«

Rosenthal Studio Prize
Competition 1976, First Prize
"The Integration of the Individual into the City"

Kirchseeon
Jugendhof Werner 1978
Hackelsberger und Partner, Architekten, München

Kirchseeon
Jugendhof Werner 1978
Hackelsberger and Partners, architects, Munich

München
TÜV Bayern Verwaltung 1. + 2. BA und Technische Prüfstelle West 1978
Lanz und Partner, Architekten, München

Munich
TÜV Bayern Administration (first and second construction phase) and Technical Testing Station West 1978
Lanz and Partners, architects, Munich

München
Theresienhöhe, Messegebäude 1979
Schulz-Brauns, Architekt, München

Munich
Theresienhöhe, Trade Fair Building 1979
Schulz-Brauns, architect, Munich

Erlangen
Fußgängerzone, Nürnbergerstraße
Wettbewerb 1980, 1. Preis
Thomas Sieverts, Architekt, Bonn

Erlangen
Pedestrian Zone, Nürnbergerstrasse
Competition 1980, First Prize
Thomas Sieverts, architect, Bonn

München-Ottobrunn
Ortszentrum 1981
Georgens und Miklautz, Architekten, München

Munich-Ottobrunn
Town Centre 1981
Georgens and Miklautz, architects, Munich

München
WWAG-Wohnanlage, Eugen-Papst-Straße 1982
Ackermann und Partner, Architekten, München

Munich
WWAG residential complex, Eugen-Papst-Strasse 1982
Ackermann and Partners, architects, Munich

München
Optimalgrund, Büro- und Wohngebäude, Pestalozzistraße 1982
Wohnanlage Westermühlstraße und Holzstraße 1983
Braun und Hesselberger, Architekten, München

Munich
Optimalgrund, office and residential building, Pestalozzistrasse 1982
Westermühlstrasse and Holzstrasse housing estate 1983
Braun and Hesselberger, architects, Munich

München-Obermenzing
Hausgarten 1983
Adolf Schnierle, Architekt, München

Munich-Obermenzing
Private garden 1983
Adolf Schnierle, architect, Munich

Berlin-Kreuzberg
»Görlitzer Park«
Wettbewerb 1984, 2. Preis
Herrmann Schröder, Architekt, München

Berlin-Kreuzberg
"Görlitzer Park"
Competition 1984, Second Prize
Herrmann Schröder, architect, Munich

Budapest
Deutsche Botschaft 1984 (1989 abgebrochen)
Laage, Architekt, Hamburg

Budapest
German Embassy 1984 (cancelled 1989)
Laage, architect, Hamburg

Dortmund
Wohnstift Collegium Augustinum 1984

Dortmund
Collegium Augustinum Residential Home 1984

München-Laim
Bürgerhaus 1984
Ackermann und Partner, Architekten, München

Munich-Laim
Community Centre 1984
Ackermann and Partners, architects, Munich

Schongau
Heiliggeist-Spital-Stiftung, Altenheim
Wettbewerb 1984, 1. Preis
Roemich Ott Zehentner, Architekten, München

Schongau
Heiliggeist-Spital-Stiftung, Residential Home for the Elderly
Competition 1984, First Prize
Roemich Ott Zehentner, architects, Munich

Seefeld (Oberbayern)
ESPE Verwaltungs- und Schulungsgebäude 1984
Hesselberger, Architekt, München

Seefeld (Upper Bavaria)
ESPE Administrative and Training Building 1984
Hesselberger, architect, Munich

München
Herzzentrum
Wettbewerb 1985, 2. Preis
Koch + Partner, Architekten und Stadtplaner, München

Munich
Heart Centre
Competition 1985, Second Prize
Koch + Partners, architects and town planners, Munich

München
Siemens, Bürogebäude, Rechenzentrum und Parkhaus, Sankt-Martin-Straße 1985
Hans Maurer, Architekt, München

Munich
Siemens, office building, computer centre and multi-storey car park, Sankt-Martin-Strasse 1985
Hans Maurer, architect, Munich

Sonthofen
Sport- und Kurhotel Sonnenalp 1985
Neumann, Architekt, Sonthofen

Sonthofen
Sport- und Kurhotel Sonnenalp 1985
Neumann, architect, Sonthofen

Würzburg
Landesgartenschau
Wettbewerb 1985, 4. Preis

Würzburg
Regional Horticultural Show
Competition 1985, Fourth Prize

Augsburg
Evangelische Diakonissenanstalt 1986
Endres und Partner, Architekten, Augsburg

Augsburg
Protestant deaconess home 1986
Endres and Partners, architects, Augsburg

Bad Windsheim
Fußgängerbrücke und Bahnhofsvorplatz
Wettbewerb 1986
Eberhard Schunk, Architekt, München

Bad Windsheim
Footbridge and station forecourt
Competition 1986
Eberhard Schunk, architect, Munich

Erlangen
Neustädter Kirchplatz 1986

Erlangen
Neustädter Kirchplatz 1986

Kassel
Gesamthochschule Technik III
Wettbewerb 1986, 1. Preis
Ackermann und Partner, Architekten, München

Kassel
Technical College Technology III
Competition 1986, First Prize
Ackermann and Partners, architects, Munich

Straubing
»Landesgartenschau 1989«
Wettbewerb 1986, 4. Preis
Franz Dirtheuer, Architekt, München

Straubing
District Horticultural Show 1989
Competition 1986, Fourth Prize
Franz Dirtheuer, architect, Munich

Ingolstadt
Landesgartenschau
Wettbewerb 1987, 2. Preis
Ackermann und Partner, Architekten, München
Schlaich, Bergermann und Partner, Tragwerksplaner, Stuttgart

Ingolstadt
Regional Horticultural Show
Competition 1987, Second Prize
Ackermann and Partners, architects, Munich
Schlaich, Bergermann and Partners, structural engineers, Stuttgart

München
Krankenhaus und Seniorenheim Martha-Maria 1987
Ottow Bachmann, Marx Brechensbauer, Architekten, München

Munich
Martha-Maria Hospital and Home for the Elderly 1987
Ottow Bachmann, Marx Brechensbauer, architects, Munich

München
Technische Hochschule und Universität, Bebauung der ehemaligen Türkenkaserne
Wettbewerb 1987, 1. Preis
Von Werz, Ottow Bachmann, Marx Brechensbauer, Architekten, München

Munich
Technical College and University, development on the grounds of the former Türkenkaserne
Competition 1987, First Prize
Von Werz, Ottow Bachmann, Marx Brechensbauer, architects, Munich

Ingolstadt
Müllverwertungsanlage und Freizeitbad 1988
Fred Angerer, Architekt, München

Ingolstadt
Waste treatment plant and swimming pool 1988
Fred Angerer, architect, Munich

München
DEGI-Seidlstraße, Neubau Büro- und Verwaltungshaus 1988
Lanz und Partner, Architekten, München

Munich
DEGI-Seidlstrasse, new office and administration building 1988
Lanz and Partners, architects, Munich

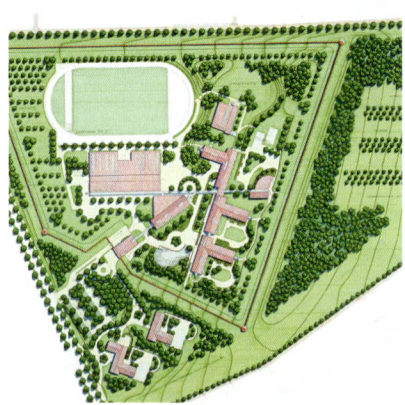

München
Lärmschutzbrücke, Lindauer Autobahn A96 1988
Schmidt-Schicketanz + Partner, Architekten, München

Munich
Noise protection bridge, Lindau Motorway A96 1988
Schmidt-Schicketanz + Partners, architects, Munich

München
Lärmschutzmaßnahmen, Landsbergerstraße 1988
Schmidt-Schicketanz + Partner, Architekten, München

Munich
Noise protection measures, Landsberger Strasse 1988
Schmidt-Schicketanz + Partners, architects, Munich

Regensburg
Neubau Postamt 1988
Ackermann und Partner, Architekten, München

Regensburg
New post office 1988
Ackermann and Partners, architects, Munich

Starnberg
Bahnhofplatz »Seearkaden«, Innenhof 1988
Lanz und Partner, Architekten, München

Starnberg
Bahnhofplatz "Seearkaden", Inner courtyard 1988
Lanz and Partners, architects, Munich

Würzburg
Justizvollzugsanstalt 1988
Ganzer Hajek Unterholzner, Architekten, München

Würzburg
Correctional facility 1988
Ganzer Hajek Unterholzner, architects, Munich

Markt Indersdorf
Erweiterung Realschule 1989
Kaupp, Scholz, Jesse und Partner, Architekten, München

Markt Indersdorf
Secondary school extension 1989
Kaupp, Scholz, Jesse and Partners, architects, Munich

München
Dreifachturnhalle und Schulsportanlage, Implerstraße 1989
Kaupp, Scholz, Jesse und Partner, Architekten, München

Munich
Triple Sports Hall and School Sports Site, Implerstrasse 1989
Kaupp, Scholz, Jesse and Partners, architects, Munich

München
Landesschule für Körperbehinderte 1989
Busso von Busse, Architekt, München

Munich
State School for the Physically Handicapped 1989
Busso von Busse, architect, Munich

Höhenstadt-Fürstenzell
Kurzentrum
Wettbewerb 1990, 2. Preis
Betz und Bea Betz, Architekten, München

Höhenstadt-Fürstenzell
Health Resort
Competition 1990, Second Prize
Betz and Bea Betz, architects, Munich

München
Herzog-Max-Burg-Anlage, Neugestaltung Innenhof 1990
Staatliches Bauamt München 1

Munich
Herzog-Max-Burg complex, redesign of the inner courtyard 1990
State Building Authority Munich 1

Leipzig
Neubau Postgiroamt 1991
Koch + Partner, Architekten und Stadtplaner, München

Leipzig
New building Postgiroamt 1991
Koch + Partners, architects and town planners, Munich

München
KFZ-Zulassungsstelle 1991
Kaupp, Scholz, Jesse und Partner, Architekten, München

Munich
Vehicle licensing centre 1991
Kaupp, Scholz, Jesse and Partners, architects, Munich

Deggendorf
Evangelisch-Lutherisches Gemeindezentrum 1992
Georg und Ingrid Küttinger, Architekten, München

Deggendorf
Protestant-Lutheran Community Centre 1992
Georg and Ingrid Küttinger, architects, Munich

München
Krankenhaus für Naturheilwesen mit Dachbegrünung 1992
Bachmann Marx Brechensbauer, Architekten, München

Munich
Hospital for Natural Medicine with rooftop greening 1992
Bachmann Marx Brechensbauer, architects, Munich

München
Neue Messe in Riem
Wettbewerb 1992, 1. Phase, 4. Preis
Koch + Partner, Architekten und Stadtplaner, München

Munich
New Trade Fair Centre in Riem
Competition 1992, First Phase, 4th Prize
Koch + Partners, architects and town planners, Munich

München
Berufsbildungszentrum, Bergsonstraße 1992
Kurz Stockburger und Partner, Architekten, München

Munich
Vocational Training Centre, Bergsonstrasse 1992
Kurz Stockburger and Partners, architects, Munich

Ottobeuren
Benediktinerabtei 1992
Staatliches Bauamt Kempten

Ottobeuren
Benedictine Abbey 1992
State Building Authority Kempten

Dresden
Regierungsviertel Neustadt
Wettbewerb 1993, 1. Preis
Koch + Partner, Architekten und Stadtplaner, München

Dresden
Government District Neustadt
Competition 1993, First Prize
Koch + Partners, architects and town planners, Munich

München
Amt für Abfallwirtschaft
Wettbewerb 1993, 1. Preis
Ackermann und Partner, Architekten, München

Munich
Refuse Management Offices
Competition 1993, First Prize
Ackermann and Partners, architects, Munich

München
Jugendwohnheim Marie-Luise-Schattenmann-Haus 1993
Georg und Ingrid Küttinger, Architekten, München

Munich
Marie Luise Schattenmann House, young people's residential home 1993
Georg and Ingrid Küttinger, architects, Munich

München-Riem
Neue Messe
Wettbewerb 1993, 3. Preis
Koch + Partner, Architekten und Stadtplaner, München

Munich-Riem
New Trade Fair Centre
Competition 1993, 3rd Prize
Koch + Partner, architects and town planners, Munich

Jena
Max-Planck-Institut für Erforschung von Wirtschaftssystemen 1994
Ulf und Claudia Decker, Architekten, Darmstadt

Jena
Max Planck Institute of Economics 1994
Ulf and Claudia Decker, architects, Darmstadt

Leipzig
Universität, Fakultäten Chemie, Mineralogie, Physik, Geowissenschaft
Wettbewerb 1994, 1. Preis
Koch + Partner, Architekten und Stadtplaner, München

Leipzig
University, Faculties of Chemistry, Mineralogy, Physics, Geoscience
Competition 1994, First Prize
Koch + Partner, architects and town planners, Munich

München
Max-Planck-Gesellschaft,
Hauptverwaltung, Marstallplatz 1994
Popp Streit Graf, Architekten, München

Munich
Max Planck Society,
headquarters, Marstallplatz 1994
Popp Streit Graf, architects, Munich

München
Theresienhöhe, Karstadt, Umbau
Hackerkeller, Saturn Hansa, Central-Hotel
1994
Fred Angerer, Architekt, München

Munich
Theresienhöhe Karstadt, renovation of
Hackerkeller, Saturn Hansa and Central
Hotel 1994
Fred Angerer, architect, Munich

Weiden (Oberpfalz)
Waldsassener Kasten 1994
Hückmann Lehnert, Architekten, Weiden

Weiden (Upper Palatinate)
Waldsassener Kasten 1994
Hückmann Lehnert, architects, Weiden

Dresden
Neustadt, Elbufer, Tribünenanlage,
Teilumbau 1995

Dresden
Neustadt, Elbe riverside, partial
rebuilding of stands 1995

Erlangen
Neustadt-Ost, Röthelheimpark, Universitätsnachnutzung 1996
Universitätsbauamt Erlangen

Erlangen
Neustadt-Ost, Röthelheimpark,
University re-use 1996
University Building Authority Erlangen

München
Postbank, Sonnenstraße 1996
Koch + Partner, Architekten und
Stadtplaner, München

Munich
Postbank, Sonnenstrasse 1996
Koch + Partner, architects and town
planners, Munich

Bad Windsheim
Kur- und Kongresszentrum 1997
Bernhard und Volker Haid, Architekten,
Fürth

Bad Windsheim
Health Resort and Congress Centre 1997
Bernhard and Volker Haid, architects, Fürth

München-Garching
Max-Planck-Institut für Extraterrestrische
Physik 1997
Büro J. Sütfels, Architekten, Germering

Munich-Garching
Max Planck Institute for Extraterrestrial
Physics 1997
Büro J. Sütfels, architects, Germering

Regensburg
Fachhochschule, Neubau Mensa, Bibliothek, zentraler Bereich
Wettbewerb 1998, 1. Preis
Hans-Dieter Hecker und Partner, Architekten, Freiburg

Regensburg
Technical University, New Students' Canteen, Library, Central Area
Competition 1998, First Prize
Hans-Dieter Hecker and Partners,
architects, Freiburg

Hannover
Krankenhaus Nordstadt Neubau Chirurgie
Wettbewerb 1999, 1. Preis
Nickl & Partner, Architekten, München

Hanover
Northern Hospital, new surgery building
Competition 1999, First Prize
Nickl & Partners, architects, Munich

Ingolstadt
Anschluss Glacisbrücke, Ausbau Gustav-Adolf-Straße 1999
Schlaich, Bergermann und Partner,
Tragwerksplanung, Stuttgart
Obermeyer, Ingenieurbüro, München

Ingolstadt
Glacis Bridge junction, Gustav-Adolf-Strasse extension 1999
Schlaich, Bergermann and Partners,
structural planning, Stuttgart
Obermeyer, consulting engineers, Munich

Coburg
Lauterer Höhe, städtebaulicher
Strukturplan 2001
Fred Angerer und Gerald Hadler,
Architekten, München

Coburg
Lauterer Höhe, urban structure plan 2001
Fred Angerer and Gerald Hadler, architects,
Munich

Ingolstadt
Westliche Ringstraße und
Lärmschutzwand
Wettbewerb 2001, 1. Preis
Rudolf + Sohn, Architekten, München

Ingolstadt
Western Ring Road and noise protection
wall
Competition 2001, First Prize
Rudolf + Sohn, architects, Munich

Jena
Hochtechnologiepark »JenArea 21«
Wettbewerb 2001, 1. Preis
Nickl & Partner, Architekten, München

Jena
High Technology Park "JenArea 21"
Competition 2001, First Prize
Nickl & Partners, architects, Munich

Passau
Straßenbauamt
Wettbewerb 2001, 1. Preis
Volker Staab, Architekten, Berlin

Passau
Department of Road Construction
Competition 2001, First Prize
Volker Staab, architects, Berlin

Herzogenaurach
Wohngebiet »Herzo-Base«
Wettbewerb 2002, 5. Preis
Steidle und Partner, Architekten, Berlin

Herzogenaurach
"Herzo-Base" residential complex
Competition 2002, Fifth Prize
Steidle and Partners, architects, Berlin

München
Brandhorst Museum
Wettbewerb 2002, 5. Preis
Steidle und Partner, Architekten, München

Munich
Brandhorst Museum
Competition 2002, Fifth Prize
Steidle and Partners, architects, Munich

München
Süddeutscher Verlag, Hauptverwaltung
Wettbewerb 2002, 5. Preis
gmp von Gerkan, Marg und Partner,
Architekten, Hamburg

Munich
Süddeutscher Verlag, headquarters
Competition 2002, 5th Prize
gmp von Gerkan, Marg and Partners,
architects, Hamburg

Hamburg-Eppendorf
Universitätsklinikum
Wettbewerb 2003, 1. Preis Entwurf
Nickl & Partner, Architekten, München

Hamburg-Eppendorf
University Hospital
Competition 2003, First Prize preliminary drawing
Nickl & Partners, architects, Munich

Lohr am Main
Stadthalle
Wettbewerb 2003, 4. Preis
Auer + Weber, Architekten, München

Lohr am Main
Civic Centre
Competition, Fourth Prize 2003
Auer + Weber, architects, Munich

Minden
Neubau Klinikum
Wettbewerb 2003, 3. Preis
Nickl & Partner, Architekten, München

Minden
New hospital building
Competition 2003, Third Prize
Nickl & Partners, architects, Munich

München-Giesing
Bahnhofsvorplatz
Wettbewerb 2003, 4. Preis
Steidle und Partner, Architekten, München

Munich-Giesing
Station Forecourt
Competition 2003, Fourth Prize
Steidle and Partners, architects, Munich

München
Westpark, Parkpflegewerk 2005
LH München Baureferat Abt. Gartenbau

Munich
Westpark, Park Maintenance Centre 2005
Munich Building Directorate, Parks and Gardens Department

München
Klinikum Dritter Orden, Ärztehaus 2006
Bader, Architekten, München

Munich
Dritter Orden Clinic, Medical Centre 2006
Bader, architects, Munich

Stuttgart
Robert-Bosch-GmbH SSB Stiftung 2006
Kulka und Partner, Architekten, Köln/Dresden

Stuttgart
Robert-Bosch-GmbH SSB Foundation 2006
Kulka and Partners, architects, Cologne/Dresden

Stuttgart
Bosch-Haus und Heidehof, Parkpflegewerk 2007

Stuttgart
Bosch House and Heidehof, park maintenance centre 2007

München
Grundschule und Förderzentrum Nymphenburg-Süd 2008
köhler architekten beratende ingenieure Gauting

Munich
Primary School and Support Centre Nymphenburg South 2008
köhler architekten + beratende ingenieure gmbH Gauting

München
Klinikum Dritter Orden, Cafeteria 2008

Munich
Dritter Orden Clinic, cafeteria 2008

München
Erzbischöfliches Priesterseminar, Innenhof 2009

Munich
Archiepiscopal Seminary, inner courtyard 2009

Gauting
Theaterforum Bosco 2010

Gauting
Bosco Theatre Forum 2010

Hannover
Frauenhofer Gesellschaft, HCTM Institut
Wettbewerb 2010, 1. Preis
Nickl & Partner, Architekten, München

Hanover
Frauenhofer Society, HCTM Institute
Competition 2010, First Prize
Nickl & Partners, architects, Munich

Dank

Acknowledgements

Dank an alle. Die hier dargestellten Planungen, die Projekte und Wettbewerbe umfassen eine Zeitspanne von vierzig Jahren, die von der kreativen Lust der Ideenfindung, dem Entwerfen, dem Zeichnen, geprägt waren. Diese Planungsarbeit, die mir zum Hobby wurde, und die Begegnungen, die Zusammenarbeit mit Bauherrn, Architekten, Ingenieuren und Künstlern waren immer von dem Bewusstsein getragen, dass hier etwas hineinzugeben war in das Erscheinungsbild der Welt. Mögen die Projekte noch so klein oder auch groß gewesen sein, es war immer ein Prozess des Entdeckens auf der Suche nach dem Ideal, mit dem Ziel, der Baukultur und der Freiraumkultur etwas näherzukommen und damit auch viele Menschen zu erreichen. An dieser Stelle sind auch die vielen Mitarbeiterinnen und Mitarbeiter zu nennen, die im Laufe der Jahre in meinem Büro gearbeitet und engagiert dabei mitgewirkt haben, die Planungsziele in Freiraumqualitäten umzusetzen. Ihre Mitarbeit war äußerst wertvoll. Besonders erwähnen möchte ich meine Freunde aus China, die Studentin Menglu Jiang und den jungen Absolventen Hao Li, Master of Art, die sich bei der Ausarbeitung dieses Buchs besonders aktiv eingesetzt und mitgeholfen haben. Von ganzem Herzen danke ich meiner Frau Edit Kluska-Szügyi, die in unermüdlicher Bereitschaft an den Projekten, den Wettbewerben und an diesem Buch mitgewirkt hat. **Dank an alle.**

My thanks to everyone. The plans, projects and competitions shown here cover a period of forty years and provide solid evidence of the creative pleasure of developing ideas and then drawing and designing them. This planning work, which became my hobby, and the encounters and cooperation with builders, architects, engineers and artists were always borne by the idea that we were contributing something to the appearance of the world. Regardless of how small or large the projects were, it was always a process of discovery in search of the ideal, with the aim of achieving a better fusion of architecture and open spaces, and thereby reaching large numbers of people. I should like to take this opportunity of mentioning all the many staff members who have worked with commitment in my office over the years in order to implement our planning goals to suit the open spaces in question. Their assistance was invaluable. I should like to name in particular my friends from China, the student Menglu Jiang and the young graduate Hao Li, a Master of Art, who have contributed with tremendous enthusiasm to the creation of this book. And I offer my sincere thanks to my wife, Edit Kluska-Szügyi, who also worked with untiring enthusiasm on the projects, the competitions and this book. **My thanks to everyone.**

Text credits

The text *Erbauung* (Edification) by Peter Stolte, p. 32, first appeared in *Kunst im ZDF* (Art at ZDF), published by Zweites Deutsches Fernsehen, Mainz 1991.
The jury's verdict about Peter Kluska's competition entry for Westpark – IGA 83, p. 52, was first published during the competition proceedings on 10 February 1977.
The text *Der vertikale Garten* (The Vertical Garden) by Gottfried Knapp, p. 80, was first published in the *Süddeutsche Zeitung* on 16 November 2005.
The interview *25 Jahre Westpark* (25 Years Westpark) with Ulrich Schneider, Wolfgang Czisch and Peter Kluska, led by Ursula Ammermann, pp. 88, 90, was first aired by Radio Lora in July 2008.
The text *Sommer im Park* (Summer in the Park) by Christian Schüle, pp. 92, 94 was first published in the Protestant magazine *Chrismon plus*, 7/2001.
The English translation of Johann Wolfgang Goethe's poem *Natur und Kunst* (Nature and Art) by Prof. James Taft Hatfield, p. 194, was published in: William Lord, *Noon*, vol. 1, no. 10 (Evanston, IL, 1901).
The jury's assessment of Peter Kluska's proposal for Rotteckring, Werderring, and Friedrichring, p. 242, was first published during the competition proceedings by the Freiburg Planning Department in 1998.
The quotation from the design brief for Platz der alten Synagoge, p. 246, was first published by the Freiburg Planning Department in 2006.
The verdict of the jury regarding Peter Kluska's entry for Röthelheimpark, p. 256, was first published during the competition proceedings by the Freiburg Planning Department in 1995.

All other text contributions: Peter Kluska

Picture credits

Kerschbaumer, Pichler and Partners, architects, Brixen: ill. p. 251
Bernd Böhner, Erlangen: ill. p. 259
Municipal authorities Erlangen: ill. p. 258
Hessisches Baumanagement (Hesse building authorities), Frankfurt: ill. p. 207
Hao Li, Freising/Beijing: ill. p. 219
German military barracks, Ingolstadt: ills. pp. 198, 202, 203
Gerner, Ingolstadt: ill. p. 197
Arlet Ulfers, Inning/Ammersee: ill. p. 216
Kulka and Partners, architects, Cologne/Dresden: ill. p. 267
Auer + Weber + architects, Munich: ills. pp. 247, 252
Florian Burgstaller, Munich: ills. pp. 240, 241, 243, 244, 245
Freunde der Residenz e. V., Munich: ill. p. 217
Management IGA 83, Munich: ill. p. 74
Kaup, Scholz, Jesse and Partners, architects, Munich: ill. p. 249
Myrzils and Jarisch, Munich: ills. pp. 166, 172, 173
Max Prugger, Bildverlag Prugger, Munich: ills. pp. 55, 71, 75
Christoph Stepan, Munich: ills. pp. 204, 205
Günther Wagmann and Partners, architects, Munich: ills. pp. 260, 261
Christoph Wirsing, Munich: ills. pp. 211, 214, 215
Bosch Archive, Stuttgart: ill. p. 176
Stuttgart, Filder area, competition documentation: ill. p. 248
Peter Walser, Stuttgart: ills. pp. 180, 181, 182, 183, 185, 187, 191, 192, 193, 195
Robert Bosch GmbH / Bytomsky, Würzburg: ills. p. 179, 190
JVA Würzburg: ill. p. 274

The remaining 170 photographs: Peter Kluska

List of artworks

Antes, Horst: Platz der Köpfe (Place of Heads) pp. 32, 33
Fuchs, Paul: sculpture, p. 259
Goepfert, Hermann und Johannes Peter Hölzinger: Licht-Wasser-Objekt (Light-Water Object), p. 35
König, Fritz: Flora, p. 221
Lechner, Alf: Wasserfall (Waterfall), pp. 23, 78
Matschinsky-Denninghoff, Brigitte und Martin: Wolken (Clouds), pp. 31, 34
Sax, Ursula: Rotation, p. 36
Venet, Bernar: sculpture, pp. 183, 195
Wesendonck, Otto: Spiralzeichen (Spiral Sign), p. 36
Wesendonck, Otto: Sculpture, p. 98
Wurmer, Hans: art object, p. 126

© for the illustrated works by the artists, their heirs or successor(s), with the exception of Horst Antes, Hermann Goepfert, Ursula Sax, Bernar Venet: by VG Bild-Kunst, Bonn 2013.

We have made every effort to identify all copyright holders. If there are any omissions, please contact Hirmer Publishers. Legitimate claims will be compensated accordingly.

Imprint

Published by

Hirmer Verlag GmbH
Nymphenburger Straße 84
80636 München
Germany

Conceptual design
Peter Kluska, Hao Li

English translation
Jane Michael
German copy-editing and proofreading
Stefanie Adam
English copy-editing and proofreading
Sarah Trenker
Typesetting
Tutte Druckerei GmbH, Salzweg
Layout and Production
Sabine Frohmader

Lithography
Reproline Mediateam GmbH, Unterföhring
Printing and binding
Firmengruppe Appl aprinta druck, Wemding
Paper
LuxoArt Samt 150g/qm

Printed in Germany

Bibliographic information published by
the Deutsche Nationalbibliothek
The Deutsche Nationalbibliothek lists
this publication in the Deutsche National-
bibliografie; detailed bibliographic
data are available on the Internet at
http://www.dnb.de.

© 2013 Hirmer Verlag GmbH, Munich;
Peter Kluska; the authors

www.hirmerverlag.de
www.hirmerpublishers.com

ISBN 978-3-7774-5681-2 (German Cover)
ISBN 978-3-7774-5161-9 (English Cover)